TERROR, VIOLENCE AND THE

PERSPECTIVES FROM ANALYTICAL PSYCHOLOGY

# Terror, Violence and the Impulse to Destroy

## Perspectives from Analytical Psychology

*Papers from the 2002 North American Conference
of Jungian Analysts and Candidates*

Edited by John Beebe

**DAIMON**
VERLAG

We are indebted to the Ann and Erlo van Waveren Foundation
for assistance with the publication of this book.

ISBN 3-85630-628-5

Cover image: Henri Fuseli, *The Nightmare* (1790/1791), oil.
Courtesy Freies Deutsches Hochstift/Frankfurter Goethe-Museum.

Printed in Canada

# Contents

# Preface

*John Beebe*

The papers collected in this book were originally presented at the North American Conference of Jungian Analysts and Candidates that was held at the Miyako Hotel in San Francisco, California, September 19 to 22, 2002. As the Chair of the San Francisco Program Committee for this conference, which our Institute agreed to put together for the Council of North American Societies of Jungian Analysts (CNASJA), I was fortunate to have the counsel of a committee of Jungian analysts and candidates (analysts-in-training) consisting of Mary Boyvey, Maria Chiaia, Martha Lawlor, and Bryan Wittine in designing a program to address "the psychology of violence and terror" from a Jungian standpoint.

We knew we weren't unique. Already available was Erel Shalit's 1999 book, *The Hero and his Shadow*, which looks hard at the dynamics of the ongoing conflicts in the Middle East. Two other books on our topic were in the wings. Luigi Zoja and Donald Williams's symposium *Jungian Reflections on September 11* would feature the reactions of concerned analysts on both sides of the Atlantic. *Terrorism and War: Unconscious Dynamics of Political Violence*, edited by Coline Covington, Paul Williams,

Jean Arundale, and Jean Knox, would include papers that leading British analytical psychologists, psychoanalysts, and analytically-oriented psychotherapists found, culling the literature, to be most significant.

It became clear to us, however, that rarely in North America do Jungians meet together to take up the "the impulse to destroy," and we shaped our call for proposals to be sure to get people to consider that theme. We received a very gratifying response, and in the end, we were able to schedule fifteen presentations. Only two of these could not be included here. The first was a spontaneous appreciation of John Dourley's public lecture, offered by Murray Stein, President of the International Association for Analytical Psychology. The other was a visual documentation by Patricia Sohl of her clinical work using nonverbal techniques to enable severely traumatized victims of torture to speak their feelings through art. These patients had asked that their material be contained within Dr. Sohl's circle of colleagues. The keynote address by Clarissa Pinkola Estés was spoken from the heart and appears here amplified in written form. This *cantadora* among analysts sets the tone for the very strong papers to follow.

When I decided that I would edit the conference papers for publication by Daimon Verlag, I had to create another, less formally constituted committee out of people I knew I could trust. Even with the good will of the entire Jungian world, shaping a successful, pioneering conference into a book someone would want to read is never easy, and I would like to acknowledge the practical help and the generous moral support of Robert Hinshaw, Robert Imhoff, Mary Webster, Toni D'Anca, and Adam Frey. There could be no book, however, without the authors listed in the table of contents, each of whom rose to this occasion with their very best efforts. As their editor, I have labored to let their papers speak for themselves.

# Explaining Evil

*Clarissa Pinkola Estés*

*Sometimes, darkness sharpens sight.*
*In darkness one can often see the exact shape of the soul*
*and how high its fires can truly flare.*

## Los Testigos

The Self is the ideal of wholeness. But can we, as mere humans, ever foresee every poor twist of fate coming and head it off? Can we bridge everything that needs bridging? Stopgap all evil? Defend against all mishaps? Become the curse-turners of the universe? Can we find final and completely inoculating choices to all that slips from good-enough into mild corruption, and thence to total infection? Can we set everything on a better or more righteous track?

No, we cannot. But we can consider how to contribute meaningfully to a progression of deeper and more insightful internal and cultural structures, present and future. We can wake up, pay attention, and design better-built inquiries and provisos. We can create boundaries, barriers, protections,

9

mediations *beforehand* – as well as during and after. We can propose doors and new manners. We can strive to enact ways of being that will allow and carry more humanity in ways not so likely to fall short.

We can insist on these. And keep insisting. We can show up. And keep showing up. We can learn the measure of words. And restraint. And *seeing* true. The depth of wounds. The means of repair. We can study and learn ways to outsmart the cunning forces that seek to destroy. Such destructive forces are often made, in large part, of slyness and sloth: All these have boringly predictable ways that are often lethal – that is, until one discovers the motives and methods behind them, and learns to anticipate and contravene them.

We know that having *one right answer* to all things at *all* times is rare. Some might wish for a beautiful and never-ending "moral harmony" – an ideal to which I am sympathetic. But, I also see over my lifetime that, regardless of one's faith beliefs and the strong eternal moral codes inherent in those – it is hard to always live these out. Often enough, attempting to do so turns out to be more of an in-the-mud, bare-knuckles, street scrap – with oneself – let alone others. Yet, I think the dust-ups and stand-offs against that which imposes or augurs great harm, are more than worthy of our repeated efforts to prevail with as much steadiness as possible.

There is something I have seen in my work with those who have "come back" from horrific circumstances. I see it also in those who have showed up, and stood up – at great cost. Also, in those who have gone underground in order to find the way through. It is this: what seems to matter so much in the end is that human beings *try*. *Try* to identify, describe, and weigh evil and self-governance; restraint and justice; one's own best and worst impulses; and those insightfully perceived by and about others. The considered weighing of such matters allows humane sight and action to be strengthened, and in more and more effective, fierce, and balanced ways.

To *try:* that is, to test each circumstance for what does not work and why, and for what *does work* and why. To test what will be good for the short run; what will be effective for the long term. To have integrity, one has to question one's integrity. Thus, one will find one's own ways to ask, What can I do that will allow me *afterward* to look into the mirror with self-respect and be sure that my humanity has remained intact – not by the lights of the ego alone, but especially by the lights of one's own soul?

I also mean the word *try,* not as some frail effort to put something across. But, *to try,* as in to examine and investigate. And thence to put full weight behind one's best aim, over and over again. In social justice work, one sees that it matters when we strive to weigh and enact any of these: doing the best right thing; the most effective good thing; the only good thing left; the last good thing left in the world; the most pitiful good thing available. This includes attempting the best possible outcome given the odds and the evens. The best hope given the times, the circumstances, the pain, the sorrow, the inspiriting force. One's assessment will weigh these, and more – Does this prevent or preserve humanity? Does this effectively restrain what is harmful? Does this *serve?*

It matters too when we pursue a carefully weighed course of action even when other good people might disagree. It matters that we go forward when we feel called by a force greater, even if those disliked by us *would* also *agree* to our undertaking. It matters mightily for repair of a breakdown in decency, or a brokenness in faith or faithfulness, or in the midst of a tidal wave of being pressed to long for vulgarity, that one hold to the boundaries wrought by the soul's intelligence, the mind's assistance, and with the spirit's flair.

In *curanderismo*, an ancient and time-honored Latin-American tradition of healing psyche and body, we have another name for *los guerreros*, the warrior-sentinels who strive for such consciousness. Those who hope to stand up to evil and those who *do* speak aloud toward such balance, are called *los testigos*. They are those who stand as eyewitnesses. *Los testigos* are not sightseers, nor "drive-by visitors" to sites of great horror or disaster. Nor are they those who visit for a while and then leave and never come back. They are not the ones who overlook, attempt to trivialize or rationalize critical circumstances. Instead, they are the ones who have willingly or unwillingly entered into, fallen into, been swept into an awful abyss. They have somehow managed to come back. In need of repair, ragged, shaken, certainly, but somehow still standing.

*Los testigos* are the ones who have literally lived to tell the true story, the *in-depth* story, the *first-order* story. There is so much in our culture that presses us to reflect and opine but without real participation or consciousness in and about the thing one is busy opining about. This dissociation from actual experience is not good for humans. It causes a person's view of real life to become utterly anemic psychically and creatively.

In curanderismo, a story of vital immersion, of living eye-to-eye through or against great harm, having been snagged or dragged by travail, great challenge — such direct facing off with evil is considered *un cuento sagrado*, a sacred story. To resist a great destruction, to return from having been deeply assailed, is considered *un cuento milagro*, a miracle story.

Likewise, in depth psychology, we would say the story of one who has suffered so, carries *numinosity*. This sacred quality is conveyed through a mysterious set of images and/or palpably felt perceptions. They erupt during intense episodes of life story, including horrendous ones. This milieu communicates to the person in some way, regardless of the mayhem at hand, the presence of divinity. Numinous experience stands above and outside "life as usual." It stirs the higher and deeper emotions. It can activate 'sudden knowings," and abrupt infusions of much needed strength. It often offers rare insights that cannot be had during mundane experiences.

Thus a living miracle story often awakens, reveals, and transforms. Yet its greatest effects can hardly be expressed in prose alone. Thus, the arts are often a great treasure to help those who are "returning from battle." The color, hue, timbre, tone, movement, shape, and texture possible in expression through the arts provides ways "to speak" numinosity's language. Through their mediation, *un cuento milagro*, the miracle story, with its harshness and its feats, finds its way to show above ground.

I know from hearing from many analysts and other souls via letters, that some part of each life has *un cuento milagro,* a miracle story. And that it is a story worth telling to at least one other who, at the right time and for the right purpose, needs to hear it. The *cuento milagro* is essential to lifting, guiding, healing of self and others. Essential for love's sake, and to teach balance, to turn away from what is not helpful, useful, effective or good. In this sense, a conscious record of one's *la lucha*, struggle, with difficulty, brings about *el autodominio,* a kind of self-governance that grants to the person both expansion and restraint in service of what is truly just. Thus, will the interior and external cultures benefit greatly.

## Some First-hand Learnings About Evil

Although I am not a theologian nor rhetorician – I admire those who are able in those areas. I have instead in this lifetime been given the work of poet. I hardly know a poet who is not also an activist. I have engaged in both for several decades now while working with persons whose spirits have been shattered.

I have also listened to the lives, angsts and dreams of many activists, teachers, religious, and interveners, leaders in the aggregate. The assistors and helpers of the broken, sometimes even more than the wounded they assist, need their spirits and souls called back to them and mended up also. My first trainings were in developmental psychology and ethno-clinical psychology, the study of groups and post-trauma recovery. Later, I also earned a diploma as a Jungian psychoanalyst. The views here are thus first-person soundings from that inquiry that poets try for, *and* that inquiry that psychoanalysts try for. As such I would offer to you the following as a personal document with academic explication, both.

How did I come to know something about matters of suffering and evil? Over my lifetime there has been as clear a pathway through the Inferno as any Dante ever conceived. I hesitate to tell you at any length, for it is intensely personal. But more so, I am reluctant out of concern about not being able, in the few pages accorded here, to tell the stories of many other brave souls with the fullest grace and honor they deserve. Yet, I carry a quickening sense that at this time in our larger world, it is getting to be nearly past time for those who have seen whatever they have seen – who have lived through whatever they have lived through – to drop as best they can all learned or stilted proprieties – and allow others to know they are not alone.

One of the first overlooks I had into the mystery of how people come back from having been mangled by evil, came as a child. Sometimes when I awoke at night, the newly arrived war refugees of our family would be standing at my bed in the dark. They had pretty sparkling glitters on their faces. This was not a dream. They stood over me weeping. But, not because any of us were in peril. Quite the opposite. My father explained to me that it was because, after all they had been through, it was healing for them to see a living child sleeping.

I understood these battered souls who came from so far away, suddenly appearing in our home all a shambles, and with eyes so making a constant sad sign language. Amongst many things, I learned as a child that evil had ways that caused people to leap, run, flee, overturn burning fires; hide, be captured, forced, hurt, harmed badly, give their lives so another might live. I learned too, that people so badly used could also learn to dance and love again. Time, it took much time. And a spirit of Life nearby that would love them without cease.

Years passed, and in my late teens, I worked in a hospital where lived children so damaged and so often thrown away. Sometimes I felt I had, through their travails with those who had dominion over them, come into the anteroom of evil incarnate. Many were damaged by landlords who refused to repair decrepit ceilings filled with lead paint. Such ceilings fell, part by part – into the cribs of babies who then swallowed the poisonous chips. The subsequent damage to the children's brains was so profound that they became staring and cadaveresque for life. There too, were children whose caretakers had beaten and burnt them till they were harmed beyond any earthly repair.

In those times, many parents were encouraged to abandon their children if they were not born "perfect" at birth. I, along with many other young women, washed and fed and changed these beautiful little ones. Through no fault of their own, some of these radiant faced children had been born with the conditions of hermaphroditus, microcephalus, and hydrocephalus. Some of the babies' heads weighed three times what their bodies weighed. They chortled and smiled and laughed with all the joy of any baby, even though they would never crawl or walk. Their necks were not strong enough to lift their heavy heads from the pillows. Regardless, as with all the children, we cuddled them as they lay.

It was a time when incredibly bright and handsome children with Down's syndrome and autism were "put away." Little ones with epilepsy lay through wave after wave of convulsions every few minutes that were not controlled with medicines. One of the worst things of all was the pathetic lack of real toys, lack of the stimulation of change, color and music; the fact that very few adults came to play with the children. There was no one to awaken their minds daily, to teach them, to show them the world outside and their own blossoming.

It was one of the premiere times in my life when I have come closest to wanting to set myself on fire to signal the entire world that many terrible wrongs had all come together in this one secret culture that existed out of sight. I used to pray, *Help. Send help. Please, let grown-ups who have power in the world find their way here. Let them be strong enough to stand to see this without turning away. Please! Send someone who can help!*

But, no one came. And no one came. It took decades before I could even begin to understand, that each of us girls who worked there, that we were the ones who would someday, each in her own way, be able to tell the stories of what we had seen there – that we, in whatever way we could, would become *the help that came.*

Yet those difficult matters were also set against mercies that were profound. I cared for babies born with hearts or spines partially outside their bodies, and also desperately ill children with frail lungs, damaged kidneys, and otherwise weak hearts, who were dying and that no family came to comfort. But, I remember one set of little parents who came and stayed at their dying child's bedside day and night.

The dying toddler was literally a golden child. He had the shiniest golden curly hair I had ever seen. As his kidneys failed, the jaundice deepened and the little one became more and more gold-colored. The night-light in the darkened room always showed the same scene. His mother and his father, alone there, older than I – but now looking back, how so very young they were. They held his tiny hands, praying out loud for angels to come take their dear child to heaven. I escaped into linen closets to not let them see me cry for them. I learned again and again that it is sometimes harder to see those who love so deeply be cut to the bone, than it already is to see an innocent little one die. From this tiny holy family too, I saw how immaculate the most tortured human heart can become.

After this, I began to work a good deal by mission, that is, by being called to a place and weighing it as spiritual commitment for a set period of time. What followed would require long books to relate to you all that occurred there. I worked at Veteran's Hospitals and what used to be called Old Soldiers' Homes. My work as an aide was portable, and I worked on suicide wards, locked wards, and what were once called drunk tanks, on locked institutions for adolescents, in hospice before it was called hospice, and in nursing and rehabilitation-homes. I worked at the "knife and gun club," the dangerous emergency room shifts on Friday and Saturday nights when gunshots and stabbings seem to erupt far more than usual. Bellowing and menacing humans still throwing punches at each other often slammed and slid right into the hospital alongside their friends on gurneys, who were bleeding to death.

When I helped to co-ordinate one of the first safe houses for battered women and children in the United States, I also began to work in the *movimientos*, the peace and justice movements, caring for souls who had painfully somehow made it to refuge from Guatemala, Nicaragua, El Salvador and the spill-over war at the borders of Honduras. Their experiences of rape and harrow were so without boundaries. At this date, it has been twenty-three years since I began a prison ministry, and twenty-some years of assisting with recovery on-site at natural disasters, thirty-three years since I first began practicing clinically. I have learned over and over again how brave people are, and how powerful, even in their pain; how sacred is the spirit and how fragile. But also I have learned how ironclad the soul is, even when a person does not feel it is so.

Since my *Católico* childhood, I have tried to live mission, regardless of all other sudden, strange, lilting, or dire challenges that have appeared inside my life, and tangential to it. Most of the time, even though there are always solemn considerations and substantial psychic and sometimes physical costs to mission, I have been able to have the wherewithal to face straight into some of the worst that can happen to humans, and the worst of inhumanity that humans can visit on other souls, including persons harmed by terrible twists of fate; child-bearing loss, horrific accidents, murders and sudden deaths of many kinds.

But one can never feel completely secure in these often nearly unbearable matters. I never could have stood by myself. Only through and in the strength of One greater. Without that "Source with out source," and *mi madre,* La Señora de Guadalupe as intercessor, I might have completely fainted away at first sight.

*Efforts to Define Evil: Unhealed Wound as Attractant for Evil*

The name of this essay is "Explaining Evil." But, I must say frankly to you that we have to say Evil cannot be explained, past a smallish counterpoint in comparison to its vast range. At least Evil cannot be explained by any purely rational means. In my studies I have noted that some doers of profound evil through-out history have had the same characteristics as monsters found in mythos. Often, there is high intelligence coupled with excel-lent intuition about others' secret desires, i.e. others' weakest points of entry. These are purposely sought out. There is an extraordinary uncanniness, a kind of psychic prescience about one's potential victims, and about human nature in general. This is put to evil use. There is personality charm that inexplicably degenerates into cruelty and atrocity for a sick pleasure's sake. This latter trait, in reality, is often especially excruciating to contemplate for anyone of sound mind.

Those are some of the descriptors of the ganglia that make up Evil. But when trying to *explain* Evil's motives, the roots of its existence, the why of it, I find that no rational explanation, explains it. Whichever way you turn it, evil cannot be elucidated in any way that makes sense to an unruined heart.

But, even so evil can be described far past the way a stone might be described as an aggregate of silica, or a car engine described as a combustion chamber. Evil's shapes, ways and effective containments can all be described. However, that statement comes with a caveat. By my sights, Evil would require infinite descriptions for us to even come close to outlining its fullest shape and many guises.

To literally write about evil would take, I think, a thousand Encyclopedias Britannica just to map its ways in and with the world and humans. Here I would only attempt to contribute the equivalent of a few paragraphs to that so larger and infinite treatise on Evil — the one humanity has been compiling for aeons. But we could anchor this discussion to an extent by visiting a working definition of evil. Evil is a word that is, like the force it describes, as old as time.

There is a saying in the family: "The Devil is not cunning because he is the Devil. The Devil is cunning because he is old." The word *evil* is old too. In essence it exists in our earliest written documents. It may also be said to be represented in one of the most ancient paintings yet known to humankind — the Paleolithic "dead man" glyph in the caves at Lascaux. Some have speculated that this petroglyph of a fallen man, stabbed with a rod, is a representation of a murder.

The word *evil* in modern times, that is, in the last 500 years, means to be morally reprehensible in such a way as to cause harm, especially to an innocent other, especially to one unawares. From various codes of law and canons of ethics, I find intentional or thoughtless harm to others to also be described in the following ways:

- Especially, to act outside of any sensible proportion so as to hurt, harm, mislead, block, corrupt or deprive self or another the basic right of humanity.
- To bar one from decency of life.
- To prevent one from living unmolested.
- To not allow one to be treated with truth and full disclosure, with fairness.
- To refuse that another be allowed to thrive, or to seek meaning, safety and life.
- To interfere with one's fair right to not be undercut by negligent or covert means.

Religion tends to identify evil via the concept of sin; and civil and criminal law, with regard to judiciary limits.

What I have learned as Chair of the Colorado State Grievance Board, where we hear cases every other month regarding allegations of misconduct and intrusions by psychotherapists, is that ethics is most concerned with *power.* There is a qualified difference in how justness and predation are weighed when there is an imbalance of power between two or more persons. It is clear that children above all – and other helpless, naive, unprotected, or ill people – cannot give the same consent as can a person whose power (or cunning) is equal to the alleged perpetrator's.

I have liked that phrase linked to the ancient Hippocratic oath that is often parsed as "If you cannot help, do no harm." When I first learned this phrase as an adult, I told it to my grandmothers, who turned an awful gargoyle-eyed look on me and said, pointedly, being *just* was far more than that: If you were to criticize another, you had a moral obligation to also help that person. If you were not willing to offer ongoing help to that soul, no criticism was allowed. What a challenge to do. ¡Ay! Yet, I suspect it is true all the way across the world, that "grandmother ethics" are higher than any other codes of law.

Some assert that there are only two forms of evil. One is a force *outside* oneself. The second is possessing elements of such *within* oneself. Some would say that evil, whether without or within, is "fallen goodness." Amongst the old believers in Catholicism, however, it is said that "the Evil one" would especially like you to think of it as having only two or three ways in which it shows up – for thence human beings will not be able to see the thousands of guises that Evil truly comes in. Such aid causes Evil to laugh with its customary unhappy joy. It is said amongst the old women who taught me, that Evil's first name was Deceiver and its second name is Divider.

What I have come to understand over these decades of working with some of the most egregious attacks and outcomes resulting from human on human malevolence, is that Evil is an exogenous force that attacks and attempts to colonize human beings. Some may be able to recognize the breach and resist utterly. Others may be in various kinds of weakened conditions and thereby be susceptible to being taken up by evil, to being devoured by it, or even led into following it.

I must admit I have never been able to think that a person in their right mind can agree to follow abject Evil. Whether by purposeful omission of voice or action, by neglect or by commission – in order to ally with evil – something of one's core humanity must be surrendered or stolen away. One's humanity is like a beacon to the psyche and the world. Without it, the person is like a lighthouse unlit on a stormy night: the dousing of such a light of consciousness will cause enormous collisions and devastations.

As portrayed in myths and legends, Evil is *hungry*. Imagine for a moment, that Evil trolls the world looking for open wounds to attach itself to and feast upon. In Asia there are "hungry ghost" rituals that spring from the stories about the gates of Hell having been negligently left open. Certain ones from that nether world are said to rise up to roam the countryside in search of earthly pleasures, gained by stealing life from others. In the most ancient tales about malignant forces, Evil promises wounded persons its protection or a sustenance of some sort – if only they will allow Evil to cunningly use their eyes, their hands, their minds, their love for life – for its own ends.

Some say that *all* who are born on earth are vulnerable to falling into the arms of evil in some part. I would differentiate this by speculating that some are more at *risk* than others, but not only by the fact of being greatly wounded in and by life. People are most especially defenseless *after* a wounding – when and if they remain *untended to*. If they remain unhealed, some significant portion of the psyche often calcifies into a defensive bitterness that can take the form of detached cruelty to self and others. In mythos, persons in such extreme conditions of despair are vulnerable to being devoured by the spirit of malevolence, for such open wounds constitute tasty treats for Evil. The milieu of the unhealed wound is understood as the exact climate that Evil finds most hospitable.

But there is another thing that Evil is traditionally hungry for. That is revealed in its chronic attraction to and predation upon Beauty.

### The Predator and Beauty: *Don Diego and La Nuestra Señora's Roses*

I further recognize Evil as a force that in some way does not value the spark of life. In tales, both fictional stories and those from real-life, human-caused holocausts, what we call Evil does not confine itself just to subverting, tarnishing, polluting, or corrupting. It is also interested in possessing and murdering beauty and the life that surrounds beauty.

The notion of a hunger to possess a beauty that one does not own, that one has not earned or created, and to which one can therefore make no valid claim, reminds me of a leitmotif in one of the episodes from the 16th century journey of Don Diego. He was the conquered Náhua / Mexican Indian man who saw a vision of Our Lady, *La Conquista*. She appeared to Don Diego several times. Amongst other things, she asked the poor man to go to the wealthy Spanish Bishop, Zumarraga. Diego was to tell the Bishop that he had seen an apparition of Blessed Mother on the Hill of Tepeyac and that Holy Mother had instructed him to please say that she would like to have a temple built in her honor there.

Don Diego, just a short little dusky Indian, told her he was a nobody. He said he was only a peasant, that he had just been converted to the new faith – by the sword, some said. Don

Diego was afraid. He asked the Beautiful Lady several times, just to make sure he had heard her instruction correctly (he secretly hoped to be let off the hook): "You want me to go tell the Bishop that you, My Lady, should have a temple built here, which incidentally you realize is the Hill of Tepeyac where once stood the enormous temple to Tonanszin, The Great Mother of the Nahua/Aztec people before the conquistadores destroyed it? And you want me to ask the Bishop to build your temple on that same exact ground under the name of Our Lady of Guadalupe?"

Our Lady tried to reassure him. But, Don Diego stuttered and said, "I cannot. You know, I'm just … I'm poor. I'm nothing."

And Our Lady said, "Do not worry. Have you forgotten? Am I not your mother? You are under my protection."

He goes to the palace of the Bishop. It is wintertime. Don Diego was wearing a *tilma*, which is like a cape. It is made of burlap. In some versions it is told that before he comes to the doors of the palace, without his knowledge, Our Lady has filled his tilma with beautiful roses. When Don Diego requests entry to see the Bishop, the big, rough guards laugh. They say, "No, no, ha ha! You filthy little peasant! You!? You cannot go in and speak to the venerable bishop. Impossible. Out, you scum!"

Don Diego hurried to leave. But the guards saw the roses in his tilma. They seized the poor man by the neck and reached into his cape. "Ah *Dio*, look! Well, we'll just take those roses from you."

And as the guards lifted the roses out – in their hands, the roses turn to ashes. The ashes fell right through their hands like sand. They sputtered, "Ha! What magic is this? What wickedness is this?" They grabbed some more roses out of the little peasant's tilma. Again the roses turned to dark ashes and fell upon the floor. The more the guards tried to seize the roses, the more the roses become ashes.

Don Diego was successful in the end. With the mystical help of Our Lady of Guadalupe, the temple was built. It still stands today on Tepeyac hill.

The story about the roses and the guards is germane to our topic. Whether it be roses or any other form of mystical or mundane splendor, there is a force loose in the world that is ravenous for Beauty. It wants to possess the roses in all things, even though it has no right to them. There is something about the predator's touch that is loathful, for it has no heart, it has no humanity. It destroys whatever it touches. And it does not stop to mourn. It only goes on to the next Beauty it finds, attempting once again to attach and prey.

In myths and tales, such a hungry and malignant force is often met with efforts to fend it off by crippling it, decreasing its strength, chasing it away, or else by attempting to transform it – but not by feeding it. In legends, sometimes a malicious force is shown to be stopped by mirroring its evil back unto itself. This is done by making an unambiguous statement or gesture that proves that the human soul fully grasps that Evil is afoot and foul, and knows irrevocably, despite Evil's seductive or horrific offers or threats, what its true nature and intentions really are.

In the ancient Greek myth about Andromeda and Perseus, the innocent and brave beauty Andromeda is saved from being murdered. She was to be torn apart by the hungry, many-armed sea monster, named Kraken. Bold Perseus, son of Zeus, is told that showing Evil what it is made of, will mediate and weaken it. So, as the Kraken rises from the boiling sea to devour chained Andromeda, Perseus raises Medusa's severed head to the Kraken. The Gorgon's horrible gaze turns the hideous monster to stone.

Yet, in other myths, it is sometimes demonstrated that Evil can neither be transformed, nor broken, but must instead, be entirely restrained, set far away, forever in containment. In *The Prose Edda*, the story goes that the Norse Gods saw no harm in Fenris the wolf when he was a pup. They allowed him to remain amongst themselves. He was fed and grew ever larger. But, as time passed, Fenris grew to such monstrous and devouring proportions, that the Áesir, the half giant-half mortal Gods, realized he should have been dealt with much earlier. If ravenous Fenris were allowed to run unfettered any longer, they feared that the entire world would be devoured.

So, they tried various means to restrain Fenris. But none held, and there was despair that it might be too late. But, finally, they asked the smithy dwarves to make a magical chain necklace that could bind Fenris. This the dwarves did, naming the neck chain, Gleipnir. And the chain bound Fenris and did not break.

The six rare, beautiful, and "impossible things" the magical chain was made of were: the sound that cat makes when it walks, the beard of a woman, the roots of a mountain, the sinews of a bear, the breath of a fish, and the spittle of a bird. Thus, with this chain, Fenris is lashed to the boulder Gjoll which is driven a mile under the earth, and an even larger boulder placed atop. It is said that Fenris, the huge hungry force is still roaring, still threatening, but unable to enact its desires as easily – at least until the very end of time.

*Hierarchy Turned Malignant Golem:*
*Redemption and Mirroring Dreams*

Even though Fenris is shackled beneath the earth, energies like his sometimes still seem to be loose on the face of the earth. And there is almost no more fertile ground for such incursive habitation as a culture, meaning any group of persons held together by customary beliefs, social forms, and material traits of one kind or another.

Within cultures, the human desire "to create order" is such a rich attribute. It often seeks to accomplish its goal by assembling a hierarchy. This is a benign and useful idea in and of itself. But because power *over* instead of *with*, is often the fundamental dynamic in a hierarchy, this common paradigm for bringing order can also attract corruptive influences easily. If such negative influences are not identified and reversed, they can cause the entire entity to fall into a trivialization and dehumanization of others that spreads throughout the entire organism. If such human factors are not consciously examined and restrained on a regular basis, the hierarchy then begins to act like an out of control golem.

A golem is the mud-creature from Hebrew mythos, which is most often created by humans for a higher purpose, especially to protect the vulnerable and the innocent. But in some old stories from Romania and Transylvania, the golem goes awry and begins to take on a life of its own. Instead of serving the original superior principle for which it was created, it begins to only perpetuate and protect itself and its most base motives. It seeks to drain the life force of other human beings in order to sustain itself.

In politics and sports too, there are many examples of ill-gotten gain through improper guile. However, amongst the early Greeks, engagement in athletic contests was measured against an ideal of equanimity – strength and evenness of mind, spirit and body. This was considered not only an honorable endeavor, but a sacred one.

To this day, a fair sports competition is far different from one in which motives and advantages are hidden. In an above-board match, there are no covert assistances and distortions used to influence. The desired outcome is not fixed beforehand. In a fair game, all rules and boundaries are overt. No person is secretly given advantage or disadvantage because all are challenged by the same hurdles and given the same breaks. In such a game, all concerned agree to engage to the best of their abilities.

But in a social contract or educational order that has fallen into a malignancy, not all players are given the rules, bona fide. In fact, the exact rules for points and fouls may be kept secret or semi-hidden, or else administered in unmeasurable ways. They may be changed according to the local hungry golem's need for keeping its power and staying alive. Thus, the exact location of the end zone may be kept secret. Or constantly moved, whenever "less desirable" players appear to be closing in on it. The advantage of special coaching is given to a select few without revealing that this help is being offered and without offering it to all. Scoring is one-sided or crookedly counted.

Unusually strong players may purposely be harmed to ensure that they are benched, effectively making them disappear from the playing field. Whoever is injured in the melees set up for this purpose is simply dropped from the line up, without recourse to any repair for what of them has been harmed. No adequate information ever surfaces officially about the nefarious means by which all this occurred.

Whether this ill and talent-killing culture is found within a family, an institution, or a governance, a syntonic psyche does not and cannot thrive in it or on it. Tellingly, in such deeply compromised situations, one's dreams will act as the consummate truthtellers. In those who have been tempted by such a golem culture to seize their own ill-gotten swag via the evil means at hand, as well as in those who have been its victims, there will concurrently be a sudden outrush of dream images that are oppositional to deceitful forces – or perhaps additionally dream images that mirror, often in nightmarish proportions, *precisely* what is occurring.

In opposition, one might dream of a redemptive force characterized by a sudden ray of light, or a small key, or other unusual object or being that carries great strength "to open" or to "reveal." Redemptive dream images can act as the exact towropes needed to help bring one back to the soul's center again, even after an experience of exile, being overwhelmed, or feeling despair.

Amongst the *sueñodoras*, the dream interpreters in our family, such liberating redemptive images are sometimes understood as personal *los símbolos sagrados*, sacred symbols. The tradition encourages that these be used for memory's sake, that is, by thinking of them one is then re-infused with memory of one's true inborn strength to resist and to move forward. Such dream images are also amplified by literally adding some symbolic representation of them to one's actual person or surroundings. These are to "remind" a person what they are truly made of and for what purpose they truly came to earth.

Via the peculiar capacity of the psyche to "copy back," like a camera's glass plate that reflects the exact image placed before its lens, the psyche can send a photograph of the unconscious directly up into consciousness through dreams. Thereby, amongst those being overwhelmed by, or being invited to participate in a golem culture of no decent intent, one of the most common images arising in their dreams is that of a monstrous non-human force – or else that of a human who, no matter which way you turn the image, can no longer be called human.

These difficult dream images signifying inhumanity are meant to be held in full consciousness and consideration, but in a different way than the redemptive ones. The horrific dream images initially and especially, are not to be "talked away" until they are little manageable "nothings." The nature of a stalwart consciousness – is that it has the strength and the will to hold daring, opposing, paradoxical, and hideous ideas up out of the slime long enough for them to be truly examined, understood at depth, and dealt with in some effective way.

Although the nuances of interpretation will vary, both these common kinds of dream images – redemptive and photographic – seem intended to lead or to roar the dreamer away from any idea that one is meant to live in, give into, slumber near, or otherwise promote a collective, or a personal milieu that thrives on subterfuge and deceit. Since time out of mind, the ambition of Evil has been to advance endarkenment. But humans are not lacking in wherewithal. The psyche appears to immediately recognize any intrusion, seductive or otherwise, from such dark might. A greater sensibility prompts about how to respond in a way that will keep the psyche most whole and able.

Anytime broadcasts of the soul's critical awarenesses are in danger of being cut off from the rest of the psyche, one will see, if one pays attention, that the aspect of psyche charged with insight and balance begins to signal quickly and clearly that alertness, discernment, and caution are required *right now*; that a broader consciousness is needed to consider, oppose, or transform whatever has intruded. Thus one begins to see *behind* the malignant force, realizing it for what it really is. And next, to weaken its hold further, its predicable methodologies must become known.

*Diagnosing Intrusion By Evil:*
*An Archetypal Map of One of its Most Predictable Patterns*

In curanderismo, such intrusions by malevolent interests that then attempt to capture and direct the entire heart and thought system of an individual, are said to be most commonly seen in persons plagued by the symptoms of chronic *envidia*, envy, as well as *el estómago vacio*, literally, "the empty stomach."

These are both understood as ever-generating and grinding hungers toward gaining *more* – to the exclusion of developing one's humanity in honest and equal proportions. These unmediated hungers revolve most often around *more* power, place, position, authority, admiration, and so on. None of these is recognized as simply the natural hunger of normal individuals to be seen as a person of worth. All are instead seen as the hungers of an insatiable element that has invaded the psyche without the victim's realization.

Also considered symptomatic in a person so invaded, is the presence of a nagging impulse toward *non arbítro,* a form of judgmentalness that falsifies the true picture of one's interior and exterior worlds. In curanderismo, this form of judgmental-ness is somewhat different than the kind that comes from a defensively over-strict superego. *Non arbítro*, means literally, *lack* of the presence of an insightful inner judge or arbiter. The invader of the psyche has decommissioned it entirely and now seats itself in the judge's chair. Now *it* has free reign to distort for its own ends.

This condition causes persons to insist, often aloud, that they can see, weigh, and describe deeply and accurately what-ever is before them, when in fact they have no fulcrum left for humane measurement. The "snap judgments" issuing from them that fall far short of both surface and deeper realities, actually come from what has invaded them. Thus, when given even the smallest aperture, this negatively motivated force within will attempt to blur the boundaries needed for adequate restraints and fullest expansion of peaceable life and society – mainly because the creeping force behind this syndrome wants no containment that might prevent its continued secret access to the psyche and to the cultural layers from which it is feeding.

There rises from all three of these conditions and symptoms, a fourth one, which is the drive to punish those who are yet free. These are defined as those who are able to fight, to resist, and those able to even in awkward but mostly timely ways, banish such intrusions. They are persons capable and conscious enough to secure and mend the psyche's perimeters against invasion.

The drive to punish unjustly often arises from a distortion of reality. The curanderas I have learned from say there is *el cálculodero*, "an astute counter" in the psyche that watches and knows much. Its list of facts about the conditions of the person and the world near at hand are uncorrupted. But, its data can be misused by nefarious elements within the psyche, which use that data to mislead the self and other persons. This is most often done by shading and distorting the truth, or else by telling only part of the truth with guile.

As the *cálculodero* counts and points out persons who are still free, the negative force overhears this accounting. But, instead of seeing souls who are still free, it only sees these free souls as the betrayers of itself, as enemies of its mal-intentions. Therefore, if these sovereign souls cannot be invaded easily, the destructive force tries to mark them for derision, exclusion, silencing, and other forms of castigation, all the way to annihilation – all so that the malevolent force can expand without limits.

This is like the Rumpelstiltskin who shatters the needy young girl by tricking her into giving him her first-born child and then doing everything he can to not have his malevolence called by its true name. Similarly, the detrimental drive to punish goodness and decency, once firmly rationalized and deeply attached to its host, is often heartbreakingly introjected into the true self, leaving that innocent in shatters. The destructive element even more so carries the will and the rage to protect itself by acting, through its host, to punish others also. Thus it attempts to impede individuals and whatever else in and of the world at large that it perceives is trying to name it and limit its incursions.

The heartbreaking part is this: From the outside, a person in such an eaten-up condition may seem to have consciously *chosen* evil. But the reality is far more likely that they are bearing some unconscious attractant, and thereby have been unawares invaded by and overwhelmed by such a force. Standing outside this phenomenon, many observers do not realize that the true person inside this fissioning complex is an innocent who has been challenged by an ordeal, but lost and been subsumed.

If others move to attack whatever has eaten up the true self of this person, that malevolent force will drag the true self in front of itself as a shield. It will allow that pitifully sagging and already wrecked spirit to take the brunt of all charges and remonstrations – while the real source of the problem still roams about without containment.

The cries of innocence one hears in such a situation are not those of the demon, for it is laughing that the true self is once again being seen as the miserable sub-human it has been told it is. The cries one hears are those of the truly naive self who is the desperate prisoner, the one who fervently needs the help, insight, repair and support of other stronger, more astute, more free souls.

All these conditions of such tumult and disgrace in the invaded psyche could be said to be diagnosable by one symptom that stands out higher, farther, and deeper than any other in such an eaten-up individual. All disruptions to one's humanity, when a negative force has invaded, clearly present as profound "longing without love." That is the bottom line. Rapacious hungers. No love in sight. In the discipline of curanderismo, such ongoing and unmediated symptoms in a person are considered evidence that Evil has already gained entry. It is already feasting on the marrow of its host, causing the true soul and self endless suffering. Ever more pronounced symptoms of insatiable hunger to possess and to punish, both, are the confirmation that not so subtly, evil has take up permanent residence, insisting on occupying a psychic land that it has no true claim on.

This entire malevolent pattern is an archetypal one that is found in thousands of myths and legends, in science fiction, in novels, as well as in history: the defeat of the wounded one by an evil overwhelming force; the subsequent murder, silencing or banishing of all who challenge the malignant power; and the rewarding of all who are similarly disposed or who try to save something they love by allying with evil.

At the pattern's conclusion, often, the group of villagers, the brace of knights, the hosts of Amazons or Angels, in all and any case the "imperfect, but pure hearts," show up. Their restraining or killing of the demon reveals inside its body, the frightened, but still whole – even though now bloody and bedraggled – human soul that had been devoured at the beginning.

But, the part that is often left out of the story, the true part, is that evil is not dead even though it has been killed. For the heroic human beings concerned, though feasting for happiness, and toiling with challenges are the orders of all future days, so now also is constant vigilance.

*Evil as Cursory Exclusion: The Eighth and Ninth Days of Creation*

In curanderismo, it is thought that, personified or not, Evil watches and waits for its chances. It will try to infuse with its blood hunger anything that slides to its side of the board. As my grandmother Querida used to say ... The unskilled *torero*, bullfighter, may fail to observe the bull sleeping. But *el toro*, the bull, is always watching the torero – particularly when he sleeps and throws open his most tender parts for all to see.

I come from non-literate families. I had parents for whom English was not their mother tongue, and the rest of my family could not read or write, or did so very haltingly. Most everything was handed down orally or through gesture. That included sacred scripture, of which the old people had memorized vast amounts. No one could read right out of the good Book until I laboriously learned to read. Then, I was so happy to read everything for them, including street signs and medicine bottles.

My close-in people were an earthy lot. To them, Evil was not a concept or a theory. It was not an "interesting idea." It was a known and highly finessed reality. They were shrewd observers of base human nature. Their lives in a small village of less than fifty large families, was like life in a psychology laboratory. There, one studied a small sample of subjects close up, day after day, and for years – whether you wanted to or not. My grandmother carried this story about the necessity of being aware of how the proclivity to over-impose order on even the most exquisite of things can go awry....

She would begin by saying, "You know, God created heaven and earth. And the Face of God moved over the waters of the dark and hovered over them.

"God gave out a breath and this breath divided the waters – and lo! land emerged. And then, this great Face turned slowly and breathed in another direction – and lo! light was created.

"And then, this great Face of enormous beauty, so beautiful that just by its looks and its breath, it then created all the rest of world as we see it now; this beautiful face created and created, until finally the seventh day arrived. And God rested."

Then my grandmother would continue: "And on the eighth day.... God created something else. On the eighth day, He created religion.

"And on the ninth day ..." she would conclude, "the Devil showed up – and said – 'I'll organize it for you!'"

Now, if we were to follow the inference of her story, ever since that ninth day, humans have sometimes been drawn into being busy building walls, divisions, monoliths, and cliques; the investitures of the few, of the many, of the few against the many, and of the many against the few – all since time began.

To build ordered structures is human. But there can be elements behind various "building" behaviors that require thoughtful examination for balance. How faithfully and justly one does it, and what exactly it is orchestrating truly, will be the questions each has to answer for him or herself. A most common giveaway that something has gone wrong appears when there is a move in the name of order to douse the creative psyche. This is often done by encouraging reward for the easy fitters of the preconceived mold, and by attempting to do away with all others "who do not fit" the predetermined model.

Throughout time, too rigid or subversive ways of "ordering order" have been used to hold others in contempt, as less human, unintelligent, and unworthy of praise, generosity, resource, kindness, and opportunity. Our history books are filled with unjust and fickle exclusions, leaving us to realize that some have plied these discriminations they have thinly veiled as "order," since forever – whether at university or club, or high or low tea party, in ways that pit sibling against sibling, lover against lover, colleague against colleague, and faith against faith.

These discriminations have depended on such frail divisions as: do you speak this particular language or don't you? Do you go to temple or church, or don't you go to either? Are you thin? Are you fat? Are you educated, or are you not? Are you born to this class or that one? Did you go to school here, or there? Are you one of us, or one of your own – or God help us all, one of those lone wolves we've heard about? Are you an intellectual, or are you not very bright? Are you a creative person, or are you not creative? Do you worship what I worship or not? Are you perfected in the way I say you ought be, or not?

So, so many of these divisions are temptingly held out as allyships – if only one will agree to join up on one side against the other. The acolyte is in some way assured that there will be strength in numbers and protection if they join up, that this form, place, and ordered entity will serve as bulwark against the world, and that it will be socially and economically rewarding as well – if only one will treat a certain group or a few others *as less than.* In this way, the manifestation of "the ninth day of creation" is met, when the Devil insists that he will "organize" everything. The Devil's real intent is to foil any proposition that might bring inspiriting new life. The Devil thus drives toward breaking and dividing any hope we might have, as humans, to be of one piece and peace – within ourselves and with one another.

But over the years, I see that there is a "tenth day" to the story of our Creation. On the tenth day, God gave us an infallible means to measure and illuminate any situation, and it is this: The clarifying moment for any vibrant psyche comes when all ideas and promises offered can be weighed against one's humanity, to see if any proposed division is really useful, proper, and true. For that measurement, God gave us not just a world, an ego and free will – but last, and most of all – a *soul*.


## How Humans Dehumanize Humans

The lengths to which people have gone to stabilize hierarchy in order to exclude and dehumanize others has a long history that affects us still. One such is still remembered bitterly by many. It was called miscegenation – "the wrongful mixin' of the races," as I heard some call it on the radio when I was very young. This way of thinking still holds an honored place for some people in the present. Back then, though, they were talking about us not supposed to be "marrying up into" certain groups for it would "taint the blood" of those "higher." Though one might hope those times are long past, I was recently reminded how hard these matters die away.

In the mail came a little book I had ordered – a modern Mexican book on Spanish cultural synonyms. The book turned out instead to be a startling screed that went on for two hundred pages. It listed all the words and concepts for layers of culture that essentially attested to and maintained wicked divisions between and amongst people. It named what kinds of bloodlines were acceptable, and which were not considered so; who could be counted amongst the elite; who could be dispensed with; and so on.

The work covered the exact words used to categorize who has this kind of social status, who does not; who speaks "the proper kind" of Spanish, versus those other millions of "rubes" who speak "lesser dialects" or different languages altogether. It detailed who belongs to the Jewish *Ladino* family; who belongs to the blood of the influential *España*; who belongs to *Los indios*, the Indian bloodline. There were endless differentiations about mixed blood peoples by quarters, halves, eighths and six-teenths. ¡Ay! It was exactly like the bellicose lexicon that grew up around the African American race and bloodlines in the United States and elsewhere, carrying the pejorative descriptions of "high yaller," "quadroon," "mulatto," and so on.

This judging of humans as though they are breed animals is not limited to any one country nor any one group. When you read the rolls of the old slave traders, whether they bought and sold human beings along the Yucatan Coast or along the Mississippi River, it is no different. With close attention to height, weight, condition of hair, skin, teeth, gait, and fertility, you might think you are reading about horses or cattle instead of humans. Nor is the effect different in many massacre logs, holocaust and prisoner of war camp records. The accounts of the predators are written as though they are describing wildebeests, insects, reptiles, or rodents and not people.

A drive to carry a dedicated humanity within oneself – is not just an urge, but a daily *decision* to strive toward compassion, sympathy, and consideration for humans, for living creatures. It constitutes a commitment to be concerned with striving to make social relations and structures – both interior and exterior – that will last, that will support and reflect those inner values.

To say this in the simplest way: a sense of personal humanity insists that one keep trying to see, with insight, boundaries, and mercy, the broad, inclusive spectrum of human behavior. As one studies the great humanitarians, one can see, as though via an X-ray, that *they* serve the humane architectures. These can be found within any sodality, society, or spiritual undertaking that is devoted to any of the Beatitudes; to the noble Eight-fold Path; to Mishnah; to the Ten Commandments; to the Five Pillars of Islam; or to the key principles of any belief system aimed toward seeing into, restraint, transformation and goodness.

Each of these humane architectures, in its own way, teaches a most simple philosophy at the fundament: that we and others, within reason, are just human beings struggling along trying to make our best contributions and hopefully with the least amount of harm in and to life. The instruction goes: that if we fail in some way, we are to regroup by fleeing into a wiser and more loving Force greater; that it behooves us to make effort to give repair; that if such cannot be made, that we will lay a memorial of some kind at that place where a precious chance was lost and can no longer be mediated; and that we will proceed thence with a new and different resolve to go forward and to try once again to live as humanely as we can. The humanity of the world rests on these kinds of commitments to action – commitments that are rooted in an understanding of our limitations and capacities for both evil and for goodness.

Through study and practice, these internal and worldly prompts to decency are strengthened and made conscious, more and more, over time. In working with many who have come back to life after a long wounding sojourn in hell, I have come to see that one's humanity is kept from fading by at least five means:

- Humanity is enlarged by inspiration from others.
- It is kept close through conscience.
- It is open to eruptions of promptings, reminders, and corrections from the Self on one's higher nature.
- It is maintained by societal support.
- It is responsive to social sanctions.

Humanity thus has checks and cross-checks so that it does not fail or be wrested away easily. If any of these five ways of keeping decency alive are missing or greatly weakened, one's humanity is vulnerable to becoming fragmented or to winding up missing.

### Humans Imagined As Degraded Beasts

As one reads through page after page of the histories of atrocities, enslavements, oppressions, grotesque injustices, inhumane negligences, and other oversights, it is clear that in order to do grave and purposeful harm to another without limit, one must somehow surrender one's humanity. These documents might give us insight into the normally private workings of an individual mind that is losing its ability to see others as truly human and instead is sliding toward what some call "evil outcome."

One particular oddity I have observed and studied in groups that are antagonistic toward one another, is that when mutual or unilateral humanity is lost or removed by the machinations of Evil, each group begins drawing literal, soulless pictures of the other. One will portray "the other" as subhuman in some way, and often negatively animal-like in particular. In historical documents, one often sees the same "bad animal" attributions and images made in written descriptions about anyone who does not fit the ruling power's mean.

Propagandists' posters and writings are also rife with images like these; the large teeth of the devouring wolf affixed to a human's face; the forked tail of the dragon snaking from a man's body; the ape-woman whore; the greedy pig; giant insects in human clothing portrayed as murderers of children; the man-serpent who strangles the innocent; the demon birds of prey with ethnic faces who feast on human flesh. The images and words depict these "non-human" humans as abandoning the young, being cunning, ready to strike, thieving, reproducing rapidly, sneaky, raiding, insatiable, invasive, infecting, diseased, not measuring up to their true potential, in need of whipping, beating, exiling, killing, as having no souls.

As I studied these materials of vitriolic exhortation I began to see how they have been used over the centuries by one group of persons to dehumanize another group. In them are found echoes from ancient times forward in their calls for slavery, for unjust wars, for the attrition of groups by harassment or starvation, or sporadic massacres; or by sending certain ones, but not others, to the front lines under impossible orders. Whether the materials call for the desecration of what "the other" holds most sacred, or for complete annihilation, the underlying archetypal motif often appears to be that of "cleansing" something.

By reducing "the other," to *a stain* that needs to be rubbed out, one may be lured into feeling righteously able to rationalize theft, torment, punishment, exclusion, enslavement, and the murdering of that life. In such a single-point schema incubated by contempt and fear of "the other," humane action is forbidden. This includes any means of meeting whatever behaviors might call for intervention with a just objectivity, moderation, mediation, negotiation, and other means that do not dehumanize others in the process of finding the best possible balances.

The old believers of my family used to say that one of Evil's favorite subterfuges is to infect the mind with the idea that doing something evil will banish Evil. This is a logic that is sometimes wrongly attributed to those in the military. In my work, long ago, with World War II, Korean War, and Viet Nam War soldiers at the Veteran's Administration hospitals, I learned that amongst warriors in real war, there is an honor code. There are things warriors in possession of their humanity during war will do, or not do, regardless – unless it is a clear matter of kill or be killed. Holding to one's humanity, even in war, has for aeons been considered honorable.

You may have noticed too, that in modern times there is sometimes a lack of humanity applied toward persons who have been sorely wounded. Some people do indeed think those who have suffered harsh wounds are tiresome. They can be heard to snap that "life is not fair," that people should just "get over it," "move on already," and "what are they whining about now?" They may voice an assortment of other bromidic distortions, and to be fair, these judgments may issue too easily from them for they themselves were once wounded and treated in the same harshly dismissive manner.

But for a genuine victim, that is, one who has been ambushed or intruded upon in some way, misled, and without adequate foreknowledge and without proper means of defense or support, and thereby injured, abandoned without resource, or forced to egregious conditions, or suddenly faced with a grievous loss – in all these matters, coldness can never help to mend this person, for it misses the point of meeting humanity with humanity, the very touch that allows one person to patiently attend to the suffering of another.


## Hope and Humanity

*Las curanderas* say the one thing that must never be done, no matter how angry, confused, disappointed, betrayed, alone a person feels, is to execute Hope. For oneself, or for another. Hope is thought by most to be an expectation of a cherished occurrence. But it is more than that. It is the capacity to dream aloud, to rearrange the molecules in a new way, to see what will and can fly, to experiment, to find one's way through, to make the way for others, to fall down perhaps, to be pushed down, but ever and ever and ever, *to come back.*

The repair of so much begins with clearly stated Hope. It is not out of fashion to do so. Hope, that small winged creature found at the bottom of Pandora's box after all the pestilences of evil, sickness, and hatred have flown out – Hope is that small red beating heart that allies with Humanity. Thus humanity, with hope intact, is strong, muscular in essence, but also delicate in spirit – tearable, mistreatable. We see in post-trauma work that if a wounded person rejects learning to heal her or himself, then both Hope and Humanity – toward self and often toward others too – will also flee for their lives.

They will dive away into the deepest recesses of the psyche to escape that once rich psychic terrain which is now every day being salted with antipathy, and sown with dust, and thus made into a wasteland. Far away then, Hope and Humanity will eke out their existence, nearly invisible, out of reach ... until one day ... if that land, wounded by fate and fallowed by bitterness, is ever ungated, Hope and Humanity will creep back, weeping over the devastations that have taken place in their absence.

But such ability to bear sorrow ought never be confused with weakness. Humanity and Hope, even in the most devastated person, with time, reassertion of conscience, mercy for self and others, with sustained ritual and care, can retake all that formerly lost ground again almost totally.

Yet, one has to ask why this ground is so regularly lost and what we can do about that? The recurring experience of people being tempted to inhumanity has made me wonder if there are innate and predictable patterns of behavior for the ordering of things in malignant ways, already positioned, spring-loaded and fully-formed in the psyche – similar to the archetypal nodes of complexes that Jung wrote about as being inborn. If these fragmenting patterns are not consciously suppressed, mediated, rendered harmless, or transformed *before the fact*, do they, indeed *must* they, leap to life in predicable patterns, wreaking destruction all around – as evidenced by repetitive events throughout history over the aeons?

Is every new generation that forgets, or is never told about these patterns or potentials for so easily assigning inhumanity to self and others, somehow directed by the unconsciousness of the generations that preceded them? Do we, in other words, act out our own ancestors' lack of development – as well as their demonstrated gifts? And, if so, we *must* teach the young better ways, and sooner, and with crystal clarity. Surely it is not meant for every new life on earth to keep repeating the worst of what can be, over and over again. Do we, as elders in the flesh for the next three generations owe self-development and the teaching of discernment and consciousness to those who have to come after us? I would propose *yes*. Though I am not certain about the complete details, I can envision something we can do for the present and future generations now.

Consider this image: somehow, before we are even weaned from our mother's milk, we have already had a gigantic net cast over us by culture. We find that if we poke our heads up, we are caught in one little square that says we can only occupy this one tiny space during a lifetime, and none other. There is often an extreme pressure to set aside multiplicity in thought and ways of being, and instead to make oneself "more manageable" by living in a one-sided way only. But what if one saw that the way of moving ideas into real actions is through the ability to consider multiple new strategies constantly – as water continues to find its way to flow regardless of the obstacles in its path? Then it would become one's absolute duty to transgress this only-one-square-to-a-person mentality any way one could, and to give serious thought to what it means to be fluid, rather than static, in thinking, discerning and feeling.

I do not find it a good thing to capture a person like an animal, and cause him or her to be unable to move, forbidden to learn more than one point of view. It appears that a plethora of ideas to choose from, rather than one unexamined and/ or solely repetitive way of thinking, allows the psyche to strengthen to its fullest humanity possible. The only time to make yourself small, is to make yourself sleek, so as to (often along with a group of like-minded others) leak under, leap over, flow into the interstices – or else make an end run around any wall built against the life of the soul. Revolution and evolution have arteries in common; they are both visionary and willing to behave, think and see differently than ever before. They do not agree to be limited to one generalized or generic way of realizing the world.... They carry new life and refuse to repress that treasure. Near perfect definitions of Hope and Humanity.

*Blame Can Be Used To Steal Consciousness Away Rather Than Augmenting It*

It is true that in order to set aright imbalances in psyche, relationship, or culture, the parts causing such have to be named with precision and brought under a measured control in some way. However, there is a potential snag waiting for naïve persons if they go no further than asserting blame, or generalizing such – whether for what has gone inconveniently wrong and for egregious and purposely twisted aggressions as well. My grandmother used to say, When the Devil hears the word "blame," he considers it an invitation to dinner. Why? Because traditionally, the Devil is the distorter of facts. He is said to be geared up to commandeer the proper blame "of one" in order to urge condemnation and murder "of the many" – just to be entertained by the ensuing bloodshed.

Throughout history, we have seen that malignant forces can seize on undifferentiated blame and use it to distort truth. A simple situation gone awry that only calls for inquiry, veracity, recompense and repair, can suddenly become an inquisition. Evil can inflate the spark of a flawed imagination into a conflagration. It can make "the true guilt of one" seem like "the guilt of all." If not held in check, it can, has, and will justify unleashing a call for punitive mayhem that will scorch the entire earth black as a cinder.

In trauma work, I find that it is more effective in most cases, for the aggrieved one to be held with care until eventually, when the time is right, they can consider many points of view about the nature of their worldly life, the hidden world of soul and psyche, and the meanings to be found in their own personal suffering. Such multiple viewpoints, including precision about blaming, offer a psychological heart-stance that builds a sturdy long-term sense of peace for and in the person who has suffered so. Each wounded person arrives at these kinds of evaluations and conclusions in his or her own way. The entire point however, is not to poison one's own heart because of the agonizing event that one managed to live through, but to insist that one will live again, not only capable of, but willfully blooming in every direction possible.

Likewise, the psyche in its usual individuation process, prompts the person to differentiate well and *then* act after suitable consideration. This is to counter the immaturity of the ego, which when unharnessed will often only pounce on and blurt out whatever first comes to mind. All persons on earth have often enough found themselves doing just that. That may succeed in marking the hazard on the map. But, it will not set up a thoughtful treatment of whatever the issue really is. When the psyche reacts in an unconsidered and one-sided way, it will not have given useful thought to what aspects of the situation, if any, ought be preserved because they are useful and good; which aspects might be transformed; which require distance; which must be ejected; and which must just be let go with the fullest heart one can muster.

For some years now I have been doing an anecdotal study of how we as humans attribute blame for "evil." I can see that to make a complaint about a state of affairs, or to name a wound a wound indeed, is not enough to mediate and mend whatever has lost its vitality or shape. To solely name evil, but to not do something to lessen its effects, tends to register in the psyche as impotence. To name a broken leg a broken leg is almost nothing, if the leg is not also set into a cast for healing.

As you can see from the preceding pages, I have been especially interested in how the blame for evil can be wrongly projected, or too broadly projected, onto either those of the so-called ruling or dominant group, or onto those belonging to the sub-dominant group – and for the same reason, because the members of one group simply do not like, or else fear the members of the other. There is also the matter of individuals belonging to a single group aggressing and trespassing upon one another within the group itself. There is no doubt that through-out history there have been true evils loosed between groups and between individual members of the same group by these and other means.

Studying their patterns, we can see that within many group structures there are provided many over-ripe opportunities for scapegoating, various kinds of assault, and extermination of "the stranger." Reading the diaries of dictators and madmen, such as Hitler's prison writings and Ted Kaczynski's materials, as well as the writings that certain despots, like Idi Amin, caused their subordinates to write about them, which are filled with an evil braggadocio about their bosses' horrors and tortures of others – one is struck by two things. The first is how a dislike of "the other," over time, progresses relentlessly from a daily dislike to an abhorrence without limits. The second is how the now despised "other" is then projected onto as irreparably deficient, and thereby deserving of the worst maltreatment imaginable.

Amongst documents from various civil strifes, I have studied the diaries of *conquistadores* such as Bernal Diaz and others who overran, or accompanied those who overran, various cultures. I have studied the 15th century witch-hunter's bible, the *Malleus Maleficarum*, The Hammer of Malevolent Influence, also sometimes called The Witch's Hammer. Perusing such documents, we can see across the aeons how their authors nervously or violently assigned blame to various groups and ideas in ways that ended up causing slaughter after slaughter.

We also see that the ultimate annihilation of these increasingly despised groups marked as detritus to be strewn away, did not start out in a massively violent way. The hatred ultimately expressed began only by throwing off a few sparks. A few condemning words here and there. Evil projections made. Subsequent suspicions based on those false attributions. Innuendos made up out of whole cloth. Whispers creating distrust and envy. More supposings. Rumors purposely spread. False accusations made. One's own lust or covetousness ignored. Muddy absolutes insisted upon. Unrighteous rage unleashed. Not till others joined in these expressions, via collusion in these sentiments or simply out of fear, or via silence, did the spark of fear be cooked into an incendiary hatred that exploded, setting a fire that could jump from person to person, and not be easily stopped.

In colloquial terms, the process of how such a destructive psychic eruption came into being was once termed "mob psychology" – systemic cultural infection via an idea transferred from the one to the many. Each one so infected, then passed it on to one or more vulnerable others, so that in aggregate, all lost their wits together, and acted unconscionably. Then afterward, many sat in the midst of the resulting rubble, wondering how did this all happen in the blink of an eye? How did such far-reaching ruin come to be? But ancestral people would say, perhaps there is another factor, one that is made insanely happy when all evil is attributed only to humans. There is a saying in curanderismo, that if you scratch the devil's smile, you will find behind it unmitigated rage.

Recently, I studied a day of CNN reportage on television, and another day of MSNBC and still another day of Fox News. I listened to all the ways our contemporaries infer, attribute, and accuse. I took note of what kinds of projected stereotypes were held up in scorn and which ones were held up to worship, as though both were unquestionably worthy of such. I noted which topics seemed most often to cause outbreaks of screeching over-talking.

I have to say that although there are a good number of those who broadcast with dynamic equanimity, far too much of what I heard sounded like a long road trip with four little tattletale preschoolers in the back seat: "You started it first," and "He touched me first mom, he did it first!" Can such childish perseverations without variation possibly be called "discussion" and real reportage? These "entertainments," as some call such intervals, might seem humorous, if they weren't also a seeming prodromal syndrome of spark-throwing that can, without anyone meaning to, attract and rally massive amounts of psychic tinder from the culture.

When a collective is under great duress it is truly the time for, as they say, cooler heads to prevail. As Jung noted in his 1938 interview, "Diagnosing the Dictators," when a culture suffers from loss and lack of economic work, deflation of its sense of superiority, when it lacks its usual ability to influence outcomes that affect the personal economic and social lives of its citizenry, there rises up a collectively unconscious desire for a "savior" who will reverse all these events and make life "right" again. History is filled with the stories of cultures that chose to gratify these unrealized longings – by choosing a predator to lead, one whose inhumanity created an uncontrollable and profligate blaze that went out of control till nothing of honor nor compassion was left standing.

Cultures do not blame cultures. The proclivity to condemn an entire swath of culture – interior or exterior – is assignable to individuals rather than assignable to a nation. Nations cannot act. Individuals act. One of my uncles who was held in a Russian forced labor camp, used to say, "Evil has no nationality, no country." The issue of undifferentiated blame is a serious one. The elders in my old-country family taught, If you see devils everywhere you look, you won't see the real one when it arrives.

As we touched on earlier, it appears that when we feel threatened, or fear we may lose control, or see Evil in everything, that one of the first things we may do is attempt to order it all by "buck-shotting" the target. This causes the ego to feel it has really done some hard work. The problem is, that if we stop at blame without differentiating carefully, then there may never be a required, merciful and useful emendation, nor a lasting resolution.

The "attributions" in the following *el canto*, chant-poem, are ordered as an oratorical rant. In curanderismo, this kind of "rant" is not a brittle bombast, but a calling out into the world, a "naming" intervention used to elevate consciousness about the issues under investigation.

The following ascriptions have often been incorporated into the rallying cries for profound bloodshed and falls from basic human decency throughout history. They are found in various

historical documents from and about roughly 50 C.E. forward
to the present.

## In The Kingdom of the Blind, The One-Eyed Man is King

Blame the foreigners, blame the time-honored enemy
whoever that is,
blame apathy, blame atheism, blame decadent art,
blame media, blame pestilence, blame the lack of propitiation
to the proper gods,
blame indecency, blame disobedient children,
blame immigrants, blame the military.
Blame it on the old men who send young men to war,
blame it on those lacking manhood ritual so that war
is somehow seen as pristine.
Blame it on "devils" of various skin colors,
blame it on not being able to think clearly,
blame it on whoever the new pagan is,
blame it on people not taking responsibility,
blame it on the turn of the millennium.
Blame it on the peril of crossing into a new year,
blame it on the clergy,
blame it on those who are watching and being ineffective,
blame it on those who are not watching
and busy having sybaritic fun.
Blame it on the intelligentsia, blame it on astrology,
blame it on biological reason.
Blame it on bigotry, despotism, racism, sexism, adultism,
blame it on the lack of feeling in teachers,
blame it on the lack of rigor in education,
blame it on fervency, on zealots, blame it on nature,
blame it on books.
Blame it on education, blame it on ignorance, blame it on the police.

Blame it on the laws, blame it on the poisoning
of something valuable,
blame it on the poor.
Blame it on the rich, blame it on the monarchy,
blame it on the relics, and on the rights others hold dear.
Blame it on being too personal,
blame it on not being personal enough,
blame it on being progressive,
blame it on not being progressive enough,
blame it on scientific explanations that fall short,
blame it on the dead, on dark people, on light people,
on native people, on non-native people,
on those with ambition, on those with vision.
Blame it on the previous generations, administrations, and leaders.
Blame it on the landowners and the landlords.
Blame it on the peasants, blame it on abandonment,
blame it on rejection, blame it on suffocation.
Blame it on writers, blame it on hedonism, blame it on sin.
Blame it on the dreamers, blame it on Christians, blame it on Jews,
blame it on Arabs, on Muslims, on Buddhists, on Jainists,
blame it on piety, blame it on sloth.
Blame it on selfishness, blame it on guilt, on vulnerability,
on sensitivity.
Blame it on ennui, blame it on the end of the world,
blame it on the decline of civilization as we know it.
Blame it on the anti-environmentalists, blame it on pollution,
blame it on nihilism,
existentialism, Marxism, Catholicism, on inborn antagonism.
Blame it on those who find everything repulsive,
blame it on those who love,
blame it on fleas and rats and animals one finds revolting,
blame it on greed and on scorn and on the homeless.
Blame it on malice and vengeance, blame it on dancing.
Blame it on God needing to jolt families out of bad living
by killing their children,
blame it on cruelty, on needing to provide examples.

Blame it on laziness.
Blame it on Frankensteinian inventors who did not realize
what they were inventing, or else, did.
Blame it on a city group or a nation, a bad part of town,
blame it on imports, on spices, on ships unaffiliated,
on goods, on the workers. Blame it on stupidity, on weakness,
on lack of foresight, on sickness, on mental depravity,
on mental illness.
Blame the mindset, the paradigm,
the *zeitgeist*, the spirit of the times.
Blame it on the property holders, blame it on the pop culture,
blame it on sex,
blame it on guns, blame it on "the primitive."
Blame it on mothers, on fathers, on moralists.
Blame it on the occult, on Divine vengeance,
on belonging to this ethnic group, or that one.
Accuse any one, any tribe, any gathering or group
of being, comprising or giving comfort to the Evil one,
of being spawn of the Devil, of killing the children
and drinking their blood.
Blame it on the empire, on the "not-empire," blame it on politicians,
blame it on management, on mullahs, on crime, on the Pope,
on gypsies, on homosexuals, on women, on men, on children,
on teenagers, on historians, on cars, on modernity, on elders.
All of these. Any of these. And more. Blame them all.


Blame is different from discernment. As you can see from
the preceding piece, blaming can be a kind of baleful and hostile
set of assertions that often take only one side vociferously, as
one seeks "to build a case against" and viciously so.

Discernment, however, does not interest itself in trying to
be "right," or in making itself feel utterly safe, or in winning
something of great value to the ego that may be of only dubious
value to the soul. People cannot repair themselves or anything

else by being inhumane. The soul simply will not agree to it, and will not thrive in it. Anyone who says it does, is misspeaking for the soul. Discernment is the magnetic compass that points to the true north of the Self.

The Baba Yaga is the fearsome Mother of all of Creation in Russian, Slavic, and Eastern European mythos. She sets the naïve girl Vasalisa to picking out tiny poppy seeds from a huge pile of dirt. She does this to teach the girl to look carefully at small things that resemble but are actually quite different from one another. Differentiating means to inquire, to see what remedy can be applied to each issue.

It asks what effect can be had by following through in a conscientious manner. By not flinching away from calling a spade a spade. By not being stopped by paradox, but rather bearing the burden of opposites willingly, and going on to the best of one's ability. Discernment does not do its job by playing, "but on the other hand," endlessly. It advances by not sticking only to philosophical favorites, but by remaining truly open to new approaches. By finding a principle that applies and sticking to it. By measuring its discriminations with and against this principle. It asks, though there need be in some cases, complete condemnation, if there can also be any merciful consideration. Can there be any conciliation? Or is a partitioning necessary?

Carrying more than one point of view changes the language. When language is changed, more solutions and mediations become clear. In the section that follows, I will tell a story that has sustained me often in my work with those who have been badly harmed. The story offers an idea about ways in which healer/helpers might think about such matters within themselves. The exegesis of the story in no way excuses, overlooks or acquits perpetrators of egregious acts. Rather, it highlights how deeply the psyche can consider and respond to the whole picture and not just to one part only.

The Monkey's Heart: *Examining Evil as Both an Outside and Inside Phenomena*

One can be driving toward goodness when all of a sudden the realization dawns that one has forgotten or strayed from the primary principle of one's discernment. Is the cause of going off track internal or external, or both? I think it is valuable to see a correction to one's trajectory in life in the same way that one might question a dream, inquiring of its subjective meaning and its objective import, both. And to see which one or if both of these, carries more meaning and momentum for the life that dreamt them.

Many of you no doubt have heard me speak of Arwind Vasavada, whom I affectionately called Vasavada. He has passed away now, but was my analyst and my teacher for twenty years. He was from Bombay. He and his wife were with Gandhi in the *Satyagraha* movement, which is sometimes misunderstood as only "passive resistance." But, as Gandhi explained it, Satyagraha is "a weapon of the strong," not the weak. It strives for a state of absolute absence of violence first *within oneself,* and then in the outer world. It believes in the fierceness of truth, gently given.

Later, Vasavada trained directly with Jung in Zurich. I met Vasavada twenty-five years ago when I first began my analytical studies. He had said one thing to me that bonded me to him instantly. After I had gone through a rather – and this is a kind way of saying it – *rigorous* application interview, he came up to me as I wandered, dazed. He said so simply, "It is alright; there are two of us." He meant that there was something unusual that he had, that he thought perhaps I might have also. And it was, I think, the storytelling function. We sometimes joked about this being the fifth function, beyond Jung's grid of four functions: thinking, feeling, intuition and sensation.

Over the years I spent with Vasavada, he had a very peculiar way of doing psychoanalysis. If you had a little problem, then you would have lunch together. Perhaps you would have Basmati rice that he fixed for you personally. Or you might go to one of the tiny restaurants in his old Indian neighborhood, where there was a deaf waiter, and no matter what I would order, something different than what I had ordered would appear. In this way, I came to taste every last thing on the menu, including one time just a plate of anise licorice.

But, if you had a big problem, then you would have *dinner* together. Vasavada would make a fragrant tea and put it in a battered melamine cup so hot you couldn't hold it for a long time. You had to lean over it without touching it with your fingers and just take sips. And you would have a special boiled egg in a dark yellow curry sauce that was cooked just right. And more sauces that sometimes smelled at first like perfume rather than food, and hot, hot naan bread with fresh garlic cloves held in place by melted ghee. And so you would have repast together. I was as filled by his humble service as by the food and his words.

He was the first soul to whom I ever revealed that I was pressed into taking accent reduction classes as a child in order to learn to speak a more standard English. "Oh yes, yes," he nodded violently, "me too!" "You too?" I marveled. Well, he meant certain people throughout his life sometimes took it upon themselves to correct his English. He was the first one that I could really open my heart to and say, "I come from a tradition that does not fit easily into the nets that I have been offered in this culture."

And he would say, "It will be alright." And then launch into his favorite discourse on the ego. He would say it like this in his beautiful high-pitched East Indian accent: "The ego is like a little monkey, do you see? And it loves every bright, shiny object.

Yes. And it is all right, just right. Because it is the ego, after all. It is all right. You are not to punish the ego. But not to follow it either."

In my work over the years with those so often unexpectedly garroted by horrendous events in life, I found that in order to stay upright, stay alive, be renewed, one had to have a guiding image – whatever it might be for each soul; to each his or her own. At least one, if not several, would be good. But these have to make sense to much more than just the little monkey ego alone.

The following story might provide a guiding image suitable for some of you, too, as it has for me. The image is this …

Once, there was a monkey who lived at the edge of an ocean. And in that ocean was a shark.

Every day the monkey came bouncing through the trees, pulling down fruit and eating it. The shark saw this and thought, "I am so sick of fish. I think I would like to have some of that fruit the monkey has. But now, come to think of it – that monkey looks mighty tasty to me too. Yum, monkey meat to eat."

So the shark swam up to the shore and spoke to the monkey, saying, "Oh Monkey, could you reach up and throw down to me some of your fruit, please?"

"I would be happy to do that," said the monkey. And he jumped up and pulled down the fruit and gave it to the shark.

"Oh yum, yum. That fruit is so gooood!" said the shark.

So, every day, the shark came to the edge of the water. And every day, the monkey pulled down the fruit for the shark. And they began to speak to each other. Then they began to share their breakfasts together. The shark would tell the monkey all about the shark kingdom under the sea. And the monkey became more and more curious about that kingdom under the waters.

Finally one day the monkey asked, "Well, Shark, could you take me down to that place, that kingdom of the sharks? It sounds sooo interesting."

The shark agreed immediately, "Why yes. I would be happy to take you there. Get on my back and I will take you right now."

So the monkey got on the shark's back, and Shark swam and swam and swam out and out and out into the center of the sea. When they were in the very middle of the ocean, the shark said, "You know, Monkey, I forgot to mention something to you."

"What is that?" asked the monkey.

"Well, the king of the sharks is very sick. And there is only one thing that will cure him."

"Oh? And what is that?"

"It is the heart of a monkey."

The monkey said, "Oh, I understand completely. But, you know, you should have told me that before we left. Because I left my heart back at the shore. But, I *do* have great sympathy for the king of the sharks, and if you had told me about his terrible condition, I would have brought my heart with me."

The shark made such a fast circle back toward land that the monkey's tail unfurled and his ears flew behind him. The shark plowed into shore and the monkey jumped up into the trees and ran away. With his heart intact. Forever and ever.

... *The way this tale is told at the end is like this:*
*The teller says,*
*"And at that time, I was the monkey.*
*And at that time, I was the shark.*
*And at that time, I was the sick king who needed the heart of the monkey."*

And so the story ends with a new beginning ...

This story, in part, puts forth the paradigm and the paradox of evil. The predicament about "explaining" such things as evil intent, fault, hunger, and decency wind as subtext throughout the story. Vasavada and I never analyzed nor amplified this tale in the archetypal manner usually associated with analytical psychology, and I would like not to do that now, but just leave it on your heart as you think about the ways that evil has perhaps presented itself to you during your lifetime – and the ways it might be mediated – transforming it sometimes, fleeing from it other times, but always striving to outwit it.

Through my work in the world, I have certainly seen abject Evil up close. I have had to count more than once the cavities in Death's back teeth. I have found in the multiple points of overview the tale offers, some hope each time for the most balancing and fruitful way of seeing where to go, what to do next.

When I have worked with people so severely wounded that one could say they already have been forced to surrender their bodies and spirits to the sick king of the sharks, the questions that are most productive and poignant, are ones like these: The story wonders out loud, what might motivate one to keep one's own heart? and for what real purpose? What might motivate one to steal what is not given freely? What waning, sick thing might hunger for more and more living flesh or living spirit? What exactly constitutes a balanced attitude of understanding in each of these matters?

The questions to ask are made even more clear at the end of the tale: How, where when, why am I the monkey? How, where, when, why am I the shark? How, where, when, why am I the sick king? How and where can I be the new beginning?

Binah: *A Special Kind of Understanding, Over and Above the Usual*

There appear to be degrees to Evil, that is, degrees of under-mining, misleading, and harming the hearts and souls of oneself and others. The measurements may, in a final analysis, be simi-lar to the weighing mechanisms used in variants of the justice system: 1st degree, premeditated and purposeful, thought out, enacted with clear intention to harm another; 2nd degree, non-premeditated, but resulting in grave or vicious harm; and the 3rd degree, which has come to mean subjecting a person to torment in order to extract something from him or her and/or force something onto that person, or to close some option off entirely.

There are also degrees of *understanding* regarding such matters as hearing from evil, reversing evil, and mediating evil. Overall in these matters, to come to your own conclusions, I suggest to you this moderating idea from the Hebrew. I sometimes study Kabbalah in relationship to curanderismo because they have a common root mother. Curanderismo was brought, in part, to the new world via the Sephardic women's' healing practices from Spain. These were then added to greatly by the later Indian and then African / German / French / Chinese / Japanese cultures brought by slavery, colonization, and immigration, into the Americas.

One word from Kabbalah that I find great moment in is *binah*. Binah means understanding – but of a certain kind. In exegesis, the concept of binah carries the idea of adding extreme depth to a normally more superficial human perception. Binah has to do with depth and intensity of experience; with one's ability to describe and to acutely remember those experiences, to be able to recall them, parse them, glean them, put what is useful to use – to not just archive them, or allow them to simply dry to hay and straw.

I would put it to you this way: Imagine a bowl of water. Imagine you say to yourself, "I wish to understand water." You are not in *extremis*, not starving, water is abundant. So, you pass your hand through the water. You say, "Ah yes, wet." "Ah yes, cold" – or "warm" – but you do not examine the water further. You remember this experience afterward, but vaguely. It may have been interesting, but not have made much of an impression. This is one form of understanding water.

But, binah implies that to understand water you would have to not only pass your hand through the water in the bowl. You would have to use water in many different ways, to test it, trade it, pour it through matter, find many of its uses. You would *also* have to go to the edge of the ocean and dive in. And not only that, but allow yourself also to go out into the unknown currents, to fight your way up and down those watery aisles, and perhaps nearly drown. Then, after all that, as you now report back, you will have *understanding* of water. That is *binah*, an understanding that can be put to far more use, a kind of depth that drives one to action, one which matches up in intensity equal to what has been experienced and learned by immersion.

This experience of engagement with something real and at depth, allows one to know and to act – a most powerful combination. It allows one to see many viewpoints and still take steps with purpose. Wholesale blaming with no real action to mediate what has gone wrong can, too often, be a form of, well, only putting the hand in the water, swishing it around, and then leaving, saying, "There, that was water alright."

As fragile as our abilities often are to realize things before they are upon us; as frail as reason can sometimes be to find a way through to answers that accurately hold the mind, spirit, and soul to their true and stated works and needs; as easy as it is to sometimes only find the fault instead of the bounty; as easy as it is to be only contentious or ambitious and not just able – those who have been to hell and back still find it worthy to start every new day vowing once again to reverse or moderate the least of what we are. They draw back their bows in the aim to live out, if not the best, than the better of ourselves. In this way, they press themselves to develop more binah. Pursuit of binah is a practice that builds a Self-philosophy that can both transform and sustain life – one that does not punitively withhold new life from that which so sorely needs it and has capacity for it.

## Tikkun Olam: *A Community of Hearts*

From watching so many good and decent persons at work in the world, I have seen how conscious efforts to go father than just passing one's hand through water are truly humane attempts to be noble. There is a drive in the psyche toward such nobility, one that is good to examine closely. A noble thought or idea can inspire one to action, can cause one to immerse fully in the timeless ways of being human, and to bring something of use out of one's struggles there.

In the other direction, there lies another kind of strength. John Beebe had told me the following, and I agreed with its goodness: "Helplessness is a hallmark of a person who cares." Helplessness is the sensation of feeling or thinking that one is profoundly unable to imagine what to do next; that one cannot think of what to do that would aid; that one is having trouble about how to even begin to deconstruct into parts the magnitude of what it will take to create something constructive, to turn the situation around. "Well, what can I do? Oh my. I can hardly do anything, hardly anything." And the would-be helper's heart is then even more troubled and sad.

But buried in that helplessness is an eternal recognition that there is much that one can do. In the rural community where I grew up, sometimes the fields and gardens we depended on were ravaged by summer hail storms that came down sideways like icy monsoons. Afterward, in the "snow" that was left on the ground, everyone would come out to start lifting and repairing whatever could be saved. My grandmother and others would bend down and start cutting the wounded leaves away, staking the bent and broken plants, putting mud poultices on certain stems, bandaging with gauze others, patting and singing and talking to the plants. Some family member or other would usually be in tears, and another one so angry, or both. My grandmother would say to them, "Any little thing you can do will help. Work now."

In Hebrew, there is a beautiful phrase that I think of as a complementary concept to *binah*. It is *tikkun olam*. It means *the repair of the world's soul*. Imagine the entire world in aggregate as having a soul. Imagine it is our work to reach out to repair the part of the world soul that is within our reach – the edge that belongs to self and the corresponding part that belongs to the world. The key words are "to repair that which is within your reach."

So we ask ourselves, "What is within my reach?"

I am! I am within my own reach.

I initially thought what Jung is reported to have said about "speaking out" might have, as we say in the northwoods, sold too cheap. As the story goes, when people came to him in the 1930s saying, "Speak out about the fascist party," he is supposed to have said, amongst other things, the equivalent of, "I will deal with this evil inside myself."

I heard this story in my late twenties when I first entered psychoanalytic training. I had just managed to move away to a little bit better economic and education level. I was no longer a welfare mother. I was no longer living in a neighborhood where I feared for the life of my family and myself every day. Hearing Jung's response to such a serious question, I remember thinking, "Well, yes. Just tell the guy down the street, who is not only armed with weapons, but who is also an addict, who would kill you at the drop of a hat – tell him that you're dealing with your "inner drug addict" – and that somehow that is going to mediate everything!"

But then, I found other concepts in his work that elucidated his statement and gave it rich meaning. My adult entry into Jung's work as a very young woman had come about by reading what in my opinion is his most sociological work, *Civilization in Transition*, Volume X in the Collected Works. There I was able to take in another idea that I knew to be electrifyingly true – expressed by Jung in a way that was very simple and thereby very powerful. He said, "Individuation brings you closer to the world, not father away."

I understood this to mean a demand for action, a statement that individuating souls have a moral obligation to involve themselves with the woes and worries, the constructions and triumphs of the world, each in his or her own way. The process of individuation urges one to examine one's own psyche, *and also to act* in the outer world one's greatest consciousness, without cease – or else to feel ill by having done *nothing* in ways that matter to "The Measurer," the Self.

We can explicate Jung's idea of individuation as something that brings a self closer to the world, as giving no permission for us to retreat from the world, nor to go and hide, whether out in the cave or up in the ivory tower. I understood his inference: that people who are doing individuation work are so valuable, that their lives *no longer belong to them alone*. It ought be said, and often, that we literally owe some portion of our lives to *tikkun olam,* repair of the world soul. We literally owe some dedicated circuitry of the heart to the repair of the cultural milieu, each in our own way.

If "the best of the best," if the most knowing, the most powerful, the most wise, the most kind, the most heartful – of which there are millions of such souls on earth – if all these were to stay away from the mending looms, then what chance would there be to effect change, to repair the unraveling of the world's soul that is within our reach? Forever and always may the venerable 1st century BCE Rabbi Hillel's gentle but insistent voice from his Mishnah 14, hover over the world – especially the last phrase: "... If not now, when?"

## Santa Sombra

Long ago, during my Jungian studies in preparation to become a psychoanalyst, but also previous to that in my developmental psych training, my grandmothers, aunts and other relatives from the old countries were still alive. I would go home or talk to them on the telephone. I would tell them everything I was learning in the analytic seminar. And they would all correct it all – especially about dream analysis.

Once I told them that a supervising professor had said my patient's dream of sailing across the ocean on a violin was a sign of the patient's unrealistic expectations in life. Once again, the grandmothers morphed into creatures with those scary reptilian eyes, and said that one could cross *any* ocean on the strings of *any* violin, a thousand times if necessary. They said that the strings of the violin are made of tough sinew that will support the soul to row across any divide. So perhaps I have a dual training: a classical psychoanalytic training, and the training of the *abuelitas*, that is – "the psychoanalytical training of the grandmothers" as well.

Amongst my family people in most directions, there is hardly a one who is not a refugee, displaced person, deportee, forced labor camp survivor. I come from and grew up with those who went through a great travail in order to remain alive, and to arrive and stay in America. In our family we have a deep gratitude toward the United States for these reasons. That was why, regarding the hard road back from having been deeply wounded, the old people would assert a philosophy that had these tenets: When you have a great difficulty on the face of this earth, when things go very wrong, then you no longer belong to yourself anymore. You now belong to your whole community. When you face Evil, you are facing it not only for yourself, but for all who live, all who once lived, and for all who will one day be born.

And: You have a heart. Inside it is an entire community of beating hearts. How you act in this moment will affect those hearts for good or for ill. Those hearts let you know you are not alone. Their strength is your strength. Your condition will be reflected in them. You will face the travail together in some way, whether those other hearts are known to each other, or to you, or not; whether they ever meet one another or not; whether they ever overtly speak to each other, or not. In the midst of travail, all the hearts beating and flaring congregate in some way, to light the common darkness.

And if you are lucky, you might meet one of these great blazing hearts when and where you least expect it. One that carries you as you carry others. And this one will show up in out of the way places and act in ways usually reserved for angels. And then afterward, this out-of-the-ordinary person will often fade far away.

We have a concept for this in curanderismo. It is a force to be respected. It too, colonizes people, but unlike Evil that subverts humanity, this force augments humanity. This force causes human beings to occasionally act, at private and public levels, in extra-ordinary ways that are better than what they seem capable of at most other times. This force is called *El viento de bondad,* literally, the wind of Goodness. It too trolls the world, looking for likely apertures through which it can cause decency to be lived out in real time.

There is a second concept that is derived from this force of Goodness. It is not one to be bandied about as an intriguing principle, or to be peered at as a curiosity, or to be played around with intellectually. It is a concept that contains a powerful force. It is the might of *Santa Sombra.* Santa Sombra translated into English would be something like Saint Shadow. Saint Shadow, the Lighted Darkening One. The way this is spoken about in curanderismo is that such is a state of being, a way of living that one aspires to. In this tradition, one is supposed to strive toward the essential attitudes represented by Santa Sombra, to be of enough light to cast a shadow. I will explain this further.

I know this may sound odd, because in Jungian psychology "the shadow" is proffered as a different concept, but here, the obscurity of Santa Sombra, means the ability to draw a darkness over one's own good actions, specifically to have a special kind of lack of memory. This deliberate non-remembering associated to Santa Sombra serves a unique role.

Recall for a moment, a time when you may have met a person who suffers from lack of conscience. In the lexicon of psychology these mysterious conditions are called by fixed monikers without much ruth: sociopathy, character disorder, psychopathy, non-empathic narcissism, and other terms. A person who has this condition of soul can also be described as suffering from a "loss of memory" – about caring for more than their own appetites, for instance. They register no remembered feeling-toned responses to whatever they thought, said or did yesterday, last week, or in the last moment. Persons so afflicted cannot even consider how they might affect, help, hurt or harm another soul. They appear not so much to be carrying a defense as living a single deficient reality. In many such persons, by my sights, at bottom appears no psychologically based cause, but rather their conditions seem to derive from some kind of organic brain chemical disorder. If this lack of memory is chemicalogical in etiology instead of wanton, it may be that some day, a cure for senility, Alzheimer's and late adult onset of dementia will give some astute clues to abject lack of conscience as well – this being defined here as a deep forgetting about principles in regard to so much that is precious.

Santa Sombra is not without conscience, but is, in fact, of heightened conscience. Santa Sombra enacts directions that are said to arrive in a great wind blowing suddenly through what might be called the heart/soul axis, that which maintains conscience and regard for life. This phenomenon appears to flow through an ordinary human being as wholly impeccable force passing through a wholly imperfect human being, which – in that moment – causes an ordinary person to act more largely than his or her usual self normally allows.

I know you may have had such experiences yourself. Analysts, artists, orators, preachers, teachers, healers, and others responding to a person or situation that needs them, have, since time immemorial, on occasion felt prompted to suddenly say things, enact things, that are greater and better than what they have normally been able to conceive – and often just at the right and rather astonishing time. In curanderismo, we would call this experience entering the realm of Santa Sombra.

This experience is one of being filled with something that is wiser, more insightful, even somewhat more dangerous than we usually are. Santa Sombra is a truth teller and is believed to have supra-ordinary grasp of the moment, *and* a sudden visionary glimpse of the future *as it will be* if nothing is done. At the same time, Santa Sombra also sees the situation *as it can be* if something *is* launched right now. This is a vision that is considered eminently useful. We must underline the word *useful*. To find what *usefully* contributes to the repair of psyche, soma, and community is the work of Santa Sombra.

The aspect of "forgetting" that is required in Santa Sombra's milieu is that the person so infused, afterwards, "forgets" what he or she did that was of help or good, and instead just travels onward. The Santa Sombras of the world do not dwell on what they just did; instead they overlook what they did that was so useful. Santa Sombras are called, collectively, Saint Shadow because it is said that as they walk onward, they allow their shadows to trail over those they just passed. The falling of the gentle shadow wipes out Santa Sombra's memory tracks of what grace has just occurred. Santa Sombra does not look back, just continues to walk forward.

The idea is that one walks through the "part of the world that is within one's reach," and enacts in one's best ways whenever and whatever one can — the way you clasp someone's hand, say some words because you see a heart suffering, or place a story on another's heart that they can feast on for a few days, that will sustain some part of them that is very hungry and without. You remember that a person needs to be seen as a human, just as a human. But when these matters are useful, one then forgets, on purpose. No going home and allowing oneself to be caught up in some self-congratulatory complex over it all. "Ah I did good today, I really did good. I did this and I did ..." No, no. Santa Sombra doesn't think about those things. Santa Sombra just keeps walking.

Santa Sombra lets its shadow cover people in order to protect, engender, and help them. I have seen many Santa Sombras who have helped many others.... They were most often the most unassuming but also massively merciful beings who suddenly stepped out from the side of the road to give water or nourishment, to save or help, or to shout Beware!

I have been helped in my life by several Santa Sombras too. You never know how and in what condition Santa Sombra will show up. My own have been drunkards and poor people, dying people, children, hags, old people, and crazy people. They have on occasion been persons who live on the planet Corporate and more often those who come from the planet Artful. Most of all, in some way, always, they have been, I think, powerful poets with blood red hearts in one way or another. They have always, in my experience, appeared in disguise.


*The Santa Sombra Is The One Who is Least Anticipated, Appearing Where Least Expected, and Who Does What Is Least Imagined: Glory To God In The Highest*


There is a person I met in recent time, who continues to be an exemplar of Santa Sombra for me. People often ask me about my work at Columbine High School. Much remains to be said about what occurred there, for it takes a good twenty years after such a tragic event for all the stories to be truly told; to see outcomes; to evaluate what really transpired, the hows and whys it took place, what happened to the souls next, and then next. But memory of one of the Santa Sombras there remains with me.

My experience at Columbine High, in toto, impressed me further about the valor of teachers, and also about the power of coincidence, *memoria*, and synchronicity. I had moved to Littleton three months prior to the massacre. I'd lived in another city for most of three decades and wanted more than anything to see the sky again. I had lived in Littleton once before, almost thirty years previous, raising family there. As a result I knew the lay of the semi-rural land well. So in 1999, I found a small town house where I could look out and see the beautiful sky.

On April 20th 1999, one of the staff members in my office told me that there was a report on the radio about some trouble at some schools west of town. In a bit, as I was sitting at my desk writing, I suddenly heard a repetitive noise, thap-a-pa, thap-a-pa, thap-a-pa … I looked up into the sky, this beautiful sky that I had moved my life to be near, and it was filled with helicopters! So many helicopters in the sky. ABC, NBC affiliates, Flight For Life Air Lift, Police helicopters, circling around and around like raptors over the land parcel where Columbine High School sits next to a park.

I turned on the television. There was a lockdown at every school in the vicinity. Something particularly bad was coming down at the high school. Shooters were believed to be on the roof, maybe out in the surrounding fields, and also inside the building where there were at least 900-plus children and teachers. Police from many different districts were responding. All aid was called into action: ambulances, firemen, all helpers were to respond immediately.

I ran hot in my car. Blockades were being thrown up everywhere. I abandoned my car and followed the back ways I knew from having lived there so long ago. I ran on foot down the creek bed and then through the backs of housing developments I had known so well long ago. I came to Leawood Elementary School, where my youngest child had gone to school many years before. Now it was at that building that hysterical parents were gathered, waiting to know the glory of which children were still alive, the deep anxiety and hope about those who had been wounded, and the utter devastation of learning which children had been lost utterly.

The points the psyche remembers after times of disaster are often unpredictable and dream-like. Many of my memories of that first day and evening that went by with people sprinting, screaming, weeping, running, leaping, staggering, pacing, falling down and falling deathly silent in all directions, since then sometimes play in my mind in slow motion – several families receiving the worst possible news and their immediate reaction, as though physically gut-shot themselves; children playing hooky that day were not accounted for until late into the day and night; their searching parents fainting with fear and sorrow; the truant children finally appearing; their parents falling upon them with the most completely broken-open love imaginable....

What happened at Columbine High School that day has a long "back story." The events that would take place had been building for months, even years, previous. The crime revolved around two young men – about whom, some insist we can never discover why they carried out their monstrous attacks. But this, in my opinion from looking at the facts in depth, is not so. It is so very comprehensible, I think. It takes adding up a number of specific factors – certain psychological ones, some spiritual, some physical, some social, that all came together in one place, like the "perfect storm" that discharges itself in the most damaging ways imaginable.

On that day, these two young men, beautiful physically and smart, came into the school with propane bombs in big duffel bags. They were stronger than usual, being filled as they were with the adrenalin of their idea of doom. They carried the incendiaries into the school cafeteria, knowing that soon that large room would be filled with close to a thousand also beautiful and smart young men and women. The two young men brought in assault rifles and sawed off shotguns. They brought in twisted minds and twisted hearts. And the rest is the saddest of sad story for all concerned.

By the time the police first arrived, all twelve of the students and a teacher who would die that day were quite likely already dead, including the two young men who were the shooters. At the end of their murderous rampage, the shooters had killed themselves.

The scene at the school was described by students and teachers alike, as "Hell." The fire alarm system was blaring its horrible Brrrrrng. Imagine a huge, cavernous building with that continuous shrill sound bouncing off every wall for hours before the school was finally entered, secured and evacuated by law officers. Bombs had been detonated in the cafeteria, but fizzled at the last moment, thereby creating huge amounts of smoke.

This triggered the sprinkler systems in the ceilings. So now areas of the building were being drenched with water as well. The school was filled with smoke, with fire, with shrieking alarms, human screams, cries, and the terrible moaning of the more than twenty students who were down, severely injured by gunshot blasts but still alive. Later, one student said to me something that we often hear from those who have lived through a huge disaster: that in the midst of that horrendous cacophony was "a silence of the worst kind."

By the time this horrific ambush was over, if ever an egregious act like this is *ever* over, those two dozen gunshot students would live, but some would remain physically injured for life, some now partially or fully paralyzed. It was said afterward, that the idea in the mad minds of the shooters was to blow up the entire cafeteria and kill all the students, teachers, and workers, or else to set the bombs off and stand outside and shoot all the students and staff as they fled the school. Had the bombs detonated as planned, the death toll would have been inconceivable.

There was a man at Columbine who was a janitor there at the time. When you met him, you might not relate to him right away because he often said one or two things in a sort of nervous mantra, "Hi, Hi, Howya doin? Howya doin? Good? Good? OK! OK!" Others at the school told me they sometimes wanted to say to him, "Alright, enough already. We already said hello, and how are you, twice now at least."

Some of the students seemed to not like this little janitor. They seemed annoyed by him. I was told some would make fun and imitate him. Students told how some other students would turn the janitor's rolling trash barrel over, spilling all the refuse he had collected so humbly. He was in many ways a very patient man. I once saw him pick up his overturned barrel, set it back up right, pat it all back together again, and say to those who had overturned it, "Hi! Hi! Howya doin? Howya doin?"

In the cafeteria surveillance films, the silent video of the day of the shootings, you see fire and smoke. You see students, some of whom are truly rooted to the spot like deer in head-lights. You see that they have been startled and cannot immedi-ately grasp what is occurring. They cannot think where, what to do next. We cannot hear them, but shots are being fired. Then, you see suddenly, this huge milling of students. It looks like a whirlpool made of human beings. Some are still wearing their backpacks. Some are wearing baggy trousers. Some are wear-ing white baseball caps. Later the students will tell me you can see at the edge, this figure, blurred, coming in, that this figure is yelling at the stunned students to "Get down!" In the next few minutes, this figure begins grabbing shocked students and throwing them out of the picture.

The students will report later that this blurred figure, this person running back and forth so fast, who began grabbing students by the seats of their pants, by their shirts, their arms, their shoulders, and just throwing them out the door, that this blur of muscle, certainty and eternity ... was the little janitor.

The students tell me that this janitor was somehow able to grasp what was going on immediately. While many students were still wondering if this was a stage play by the theatrical department, or a spoof from the computer video class, the janitor was able to throw students toward the doors that were not locked. He was yelling, "Run! Run for your lives! Run!" Many lives were saved that day by a fellow who usually just likes to say "Hi! Hi! Howya doin? Howya doin?"

After the conflagration in the cafeteria, then, with his big skeleton key set, the same keys that some of the kids used to hide from him to trick him, with those in hand, he, in the midst of all the smoke and all the horror, went up and down all the halls, up and down stairwells, completely unguarded with his little chest wide open, locking all the doors of the classrooms, sequestering away many of the terrorized students into classrooms so the shooters could not easily enter and attack them.

Then, because he was a janitor and knew his way around the school, he did something else. It was said later that the police and the emergency personnel may not have had a precise map on file of the layout of the school. Some say that this, in part, is why they did not go into the building immediately, for they did not know the configuration of it, and thereby the many reported locations of the shooters, or the students and teachers who were flooding 911 dispatch operators from their cell phones with pleas for help. You may have heard that it took many hours before the police and the SWAT teams entered the building. It is true, and during those horrible long hours, many students and teachers were in anguished hiding inside.

The little janitor could have fled the school, but he did not. Instead, he removed some ceiling tiles and started crawling through the ceilings of the school. A group of students and teachers had rushed into a tiny closet and were standing butt to belly, hour after hour, with the fire alarms going, with the smoke and water, and not knowing whether they would live or die. A student told me that all of the sudden, in that closet, the frightened group huddled there saw fingers coming through the seams of the ceiling overhead. They were terrified. One of the ceiling tiles lifted up. It was the little janitor: "Hi! Hi! Howya doin! Howya doin!"

This was the Santa Sombra in the flesh. He did more than there is room here to tell you. But in the end, as days passed, and as he and others at the school received their very few moments of thanks, his story remained for me, written hard in memory, along with those many others who rose to the call, and then too, like Santa Sombra, also just faded away afterward.

The years of aftermath are difficult, but for most, the first year after a horrific event is especially hard. The teachers and staff were heroic, for they would, four months hence in the next autumn, come back to the massacre site day after day, to teach, to work, to care for the children. Most persons who have been hurt by a huge travail do not have to go back to the scene of the crime. But this was a school, and there was no other for students to attend.

So, other Santa Sombras came to the site during the summer before school began again. They ever so carefully washed up the blood, and took down walls, and tore out and built back up with the tenderest of hearts, so there would not be one speck of red to throw a young daughter or son into another round of flashback horror – at least via preventable catalysts. So, all the teachers, the students, and the staff went back to trying to normalize life insofar and in the best ways they could. It was a huge moral accomplishment, because for a long time after a horrific event, there seem to be what we call "ghost" or after-images hanging in the air, displaying the hurt that happened there. These after-images can be unsettling even as they fade over time.

Too, there is a small after-story, a hidden aspect about the janitor who was so brave that day. Some told me that he has overcome a great challenge in his own life, one that few knew anything about. He had what are sometimes called "special learning needs," or what some used to call "learning disabilities," which meant in his case a person who has had a different and perhaps difficult time learning in standardized ways, in knowing the boundaries, in grasping certain complex concepts, throughout his life.

I do not know at depth or judge any of those appraisals. But, what I do know is a Santa Sombra when I see one. This man was able to instantly step out of the little self, his usual self, and roar into an enormous self. He embodied *tikkun olam*. He helped to repair the unraveled soul of the world within his reach. He did not spend a moment talking about the merits and demerits, nor over-long analyzing anything. He allowed the divine wind to whip through him, and he acted. Little Big Santa Sombra.

This would then be my benediction on us all. Could each of us, in some way, be Santa Sombra to someone? Today? Tomorrow. Any day? Think about it: Hmmmm.... How could I be, do something like that? What does it take to be open to habitation by *El viento de bondad*, the force of Goodness?


*And What If Despair?*

What might be one of the greatest dangers of falling into the kinds of evil inherent in human nature? If someone asked me, I would say the syndrome that might most easily lead one away from one's calling, is to feel unmediated despair. Some ask, what can I do, for I feel so despairing? In my own language it would help to clarify if one could remember that despair means to be without God. In my personal experience, God and despair cannot exist at the same time. I think that Jung ... I always hate it when people say, "Well, I think Jung would have said ..." (I always think, "Well, what the heck, you don't know what Jung would have said....")

But please allow me break my own aversion for a moment and say, *maybe* Jung *would* have said about despair, something like this: that to forget that you have a Self, a huge Self, would be to fall into a negative and unmediated complex of which despair is the central poison. (This kind of despair is not the same, incidentally, as that associated with neurochemically caused depression – another matter entirely that most often responds best to medical intervention.)

Again, *memoria*, remembering the "Source without source" – however one sees this – is to bring to bear in a real way, in one's life, an inextinguishable light under which the force of, and ways of, being humane stand much more revealed. The Self ever tends toward coalescing the wholeness of the psyche – so that psyche's entirety is really held, clarified, added to for strength. One is not meant to live like an ever-morose Job, just picking at one's boils and lamenting about how no matter what one does, it will not really matter.

There's a fine story about an attitude like this, about "the inflation of such deflation" that tries to believe that everything is a hopeless cause. It is about a group of pietistic men at the Wailing Wall. They are *davening* and *davening* (saying prescribed prayers often accompanied by rocking and bowing back and forth), saying, "I am not worthy, I am not worthy." Another man approaches, one who is looked down upon by the first group of men. The lone man begins davening and davening, chanting, "I am not worthy, I am not worthy." Finally one of the men from the first group can't take it anymore, and he remarks, "Oh Look at Schwartz davening there. Look who thinks he's not worthy."

There perhaps ought to be something in the psyche which entreats that we are not even worthy to not be worthy – and by such absurdist statement, to catapult us out of feeling so inept we do not even begin before we quit. But, from working with those who have felt exiled and damned, excoriated and benumbed, and yet have made it back to useful and creative life again, I know there are more sure, albeit intense, ways to aright oneself. One can choose any of the following and keep giving one or more of them the seat at the head of the table of one's life: *Amor grande*, the great embrace of Love; *memoria*, the memory of what profound love means; the *binah* of profound Love, the *experience* of *Love without Limits* and all its paradoxes; the *tikkun olam* attached to such love; the *active heart* that moves one out into the world in useful ways for Love's sake.

In however at first hesitant or wavering ways, whichever of these is coalesced and followed in the reality of the psyche, begins to contribute the exact share needed to knitting oneself and the world soul back up again.

*A Prayer For Memory*

Returning to the old people's caution when they identified Evil by the name "Divider," I have hoped here to contribute, neither to the swale nor the swill, but to a "clear-enough" current about the subject of evil. In the main, I have parsed the subject by circling it, for since ancient times – it has been advised to not be so foolish or naïve as to try to mediate Evil by simply taunting it, or trying to trivialize it.

The work here is not the final measure of the subject by any means. There are other aspects, conditions, and considerations to be raised and discussed. However, I have tried to identify and offer from my up-close work over the decades, some of the strongest, most time-honored ways to identify, mediate, and recover from exposures to loss of humanity, whether they be sociological, political, or personal losses. Too, I have purposely put the medicine of some levity into these pages in order to give some rests between the various issues' intensities.

It has been said that evil can most easily make its incursions when people forget they have unity with one another at a basic level. It is true that it is sometimes hard to see how we are all united with one another. One psyche, ten thousand, a million psyches – each one generates an unwieldy amount of complex data that makes it seem impossible that we might sift through all that and find our most fundamental similarities. But looking for correspondences of interests and impulses might not be the most effective place to find the root of what links human beings to one another.

More so, there is a place that elicits deep empathic agreement. It is a place of wholeness that we all belong to, a field in which we can immediately realize that regardless of all our foibles and bewilderments, we are whole. Jung sees this locus as the center of each psyche and yet greater than any individual psyche. It is the mysterious psychic field that supports and amplifies our interlocking reality. In that field, we are not isolated entities, even though in the day-to-day world, we may sometimes feel lonely and set aside. In the center, *we are wholenesses set inside a larger wholeness.* There, what is fundamental to being human is not elusive or confused; it is immediately understood as our splendor as human beings.

Such a vast and nurturant center is called by various names by different people. Jungians sometimes say such is the greater

Self that resonates with the smaller self that we know as "me," or the "I." I have been thinking for a long time, when looking through an analytical psychology lens, that this locus of unity of all beings seems like an ante-room to the psychoid unconscious – a place where one can *know* and is capable of *remembering* what one has experienced of the numen there – different from entering the psychoid entirely and losing ability to mechanistically report back about its enormous eternity.

Other names for this field of unity: Some might say such a locus is the electrifying realization of substance and feeling that one finds when entering into the palpable presence of God. Some would say, this place is made of detachment from the illusory world and immersion in the compassionate source. Still others would say this center has this particular name or that different name, but in all systems, regardless, this nucleus is based on a unifying factor that is ever radiant.

So I think it can be said that endarkenment begins to creep upon us anytime a person forgets she or he belongs to this field. It is true that we are vulnerable – for, if not once, then a hundred times a day, we all forget this homeplace, and we have to pull ourselves back to remembering. This practice of remembering and return becomes a diurnal set of active contemplation, as effective as any cyclical ablutions, any daily prayer.

The Cartesian view that has so dominated much of culture over the last three hundred years, attempted to set such ideas aside in the effort to unify all knowledge as the product of clear reasoning from self-evident premises. But, that viewpoint carried only half the overview of the huge unifying center that is both within and beyond mundane human comprehension.

The other half of the field at center, comes best into sharp focus through what is often characterized as that which is "invisible but can be palpably felt," what I would call the supra-rational. There, intuition, heart vision, kinesthetic sensation, inspiriting or inspiration, calling, and the creative force are the self-evident premises. They derive from a different kind of reasoning – that of the soul. Although the Cartesian view has too often been used to demote these as imaginings without substance, they are in fact fierce and sturdy functions that derive from a cohesive pattern for individuation, and that bring forth clarity, functionality, and new life – by not only concentrating on *what is*, but often much more so, *on what can yet be*.

One of the most interesting features of holding the view these functions support is that although the Cartesian view is not large enough to hold the Supra-rational view, the Supra-rational view is large enough to hold the Cartesian. The larger perspective recognizes that the more mechanistic view and the more intuitive one rest in their own wholenesses within a field of even greater wholeness. I think persons intent on maintaining humanity in, of, and with the world cannot serve at their optimum on a half-glimpse only of their innate and extra-ordinary wholeness – they have a right to avail themselves to all.

Thus, the psyche, through dreams and spontaneous inspirations and the results of weighing matters by material means and by heart means, encourages us to rethink the old order and add to it. This synthesis of rational and supra-rational, insofar as I am capable of parsing it, constitutes the field of humanity's greatest interlinkage and fullness.

We have seen over our own lifetimes that good people sometimes seem encouraged to argue with one another over the minutiae attached to any difficult circumstance wherein evil may have imposed itself – whether it be in social, familial, or personal life. Too often, this bickering over details only delays their acting in timely ways to identify the multiple incursions a nefarious force may have made. And it keeps them from moving quickly enough to loosen evil's grip and deal with it effectively.

Too much strife over the fine points of difference also whispers that one has no faith in *El viento de bondad,* the sudden infusion of goodness from the Self that will *inspirit,* propel, and guide one through unknown waters to the better and best of what is possible.

It is true that, from a typological point of view, each person will have different reactions to the topics of good and evil – as to all else – and so will have different ways of seeing and defining evil, and of finding their good ways through. But even these differences do not override the truth of that heartful and soulful homogeneity to human beings. That harmonizing principle from the center cuts across all economic, racial, ethnic, political, religious, and philosophical differences to unite the souls of the world. Being in that center *causes us not to be afraid* of realizing and saying we are in danger as souls, and that something must be done.

Residence in that optical field of original unity that we all share, causes us not to be afraid to see that we are on the verge of extinction and yet also realize that we are on the frontier of unlocking brilliant ways of being in the world and with one another. Remembering that home place makes one not afraid to realize that our beautiful world is just now coming into a range of consciousness about complex personal, social, political, philosophical, and national interactions that have never been possible before, and that we are in a visible evolution wherein more and more we stand to insist that we will not live in a dead universe, in a deadened community, in a benumbed psyche, or a dead soul. We go gladly to our work remembering to keep what matters of the world as dynamic and alive as we can – for our own sake, for the sake of the world now, and for the generations on their way to be born here as we are speaking right now.

What is the plasma, the serum that runs through that great center? It is, I think, the reality of Love without limits, that kindness that one can touch and enter from time to time, and perhaps for longer and longer times the older and wiser one becomes – that kindness that knows that so much about humanity is compatible and can be shared. When my grandmother was in her 90s, her sight was failing, and I had told her about cornea transplants, and also heart transplants and the brand new lung transplants. She was thoughtful, and said, Oh, don't you know, these things have always been so. See, no matter a person's race, one's eyes can be given to another. See, no matter the person's age, the heart can be shared with another. See, no matter where anyone comes from, the breath of life can be shared from one to the other....

## The Field of First Memory

Beyond the places of dissention,
beyond the worlds of argumentation,
beyond the locus of clashing and crashing things:
egos, temperaments, opinions;
beyond all this, and not too far down the road,
there's a quiet field in which grow tiny, white flowers
that when walked upon, give off the fragrance of all
of God's creations in all their many forms.
It is for you, it is for me, that this place has been made –
for memory's sake –
Far away from here, but not too far down the road,
beyond the places of dissention
and the worlds upon worlds of argumentation
and the locus of crashing and clashing things:

egos and temperaments and opinions —
there is a field of calm and peace.
For seven centuries now, Rumi has been saying,
"Out beyond ideas of wrongdoing and rightdoing
there is a field. I will meet you there."
And even if seven thousand more centuries pass
with Rumi's invitation unheeded by many,
it will still never be too late,
to begin walking toward that field,
to meet one another there
in that field of shared remembrance.

# Kidnapping: Latin America's Terror

*Jacqueline Gerson*

I would like to begin with what happened to me as I began to engage with this paper. Because the fear of being kidnapped or having a loved one kidnapped is such an anxiety for Mexicans today, my resistance to taking up this really frightening topic was stronger than my intuition that it would be important to write about it for this conference on "terror, violence and the impulse to destroy." The project was almost out of my conscious thoughts when I left for Acapulco with my family on the Mexican holiday weekend of February 5, 2002 determined not to deal with the possibility of a paper until I returned.

In Acapulco, however, while I was taking a sunbath, smelling and watching the ocean, and talking with people I love, I found myself captured by the question of what kidnapping means, about what is being communicated to and by the psyche through this ongoing evil. I became flooded by this topic, and I stopped watching the ocean, hearing the conversation, and enjoying the sun over my skin: my body and my mind were taken away into the world of kidnapping. As a way of containing the strength of the experience, I sat down to write the ideas that had come to take me away. It was only then, with my paper already begun, that I realized that I myself was actually living the experience of being kidnapped.

In recent years, in Mexico as in other countries in Latin America, such as Colombia, Venezuela, and Brazil, kidnapping has passed from being a single, occasional incident, to a more and more frequent event. Ordinary citizens like myself have gone from reading about kidnappings in the newspaper, where unknown names are mentioned, to talking about kidnapping often at home, and finally to knowing about it first hand, from victims in our own families and those of our friends. In my analytic practice in Mexico City, 80% of the patients have in one way or another spoken about kidnapping, some having themselves been kidnapped, though more often the topic comes up in relation to a child having been kidnapped or threatened with kidnapping. The segment of the population that is most vulnerable, even though not the only one exposed to this ongoing terror, is the young adult ranging in age from sixteen to twenty-six. It is usual for these young people to be kidnapped while driving alone in their cars; the kidnappers prefer that their parents be left free to obtain the money to pay the ransom that will be asked for.

The phenomenon has long outgrown single acting-out episodes by psychotically isolated personalities. Kidnapping in Mexico today involves a complex and pyramidal organization of kidnappers, with several levels of agents and a host of well-differentiated ways in which people can participate in this criminal activity. There are several well-known kidnapper bands, which keep multiplying as the existing bands fragment and regroup. The phenomenon is beyond the control of the government, the civil population, and any logic that has so far been applied to it. Since kidnapping is a very fast way to make a lot of money, an economic explanation is often offered for the phenomenon.

This literal-minded account, however, steps over the psychological process that is actually involved.

In the course of interviewing some famous Mexican lawyers, who together have intervened in over four-hundred cases of kidnapping, and always successfully (meaning that the victims were released alive), I was told that "kidnappings are custom-made events: they have complex dynamics that keep changing. There is never one like the other. Still there is a common basis for all of them: the pleasure the kidnappers take in accomplishing the kidnap. The pleasure, especially at the top of the ladder of the band of kidnappers, derives not from the money but the act of kidnapping itself." The top kidnappers feel nurtured by this act, and in a physiological sense they are, through the adrenaline that it releases, but they are also psychologically fed by the knowledge that they possess the Other.

Kidnappers need to negotiate to keep the adrenaline of high-stakes excitement running and to confirm their power. Lawyers understand this, and so always insist upon negotiation, even when the family is prepared to give all the money that the kidnappers originally ask for. "It must be understood," a lawyer specializing in kidnapping told me,

> that we are in a "game," and we must play it, because we are already in it: we "play," not to win, but to rescue a life. The kidnappers establish the rules, which we follow; and the first rule is that they should never feel threatened. A kidnapper will always communicate in indirect ways, and this must be respected. What we seek to attain is a trusting relationship between the mediator and the kidnapper.... The kidnappers must feel that we are not against them personally, that we just want to rescue the victim. This process of building trust takes an agonizing amount of time, during which the negotiation stance and situation has to be maintained.

In practical terms, this means that a schedule of telephone calls is established, always through the same phone line, with only one member of the family talking to the kidnappers' representative. This transaction, as tightly contained as psychotherapy, is really where the shifting of the power takes place from kidnapper to mediator. When that power transfer has occurred, the negotiation reaches the stage in which the money can be given. The victim will finally be released only as the outcome of a successful business transaction in which both parties have won respect, measured in tangible financial terms. In the process of coming to an agreement as to terms, the mediator making the negotiation will be tested once more to see if he is reliable. In his *News of a Kidnapping,* Gabriel Garcia Marquez notes that "for the kidnapped and the kidnapper ... the slightest noise may be confusing ..." A lawyer told me, "It takes many, many rounds and proofs of confidence and loyalty to the agreement, consuming many hours, and an absolute and precise following of directions, for the kidnappers to carry through to the last part of the game: releasing the kidnapped."

After hearing all this, I finally asked one of my informants, "Do you trust them? Can you believe kidnappers?" The expert negotiator's answer was: "Yes I do. Confidence builds up from the lack of confidence on both sides. I trust them, they trust me, and we both play our parts in a clean way. They have never failed to live up to what we agreed, and neither have I."

I looked up the verb *to kidnap,* which in my own language is *secuestrar,* and comes from the Latin *sequestrum,* which means "the action of separating or putting apart." It derives from *sequester,* meaning "trustee, receiver, mediator."

Kidnapping can be defined as the act of usurping, transgressing and violating someone's freedom to live and right to be. On a cultural level, one of the first historically recorded kidnaps in Mexico was the conquest of Tenochtitlan, capital of the Aztec civilization, by the Spanish people, who of course performed other such "kidnappings" of civilized Indian peoples in other areas of Latin America. Mexico's kidnap was synchronous with an event long anticipated in Aztec mythology, the return of the God Quetzalcoatl. Cortés, a bearded white man, was taken at first as the God Quetzalcoatl himself. But unlike Quetzalcoatl, who, according to Aztec belief, was supposed to accord protection and care to the Mexican people, Cortés and his men usurped the customs and traditions of the Aztecs, along with raping their women and taking their men as slaves.

In this kidnap of a culture, Mexican people were, as Luigi Zoja says, betrayed by their gods. A new culture and tradition simply stepped on top of theirs. The Cathedral of Mexico City is built on top of the *Templo Mayor* – the Major Temple – of Tenochtitlan, the demolished capital of the Aztec civilization.

The archetypal field of this trauma resonates even today, five-hundred years later. In more than 75% of kidnappings, guardians of the law are involved, just as they were when Tenochtitlan was handed over to the "protector" Cortés/ Quetzalcoatl. We can understand this partly as "identification with the aggressor," already recognized by Freud as a pervasive cultural mechanism. Freud's follower, Sandor Ferenczi, who emphasized love as the prime motivator in all human behavior, has an interesting elaboration of this theme: the identification "occurs when the child is unable to hate the loved father (or God) and instead identifies with him as good ... and takes the father's aggression into the inner world and comes to hate itself and its own needs." (Kalsched 1996, p. 17) Donald Kalsched thinks this fosters the creation of primitive "self-care systems" that paradoxically work against the self. I feel that a similar mechanism creates, in an entire society, a cultural complex that identifies with a violating aggressor, thus perpetuating an archetypal field in which the culture's wholeness is repeatedly conquered.

Octavio Paz has described the Mexican people as *"hijos de la chingada,"* children of the fucked one, who nevertheless want to be the *chingones,* Mexico's abusive fuckers. This fantasy may empower us in the face of our historical traumas, but it causes us to feel at the same time deep contempt towards ourselves, for, at the very same time that we are the fuckers of our cultural mother, we are the fucked ones.

To formulate the dynamic Paz is pointing out in terms Freud and Jung would have understood, when, on the basis of an outer violation, a trauma occurs in the psyche, an inner psychic factor also has to exist that permits, affiliates itself with, and in some cases even provokes the trauma. Zoja has noted that among the Aztecs was a "preexisting anxiety" reflected by their calendar-based mythology having supplied the date of the Conquest even before Cortés arrived.

The myth of Quetzalcoatl provides the context for this anticipation. Quetzalcoatl is first and foremost a creative God, the hero who brings culture – astrology, agriculture and writing – to Mexico. But he is also, like Osiris, the victim of an aggressive brother, Tezcatlipoca, who seeks to discredit Quetzalcoatl in different ways and devastate his morale. Finally Tezcatlipoca succeeds by getting him drunk. It is then that Quetzalcoatl becomes the violator of the culture he has created and suffered for. He rapes his own sister. After this terrible transgression of taboo, Quetzalcoatl's shame is so great that he leaves the land, abandoning his people, though promising to come back at a specified time, the very year when Cortés arrived.

This historical myth teaches us that through a sort of identification with the aggressor, the feminine soul of Mexico had been raped by its supposed protector even before the Spanish people arrived in Mexico. Within the cycle of time that Quetzalcoatl himself had taught his people to respect, a diabolical self-care figure of the kind Kalsched has described – one that still haunts Mexico with his destructive archetypal field – entered our psychology. Our present curse of kidnapping seems to belong to that diabolical field.

Since Quetzalcoatl is not just a culture hero, but a god, this destructive archetypal field is also a divine gift to us. So what does it do *for* us to have a diabolical self-care system involving kidnapping? In speaking of how some traumatized patients turn passive victimization into active terrorization of others and themselves, Koenigsberg writes that "by being the active agent rather than the passive victim of trauma, patients maintain a sense of being in control ... [I]mpulses to reinjure ... [arise] ... in enactments reflecting identification with the batterer (aggressor) and at the same time relief of passive victimization." (Koenigsberg *et al* 2000, p. 176) From this perspective, the myth of Quetzalcoatl/Cortés is Mexican culture's solution to the problem of passive victimization.

I read it as the story of a folk and a land where both inner and outer kidnap need to take place. Our repeatedly violated culture is like a traumatized child, and as Kalsched has observed,

> ... inasmuch as the traumatized child has *intolerable* experiences in the object world, the negative side of the Self does not personalize, remaining archaic. The internal world continues to be menaced by a diabolical, inhuman figure. Aggressive, destructive energies – ordinarily available for reality-adaptation and for healthy defense against toxic not-self objects – are directed back into the inner world. This leads to a continuation of trauma and abuse by inner objects long after the outer persecutory activity has stopped. (Kalsched 1996, p. 19)

I would note that Mexico is still under the care of a less than fully constructive government, five hundred years after the conquest, and almost two hundred years after the Mexican independence.

It is not hard to see how, through its own mythology, Mexico accommodated Cortés the aggressor. But what about the effect of the mythology Cortés brought with him to Mexico from his homeland on the Mediterranean? In the Mediterranean myth of the Rape of Persephone, we find an element not emphasized in Aztec mythology – the rage and resentment that arises in the mother of the victim. Demeter's relation to the kidnapping drama is readily found in a Mexican transposition if we look at the structure of family life in our country. Ninety to ninety-five percent of the young people that are in college remain at home while they are pursuing their studies. Many continue to live at home after graduation from college, leaving home when they get married. Kidnapping, in this cultural context, may represent a forced, Hadean process of leaving the mother's house. It can be regarded as a kind of violent initiation into autonomy, compensating for the relative devaluation of that psychological need within the present culture where Demeter seems to reign.

More interesting to me, however, because of what I see with my clients, is the *absence* of some of Demeter's energy. Kathie Carlson, in her book *Life's Daughter/Death's Bride*, interprets Demeter as the fierce preserving and reclaiming mother who refuses "to serve the authorities that fail to protect the seed life from unnatural harm and danger." She has "the power to hold accountable and transform even the distortion of 'father right' reflected in both the myth and this life contemporary drama." Demeter "will not collude with the abuser by blaming the victim or abusing [herself].... [She] has the passion for life and the power to stand against and transform what threatens the life she holds so dear." (Carlson 1997, p. 70, 80, 81)

I have seen the need for what I would call Demeter's ability to stand up to the aggressor in my analytic work with a fifty-five-year-old woman whose son was kidnapped. Because of her unremitting distress at this incident, she was referred to analysis by her psychiatrist, who told her that medication was not enough and psychological work was needed. This woman, whom I will call Pola, is the mother of four, the eldest being a twenty-six-year-old son, kidnapped when driving back home in a sports car after dinner, ten blocks away from his house. Pola received a phone call at four o'clock in the morning from the kidnappers, who told her they had her son and stated the amount of money that would be necessary in order for her to see him again. In the event, it was the father who, risking his own life, took some of the money to the kidnappers.

Pola blamed herself for the kidnapping, because her son was driving a car given to him by his parents, and because she had been sleeping rather than waiting for her son to be back home when she got the phone call. This self-blame obsessed her, even though she had warned her husband against buying a sports car for his son and even though she was very much in the house and able to respond when the call came.

As I got to know Pola, I learned that in her childhood, as the eldest daughter in a family of seven children, with a mother and father who became divorced, she was the one who adopted the parental role, even toward her parents. She still tends to become a mother to every one who appears in her life. This soon became apparent in the analytic relationship. Pola started to worry that she was talking too much, that I seemed tired or bored. Out of concern for me, she often offered to change the subject or stop talking.

Unlike Demeter, Pola is the kind of mother who tends to blame herself not only for what actually happens, but also for things that *can* happen if she is not constantly available and present. This prospective maternal anxiety applies especially to her own children, but it is also present in her toward the rest of the "adopted children" in the world, as a social attitude of concern and guilt. This tendency to assign guilt to herself is also projected: Pola has a constant fear of being blamed by others if she doesn't do or say the right thing. She prefers not to participate when important decisions are made, for instance, the decision to buy the son the sports car. She would not even participate in the selling of the sports car in which her son was kidnapped, though she had so many times wished that the family would get rid of it.

Finding out what is really right and true for Pola and sustaining her sense of what is really her responsibility and what not, has been an important part of our analytic work. Taking a position and holding it in relation to any event – the capacity Demeter embodies so impressively – is still a challenge for Pola. Such instinctive feminine assertion is deeply feared because of the blame and severe punishment Pola believes she will incur if the stand she takes is "wrong": Her ambivalence toward her feminine Self is expressed in a constant oscillation between saying yes and saying no to her own standpoint.

The kidnapping of Pola's son did not immediately constellate the outrage of Demeter in her – secure in its ground – but over time it moved her closer to this position, by leading her to a psychotherapy where she could gradually discover the authority of her own emotions.

I saw another example of the psyche's response to kidnapping in a woman, now forty-eight years old, who was kidnapped and sexually abused four years ago. She came to analysis three months ago, thinking that now that her children have grown up (they are twenty-eight, twenty-six, and twenty-four), she would like to have a space for herself in which to talk about some issues that have been "just there." She told me in our fourth session that she had been kidnapped and described the whole terrible episode, including what she felt to be the worst part of it, being sexually abused. While telling her terrible story, she repeatedly assured me of its veracity. She kept promising that it really happened, that she had actually felt the weapon of the kidnapper against her body, and that this was why she felt forced to go through the nightmare of the sexual episode. I realized that my patient was blaming herself for having allowed the kidnap to happen, castigating herself for participating in a sexual violation she couldn't have avoided. From that stance, she was protecting the kidnapper.

I have read that, although rape and violation is the second most frequent crime in Mexico, usually the abused woman does not denounce the sexual attacker or even report him, fearing that she will be blamed for provoking the attack and participating with the abuser in a sexual transgression. I felt like crying at this point in my patient's account, not only in protest at the invitation to collude with her in protecting the actual aggressor but out of shared recognition of the Mexican woman's need to make the male aggressor right at her own expense.

Another case that I saw involves what I would call the woman's inner kidnapper, by which I mean a complex within that has the power to capture and kidnap a patient's ego. Nora is a divorced forty-three-year-old woman with a controlled anorexia nervosa. She has two children, a ten-year-old boy and a four-year-old girl. After going through a surgery in her shoulder and feeling physically and emotionally weak, she arrived at a session with the following statement: "I want to take a knife and cut my children into pieces, because they make fun of me. They will not listen to me. My son is going to drown my daughter in the Jacuzzi while I am here talking to you. I know this is what is going to happen, and I am going to take a knife and chop him down."

The complex that has taken possession of this woman is a sort of *logos* vigilante, a negative animus who has kidnapped her away from her maternal capacity for holding, relating, and caring. In the name of securing order, there is a desire to mutilate her children's autonomy and integrity with the sharp unconscious knife of her fantasy, which penetrates the problematic behavior of her son, not to create a new order grounded in a mother's feminine ethic of care, but to violate and sever the boy's embodied ego with a vengeful, furious "justice."

In the safety of the analytic container, confidence has gradually been built up so that we begin to see the inner figure acting in Nora's psyche to rape her maternal femininity. Now, four years after treatment began, Nora recognizes him as a "Tyrant" – the same one that had her go through a whole day eating only half of an apple, while heavily sweating in endless exercise to keep her thin. "Where was my hunger?" Nora has asked in many sessions, while I have thought to myself: "kidnapped; in the underworld; split off from the upperworld by the rapist that invades your instinctive feminine space."

As with an outer kidnapper, a trusting relationship must also be developed with the inner kidnapper. A negotiation must take place, that will let this inner figure speak, and even (a rare experience for the negative animus) get its feelings considered, because the life of a kidnapped soul, like that of a kidnapped person, depends on this stance of negotiation: hearing, relating to, and finally learning to trust the voice of the inner figure who has kidnapped the patient, even though we instinctively hate him because he has violated someone dear to us. In working with the negative animus, a space is needed for his usually silenced resentment to express its horrible and destructive ideas and wishes, because it is only while the feeling of the destructive animus is able to talk to us, that any containment of his power can occur.

It isn't easy to listen to a rapist/kidnapper in therapy. I felt intensely protective of the children Nora's animus was describing so unfeelingly. I tried to figure out where this animus had learned its capacity for such fury. I learned of Nora's own father's physical violence, which had been repeatedly enacted, as Nora's mother, herself possessed by a cold, rigid and perfectionist animus, failed to stand up for her daughter. This helped me to understand better why Nora's inner Tyrant had abused and starved her body, causing her to fall into a severe anorexia, which, from a prospective standpoint, was not just the introjection of past aggression toward her on the part of the parents, but I think her feminine self's statement that she simply couldn't swallow any more of what was daily offered by those parents.

As I listened to Nora's description of how her hands became claws, to beat and hurt her children, feelings of fear would arise in me. Gradually I came to feel the inner kidnapper as an attack, not just on her feminine maternal capacity for holding, but on the shared mind of the analytic dyad as well. He would steal away the capacity for interpretive and empathic linking and thrust us into a timeless illogical, unethical space, governed by ruthless laws; a place that allowed no space for any other consciousness to exist. In that terrible space, I would become frightened, angry, and sad, worried about what she would do to her children and what that would do to her. But as my fear took over, I was more able to identify with the impotence of my patient's victimized ego, completely blind-folded and deaf, unable to see hear, smell, or taste. The complex kept her isolated in a world where there is no connection, and where the true victim, her own feminine ego, seemed forever unreachable.

But kidnapping would not be such a powerful psychological experience if it were only negative. The experience of being kidnapped came up as a prospective symbol in the dream of a patient of mine, who at thirty-eight years of age is still very much a *puella aeterna*. She is in her fourth marriage, having had several lovers, with no professional career achieved or business developed, living a life where nothing has been concretized. She presents, of course, a strong resistance to binding commitments, including to therapy, and in the course of analyzing this resistance she had the following dream:

> I am with my daughter and Dr. "X." I start flirting with him and he responds. My daughter says: "Well, if you want to go with him I can understand your need." I let him invite me to have a drink. We are to go down in an elevator, and I have that special energy for flirting. When the elevator door closes, he immediately starts using his surgical instruments to secure the door. I ask seductively what he is doing. He turns toward me like a monster, with the same surgical instruments in his hand. I think "Ha! This is a kidnap!" I realize that he will communicate with my family from the elevator to demand a ransom. I think to myself: "I am his hostage, how horrible!" As I finally cry out, "This is a kidnap," he nails me down against the wall of the elevator. I end up suspended by a pin from the center of my body, like a butterfly. I beg him not to hurt me, but the pain and the fear are so deep that I wake up in an agony of horror.

My patient's first association was to the "butterfly woman" in the movie *The Collector*, which led to the feeling that she herself is like a butterfly who is swept away by the currents of the winds without root or direction. The surgeon Dr. "X" reminded her of Dr. Jekyll because he maintains a very polite demeanor as a professional man, perfect as someone with whom to flirt and yet he ends up being a kidnapping Mr. Hyde.

According to Chevalier and Gheerbrant, "the butterfly is a symbol of lightness and lack of constancy. Among the Aztecs it is a symbol of the soul or the vital breath that escapes from the mouth of the one agonizing ... it is the symbol of the solar fire and of the black sun crossing through the underworld during its night journey ... is the symbol of sacrifice, death, and resurrection ..." (Chevalier and Gheerbrant 1988, p. 691-692) Murray

Stein (1998) has recently emphasized the potency of the butterfly as a symbol of transformation.

This kidnapping, though clearly against my patient's will, was the Self's way to pin her soul down, the enforced containment stopping the flying around and becoming swept away by the currents of unconscious passions and flirtatious whims for which she takes no responsibility. The dark animus figure who pins her down is both a potential lover and a potential healer. At the persona, Dr. Jekyll, level, he is a promising, if temporary, rescuer from the isolation and boredom of her life. But it is in his more demonic Mr. Hyde aspect that he appears to penetrate her darkness and make her feel something new. He uses medical tools that are normally employed to save lives in order to sequester his victim, indicating that there may be a therapeutic value to this operation. As the terrified dreamer realizes that she is being literally pinned to the wall by him, she becomes the butterfly woman, accessing the transformational possibilities in this seemingly masochistic archetypal image.

In these examples from my analytic practice, different personal meanings were found in the kidnapping theme. I find a consistent motif, however. *Kidnapping and kidnapped energy is out of the ego's control.* When we are kidnapped, our will is lost, and an unsuspected plan takes over our lives. We are part of a strategy that no longer belongs to us, and the status of our being requires renegotiation. I believe this motif hides in the archetypal background of the kidnapping phenomenon that is currently robbing the citizens in so many Latin American countries of their sense of security.

In any archetypal field there are polarities – attitudes that are not contemplating one another, neither knowing nor hearing about each other – generating such an accumulated psychic tension that something must change. One polarity, determinative of much of Latin American life, and involved in this wave of kidnappings, is the economic difference between classes. In Mexico today, rich people are very rich, and they feel like they have to be so, so they work hard to make even more money. Poor people are very poor, and they feel they cannot stop being so, so they tend to stop trying to better their condition. Both classes in this two-tier system are maintained by the economic definition of themselves that they follow. Kidnapping can be seen as a sudden reversal of this polarity, a compensatory situation in which poor people can get rich (and powerful) very fast, and rich people can rapidly be relieved of some of their wealth and of all their sense of control over what happens to them.

That more than economic reversal is involved becomes clear, however, when the kidnappers are caught: the bags of money are usually found in the exact same, unspent, condition that they were when given in ransom for someone's life days or weeks before. After a successful kidnap, within the pyramidal structure that organizes most such crimes in Mexico today, the people at the broad lowest end of the hierarchy are paid almost immediately with small amounts of money. The head of the structure is almost indifferent to the money. When caught, he is likely to comment "Game is over, you won," as he walks to jail, leaving the unspent ransom behind.

In countries that lack a psychological culture, concrete experience is overvalued, and little time is granted for reflection in the inner life of psyche. There is an enormous distance between projection and recollection and between compensatory archetypes. In Mexico, persona and shadow rarely touch each other, for our society is structured to keep them from touching. Depending on which class you are in, life is either too easy and focused in pleasure or so hard that you can only think about your daily bread. Both styles of thinking lead to a style where to act impulsively and not think about it brings a kind of adolescent excitement. And this is what I think leads to the Self's ruthless demand that the ego's will be pinned down and transformed, fixed into something with more psychological integrity.

I think that the kidnap archetype is finally bringing to the Mexican people what it has brought to some of my patients, the possibility of raising their voices, on behalf of "feminine" vulnerability in the face of "masculine" action, voices that reclaim the lost value that occurs when the dearest to us – our children, the children of our friends and neighbors, our husbands and wives – are snatched away, raped, and usurped, with no permission, no consideration, no limits, and no feelings – in a totally inhuman way. When our children, the most vulnerable aspect in this phenomenon, become a piece of merchandise to be bargained for, so that they can continue living their lives, you can be sure we deeply feel it. An outrage not unlike Demeter's is building in the Mexican soul. It may yet undo our centuries-old identification with the aggressor, when these "new conquerors," so full with greed for power and control, intimidate our loved ones in order to enrich their own empty souls to make up for the lack of love and care they never got.

When, on this archetypal stage, a mother gets a phone call at work and hears her daughter screaming and shouting on the phone that she has a gun pointing at her head as she stops for a red light in a main street in Mexico City at 5.00 o'clock in the afternoon, that mother feels the transgressive force of the violating archetype. From her cell phone, the daughter's voice cries out, saying that she is being followed by a car with three men who are carrying weapons and are pointing at her! The mother immediately calls her husband, and the girl's father begins to drive through the streets of Mexico City, desperately looking for his daughter, hoping that he can still find her before she is taken away; before he will discover only her empty car, and, after an excruciating wait, will take the call that tells him:

"We have your daughter, and if you want her back alive, you do what we say."

Meanwhile, the terrified girl manages to get hold of her brother for a life-line conversation, cellular phone to cellular phone, a conversation that goes like this: "Run, run, keep driving, don't let them take you, you can do it." "I am with you, don't stop talking to me." "Keep driving, don't stop, run, run!"

This girl escaped. The attempted kidnap had made an entire family cooperate. It brought out in them the awakening of both a sense of vulnerability and a feeling of strength, which together enabled them to overcome the danger.

I have seen other families whose child did not escape wait together for the single phone call that will give them instructions as to what to do to bring the game of kidnap to an end. Whole communities of families, and friends, and neighbors keep alive the possibility of reunion with the beloved.

These outrages are evoking in the Mexican people a capacity to experience the victimization that has been our fate for so many centuries. As a result, we are beginning to see a new way of taking care of ourselves in our culture, one that starts saying to the old diabolical self care system: "No more!"

Every citizen is concerned with the individuation of his or her country; so I beg your indulgence as I proceed to infer what the kidnapping of so many of our citizens has to do with the individuation of Mexico herself. My belief is that Mexico's transformation must come from its people and that Mexicans must find in themselves the guardians they have projected onto unsatisfactory governments.

Throughout their post-Conquest history, Mexicans have given their power to some Other: we have been ruled by the Spanish, the French, the Americans, and by our own governments, which have at times become an Other. The kidnap archetype is forcing us to reclaim our own power.

For it is in us, in each one of us, not in some well-meaning, or well-promising, government, that the guardian of the law must be awakened. It will of course be hard for the Mexican people to raise their heads and lift their voices to defend what is theirs – their children, their people, their land, their wealth – but I hear, in my practice, their desire to do so. Kidnap has transgressed our country's traditional penchant for silence and the acceptance.

Particularly in our country, women, who have long identified themselves with the archetype of the *Mater Dolorosa*, suffering with and for their children in silence, are starting to demand that their children be permitted to be. Through this act of demanding, they get to hear that they have a voice, and a say in the matter of kidnapping.

Interestingly, in the business negotiations with the kid-nappers, the theme of the "suffering mother" is frequently sounded, through references to the Virgin of Guadalupe, the mother archetype that has watched over the Mexican people since a little after the Conquest. The kidnappers are literally told that the Virgin of Guadalupe has been invoked to take care of them and the kidnapped, and that there is a mother waiting for her child to be released, a mother like Guadalupe, the Virgin, our Virgin Mother, who suffers and needs her child back. In a country like ours, with a medieval power structure, the force of the mother's sorrow cannot be overestimated. In Mexico today, however, women are becoming conscious of their power, not just to suffer, but to insist on life.

As for our men, the kidnap phenomenon is forcing them to raise their heads in order to confront the kidnappers. Men are starting to look into the eyes of the Other on the level, as the lawyers negotiating with kidnappers must do. In the drama of kidnapping, they are ready to confront the perpetrators, and their actions arise out of their feelings. I believe that Mexican men and Mexican fathers are starting to listen to their own weeping and kidnapped *animas*, so that a different connection with their own authority can be established, not through an external god who can leave them vulnerable to abuse, and then return (in human form) to actually abuse them, but through a reliable inner guardian of the totality of their being and their history, the archetypal protector that in Jungian psychology we call *Self.*

I can intuitively feel that something is moving and changing in the hearts of the people who have had to endure the horror of being constantly exposed to kidnap. As a Mexican Jungian analyst, I find in the cultural complex bedeviling our country an archetype torturing it into consciousness.

## References

Beebe J. (1988) "Primary Ambivalence Toward the Self," in Schwartz-Salant, Nathan and Murray Stein (eds.), *The Borderline Personality in Analysis.* Wilmette, IL: Chiron Publications.

Carlson, K. (1997). *Life's Daughter/Death's Bride.* Boston: Shambhala.

Caso, A. (1953). *El Pueblo del Sol.* México: Fondo de Cultura Económica.

Chevalier, J. and Gheerbrant A. (1988). *Diccionario de los Símbolos.* Barcelona: Herder.

García Marquez, G. (1996). *Noticia de un Secuestro.* México: Diana.

Gómez de Silva, G. (1995). *Breve Diccionario Etimológico de la Lengua Española.* México: Fondo de Cultura Económica.

Jacobi, J. (1959). "Complex, Archetype, Symbol," *The Psychology of C.G. Jung.* Princeton: Princeton University Press.

Kalsched, D. (1996). *The Inner World of Trauma; Archetypal Defenses of the Personal Spirit.* London: Routledge.

Koenigsberg, H., Kernberg, O., Stone, M., Appelbaum, A., Yeomans, F., Diamond, D. (2000). *Borderline Patients: Extending the Limits of Treatability.* New York: Basic Books.

León Portilla, M. (1964). *El Reverso de la Conquista.* México: Joaquín Mortiz.

Montessori, M. (1971). *La Mente Absorbente.* Barcelona: Araluce.

Paz, O. (1959). *El Laberinto de la Soledad.* México: Fondo de Cultura Económica.

Real Academia Española (1992). *Diccionario de la Lengua Española.* Madrid.

Stein, M. (1998). *Transformation: Emergence of the Self.* College Station, TX: Texas A & M University Press.

Woodman, M. (1982). *Addiction to Perfection: The Still Unravished Bride.* Toronto: Inner City Books.

Zoja, L. (2001). "Trauma and Abuse: A Psychological Approach to a Chapter of Latin American History," *Journal of Jungian Theory and Practice.* Vol. 3, Spring.

# A View from the Islamic Side: Terror, Violence, and Transformation in the Life of an Eleventh Century Muslim

*Judith Hecker*

The Islamic view I present for your observation is based on the spiritual autobiography of an eleventh century Muslim sage. He was known to Muslims as al-Ghazali and to Latin translators as Algazel. The approach I have chosen stems from my understanding that an observer/observed separation does not exist. As we know from our clinical practice (as well as from quantum physics theory), our observation is not a dispassionate act in which we stand back and keep ourselves out of the procedure. Like the quantum observer, we stand inside our observation, and in a sense help to make the world of our observations. The world we observe in this paper is the world of Islam. I propose that, as observers of Islam, we also reflect on the nature and history of our relationship with Islam.

I plan to proceed in the following manner: In the first section, I describe the birth of this paper and my personal history with it. Next, I review the life and times of al-Ghazali. In the following section I consider the history of the relationship between Jung and Jungians and Islam, and in the final section I discuss some psychological problems of intercultural observation. As you see, this view from Islam includes a look at the viewers as well.

## The Birth of this Paper and my History with It

The core of this paper is the story of the life of a Muslim jurist and theologian by the name of Abu Hamid Muhammad ibn Muhammad al-Ghazali. The paper was born twice. The first time, it appeared as a psychological study of the transformation of al-Ghazali. The second time, it took shape as the present exploration of al-Ghazali's autobiography and our community's relationship to Islam. I would like to tell you how this came about.

Initially, the paper was intended to be part of a series about Jung and Islam, which was to take place at the Jung Institute in Los Angeles. The idea was hatched in the mind of one training director, and when his tenure was cut short, he suggested it to his successor. Looking at lecture programs in other institutes, he could not find a program about Jung and Islam, although lectures about Jung and Christianity, Jung and Judaism, Jung and Buddhism had taken place regularly. He thought that a series on Jung and Islam might be of interest. The plan for the series was finalized in the year 2000. The director then proceeded to set a date for the series and scheduled the first lecture for September 12, 2001.

None of us knew the psychological turmoil we would be in on September 12th, the day after the bombing of the Twin Towers in New York. We were shocked and horrified by the unleashed destructiveness. Many were expecting further acts of mass destruction, and there were rumors that Los Angeles would be the target for the next monumental act of terror. People sat at home and watched television in zombie-like dissociation, or went about their daily activities in a disoriented daze. At the Institute, we did not know if it was safe to have a public gathering. We did not know whether people would venture out of their houses to attend a lecture. We could not tell whether a lecture on Islam might be considered a supreme act of disrespect for the dead in New York, or become a focus for an outburst of rage against Muslims. Eventually, it was decided to keep to the plan and hold the first lecture. The series thus opened with a small, disheartened audience in attendance, marveling at the power of intuition that had moved us to focus on Islam. The timing of the series was felt to be eerily, darkly impeccable.

To me it felt appropriate that al-Ghazali's life story should be discussed just at that moment. I sensed a dark correspondence between al-Ghazali's times and ours, which brought home the intensity of his experiences. There are times in life when we feel closer to the abyss, when we experience more immediately the violence and destructiveness that are headed our way. September 11th and its aftermath provided such an experience. Al-Ghazali's book *Deliverance from Error* (al-Ghazali 1980) was the outcome of another set of experiences of closeness to the abyss. It describes an individual's life in the aftermath of extreme violence and terror.

The second, current version of this paper was presented at the North American Conference of Jungian Analysts and Candidates in San Francisco one year after the first. By then there had been an awakening of interest in Islam in our collective consciousness, and many new books on Islam were published to satisfy the interest. Most of the recent books were written by journalists or by intelligence and terrorism experts, and showed little interest in, or knowledge about, deeper cultural issues. A number of scholarly books, like Cambridge University Press's *A History of Islamic Societies* (Lapidus 2002), had been revised and updated in light of the events of 2001. Such tomes (the latter weighs in at 970 pages) were mainly for use by scholars and students. My impression was that not many books had been published, which presented the views of psychologists about Islam and terrorism.

But do we need such books by psychologists? Can they contribute to our understanding of the events of September 2001 and subsequent violence and destructiveness? Does Islam have anything to teach us? I believe that the only valid approach to the study of the phenomena of terror and destructiveness is an interdisciplinary one. I have no doubt that an approach from analytical psychology, which incorporates history, teleology, cultural amplifications, archetypal, and countertransferential materials, can make an important contribution to the study of individual, societal and cultural violence. As well, I hope this paper will provide us with the opportunity to reflect on the question of what we in the West can learn from Islam in terms of reacting to violence and terror.

During the year that followed the first presentation, I gradually realized that the paper about al-Ghazali's view needed to include us as well. This realization was rooted in clinical theory and practice. In our clinical work, we know the importance of countertransference, and that observing and analyzing what happens in the psyche and soma of the therapist is integral to the work. In the case of an individual patient, it is essential to examine my reactions and note what I learn about myself, and what changes take place in me, in the process of working together. I decided to follow the same approach in my discussion of the view from Islam, by placing that view within a Jungian-historical context. My decision was also inspired by the fact that this conference took place in San Francisco, the host city of our annual history conferences.

Unexpectedly, the second birth turned out to be a twin birth. "The View from the Islamic Side" arrived entangled with another paper about viewing Islam from the Western side. Entitled "Murderous Brothers," it explored archetypal images that possess our involvement with Islam and terrorism. As it was with the arrival of the biblical twins Jacob and Esau, each of the twin papers clamored to come out first. I could empathize with Rebecca, the mother of the twins, for I was almost done in by the twins' struggle.

Yet perhaps the strangest thing about this paper is the fact that I, a Jewish woman born in Palestine to parents who emigrated from Hungary, was the one to bring 'the view from Islam' to an audience of North American psychotherapists. The only explanation I can offer is in the nature of a personal conviction that originates from feelings about my experiences. As I look back I realize that my life has taken strange twists and turns. I grew up expecting to become a professor of Islamic Studies in one of the universities in Israel, but ended up writing a doctorate and teaching at the University of California. Years later, during my analysis, I concluded that the academic life was not for me. I transitioned to clinical psychology and left the study of Islam and the academy for good. At least, that was what I thought. But the events of 2001 blasted me back into relating to Islam, no matter whether I had planned to do so or not. My life and actions seemed to be carried by events which I could not have predicted, and over which I had no control.

While reflecting on the events of my life I began to feel dimly that there might be a general plan behind them. I have not been consulted about this plan, nor have I been informed of it. I am just the individual who has been living it and who, every once in a while, gets a feeling that these events have a depth and meaning beyond my personal plans. I make my ego-decisions for the future, but the unknown plan governs what actually happens. Its strange purpose has brought me to this presentation.

Let me describe to you my first meeting with al-Ghazali's autobiography. When I was in high school I was offered a chance to opt out of a matriculation examination, if I wrote a thesis under the supervision of a university professor. My mentor turned out to be a Professor of Islamic Studies by the name of Martin (Meir) Plessner. I remember how he looked when we first met in his book-lined study. I saw an elderly man (he must have been forty years old, which for me at the time was the other side of midnight), concentrating on stuffing tobacco into his pipe. He seemed to be pondering what would be a good topic for my thesis. Finally he said he thought I could translate into Hebrew a book called *The Rescuer From Error.* He had the Arabic text, which he would lend me, and there were translations into English and French, which I could use to help with my work.

To this day I do not know why he thought this book, which describes a midlife crisis and transformation in the wake of an assassination, was appropriate for a sixteen-year-old. Yet for some unknown reason, I agreed to Professor Plessner's proposal and ended up translating the book. There was a lot to learn about the theological and philosophical background, and I struggled with the technical terms and the meaning of the text. Still, while clumsily feeling my way through the pages, and wondering what possessed me to take on the project, I was deeply moved by al-Ghazali's words. There was an exquisite feeling quality that emerged from the old text. The words conveyed the courage and humility with which he faced his suffering.

Eventually, and not without difficulty, I finished the translation and was excused from the matriculation examination in Islamic history. I was only too happy to be done with the work and did not expect to look at the book ever again. After graduating and serving in the Israeli army, I went on to study Arabic and Islamic Civilization at the Hebrew University in Jerusalem. Later, I wrote a Ph.D. dissertation at the University of California in Berkeley, which was an edition and translation of a manuscript by a 10th century theologian named 'Abd al-Jabbar. Subsequently, after some life-crises of my own, I transitioned to psychology and did not expect to look at an Islamic project ever again.

In 2001, however, it became clear that I was not finished with al-Ghazali, or that al-Ghazali was not yet done with me. For a while, my dreams during the early part of 2000 kept taking me back to him, and I could not understand their insistence. Because of these dreams, however, I felt ready to lecture on Islam when the Director of Training approached me, and I knew that my presentation would be about al-Ghazali. This time I come to his text not as a student or scholar, but as a psychologist. So far as I know, a psychological exploration of this book has not been undertaken before.

### The Life and Times of al-Ghazali

Al-Ghazali, one of the most influential writers in the history of Muslim religious thought, was trained as an Islamic jurist and theologian, and eventually became a mystic. He has been called the greatest Muslim after Muhammad, and was given the honorific title "Proof of Islam." He was born in 1058 A.D. in the city or district of Tus in northeast Persia. Together with his brother Ahmad, he followed the usual course of theological and legal studies. At first he studied in and around Tus, and later in Nishapur, under the Imam al-Juwayni, a brilliant lawyer and the leading theologian of the school of al-Ash'ari. The latter held the chair of law in the college that had been founded expressly for him by the most powerful man of the day, the vizier Nizam al-Mulk (d. 1092).

After al-Juwayni's death in 1085, al-Ghazali attracted the attention of Nizam al-Mulk. During the next years al-Ghazali became known throughout the Islamic empire as a distinguished scholar and author of works on Islamic law. In 1091, at the invitation of Nizam al-Mulk, he was appointed professor of law at the Nizamiya in Baghdad. This was one of several *madaris* or colleges founded by Nizam in various eastern Islamic cities, which served as training institutions for theologians, and were models for later colleges throughout the Muslim world. The college in Baghdad, the seat of the caliphate, was the most prestigious of the colleges. Al-Ghazali was a devoted and brilliant professor. People were amazed when, after a breakdown in 1095, he decided to leave his teaching position.

It was a time of outbreaks of violence in the Islamic Seljuk Empire, where the impulse to destroy was acted out by a group known as the Fida'is or the Hashishiyun. (Lewis 1967) These were young Shi'ites who were selected and trained by their spiritual leaders for the task of political assassination. Their bases were in remote mountain fortresses, and they would be ordered to leave those fortresses in order to carry out the assassinations. Before leaving on their missions, they were urged by their leaders to use hashish in order to be ready to perform any brutal act. The English (and French) word 'assassin' originates from Crusader references to these hashish-using killers. (Gibb & Kramers 1961)

One of these terrorists assassinated al-Ghazali's patron Nizam al-Mulk. It has been suggested that Al-Ghazali might have been, or thought he would be, the next target for assassination, and that his abrupt departure from Baghdad was motivated by fear for his safety. Most scholars, though, believe that there was no direct threat to his life, since the assassins targeted political leaders and not religious scholars. Still, Al-Ghazali may have been threatened in response to his aggressive polemics against the Shi'ites.

Looking at the events as psychologists, we know that the murder of a person who is a close associate and patron may cause post-traumatic anxiety, even if the survivor does not believe that he or she is a target. We may never know if al-Ghazali was personally at risk, or whether external events synchronistically mirrored the turmoil in his soul. But we do know that after the murder of Nizam, al-Ghazali was plunged into a deep psychological crisis. He describes the crisis and his psychological process in his autobiographical book *Al-Munqidh min al-Dalal*, translated as *The Rescuer from Error* or *Deliverance from Error.* (McCarthy 1980)

The *Munqidh*, which was composed in 1105, is an autobiography, but not a straight narrative of a life. As the title indicates, it is governed by the goal of soul rescuing. The book has, additionally, a longer title, or rather two versions of a longer title, which are indicative of what the author had in mind. The first version, in translation, is *What Saves from Error and Makes Plain the Mystical States of the Soul*, and the second version is *What Saves from Error and Unites with the Possessor of Power and Glory.* The title has also been translated as *Freedom and Fulfillment*, or *Liberation and Illumination*. The *Rescuer* is not a personal autobiographical account, but rather a spiritual autobiography, describing al-Ghazali's intellectual and spiritual evolution. The book is considered a unique document in medieval Islamic literature, where personal revelations in the form of an autobiography do not ordinarily meet with approval. Some Muslim writers feel that the book was accepted because it was thought to have didactic value.

In the book al-Ghazali describes two episodes of a spiritual crisis, which occurred within a period of four years. The first episode, which Al-Ghazali called a crisis of skepticism and an illness, occurred around the time of his move to Baghdad. Al-Ghazali reported that he tried to overcome this crisis by use of rational thinking, but was unsuccessful. He reported remaining in this illness for two months, until the crisis abated and he could return to his prior functioning. Al-Ghazali felt that he regained his balance not through thinking his way out and reaching a resolution, but because of a light that God had cast into his breast. This episode foreshadowed a deeper and more prolonged crisis four years later.

In 1095 al-Ghazali underwent a second crisis that changed the course of his life. Again it was a crisis of both body and soul, and al-Ghazali recorded some of his process in *The Rescuer.* He went through six months of mental anguish, feeling that his life was a meaningless sham, and that the time had come to care for the needs of his soul and gear his activities towards the search for true meaning. Still, he was unable to make up his mind whether to stay in his secure, prestigious academic position or leave. He suffered from severe depression, and eventually lost his ability to speak and was unable to eat, drink or continue his daily activities. At the same time, he became dissatisfied with the doctrinal and intellectual approaches to religion. He felt that these approaches bypassed the heart of the matter, which is what is known by experience. He had read the works of the Islamic mystics, became acquainted with their practices, and reached the conclusion that their path was the one that led to true knowledge. He then made up his mind to leave his academic career and follow the Sufi path.

After making arrangements to provide for his family, he left Baghdad, disguised as a Sufi. He headed for Damascus, where he secluded himself in the minaret of its great mosque. Next, he traveled to Jerusalem, where he secluded himself in the Dome of the Rock. From there he traveled to Hebron, then to Medina and to Mecca. He continued his life in seclusion for about eleven years.

To illustrate the feeling tone of al-Ghazali's writing, I quote from his description of the internal struggle that led to his decision to leave Baghdad:

> I attentively considered my circumstances, and I saw that I was immersed in attachments that had encompassed me from all sides. I also considered my activities – the best of them being public and private instruction – and saw that in them I was applying myself to sciences unimportant and useless in this pilgrimage to the hereafter. Then I reflected on my intention in my public teaching, and I saw that it was not directed purely to God, but rather was instigated and motivated by the quest for fame and widespread prestige. So I became certain that I was on the brink of a crumbling bank.... unless I set about mending my ways.
>
> I therefore reflected unceasingly on this for some time, while I still had freedom of choice. One day I would firmly resolve to leave Baghdad and disengage myself from those circumstances, and another day I would revoke my resolution. I would put one foot forward, and the other backward. In the morning I would have a sincere desire to seek the things of the afterlife; but by evening the hosts of passion would assail it and render it lukewarm.
>
> Thus I incessantly vacillated between the contending pull of worldly desires and the appeal of the afterlife for about six months … In this month the matter passed from choice to compulsion. For God put a lock upon my tongue so that I was impeded from public teaching. I struggled with myself to teach for a single day … but my tongue would not utter a single word: I was completely unable to say anything. As a result that impediment of my speech caused a sadness in my heart accompanied by an inability to digest; food and drink became unpalatable to me so that I could neither swallow broth easily nor digest a mouthful of solid food. That led to such a weakening of my powers that the physicians lost hope of

treating me and said: "This is something which has settled in his heart and crept from it into his humors; there is no way to treat it unless his heart be eased of the anxiety which has visited it."
Then, when I perceived my powerlessness and when my capacity to make a choice had completely collapsed, I had recourse to God Most High as does a hard pressed man who had no way out of his difficulty ... and He made it easy for my heart to turn away from fame and fortune, family, children, and associates. I announced that I had resolved to leave for Mecca ... (al-Ghazali 2000, p. 53-55)

According to Marie-Louise von Franz, Islamic culture was superior to the medieval Christian West in terms of the differentiation of the religious Eros. Islamic alchemists had the ability to express greater intensity of feeling in their writings than the alchemists of antiquity and later Christian alchemists. In von Franz's opinion, one of the original contributions of the Islamic world to Gnostic alchemy was the addition of a passionate feeling tone. (von Franz 1999) The above passages leave no doubt as to al-Ghazali's ability to experience and express intensity of feeling.

After eleven years of wandering, al-Ghazali was summoned to come back to Baghdad and decided to return to his family and to teaching. Out of his experiences came his greatest work, *The Revival of the Religious Sciences (Ihya' 'ulum al-din)*. It is a comprehensive work in forty chapters – forty being the number of patience and trial, the number of days of seclusion that the adept undergoes at the beginning of the mystical path.

Al-Ghazali's teachings have been called "a marriage between mysticism and law." (Schimmel 1975) He taught that it was the life of the heart that mattered. His approach combined the life of the heart with a theologically sound attitude and behavior that was in strict accord with the law. This was acceptable to the orthodox theologians as well as to the ordinary believers. As a result of his writings, a moderate Sufi outlook began to color the life of most Muslims.

Scholars of Islam are in agreement that al-Ghazali's distinction was not due to his intellectual accomplishments, nor to his originality. Rather, its source was his extraordinary character in the experiences that he had undergone. To end this section, I quote from reviews of al-Ghazali's life by two historians of Islamic theology.

> He was not a scholar who struck out a new path, but a man of intense personality who entered on a path already blazed and made it the common highway. We have here his character. Other men may have been keener logicians, more learned theologians, more gifted saints; but he, through his personal experiences, had attained so overpowering a sense of the divine realities that the force of his character – once combative and restless, now narrow and intense – swept all before it, and the Church of Islam entered on a new era of its existence. (Macdonald cited in McCarthy 1980, p. 46)
> Al-Ghazali thought himself called to be the 'renewer' of religion for the sixth Islamic century, and many, perhaps most, later Muslims have considered that he was indeed the 'renewer' of this age ... As his achievement is reviewed, it becomes clear that he was more of a prophet than a systematizer. Yet he is not simply a prophet, but is best described as a prophetic intellectual ... Above all he made the individualistic aspect of religion intellectually respectable ... but he was far from being a sheer individualist. In his theorizing he sometimes fails to make explicit allowances for the communalism of the Shari'a, but he always presupposes it, and in his practice he effects a genuine integration of individualism and communalism. This is part of his title to greatness and of his achievement in 'renewing' Islam. (Watt cited in McCarthy 1980, p. 47-48)

We might ask, what can we in the West learn from the story of al-Ghazali's life? Does it present an approach that Western culture considers alien and has yet to integrate? It seems to me that al-Ghazali's life presents a reaction to circumstances of destructiveness and violence not through a rush to action, but through deep introverted feeling and love for the Self. For us in the West, it is difficult to understand an approach that responds to destructiveness not by action, but by introversion and suffering.

## On the Relationship between Jungians and Islam

The task set for this conference was to explore psychological phenomena connected with terror, violence, and destruction. Recent events led us to direct our attention to the Islamic side, and at the same time to realize the enormous gaps and limitations in our understanding of Islamic culture. The limitations are due, in part, to the fact that Islamic materials are nearly inaccessible to the non-specialist. Still, Jungians have not been reluctant to take up cultural materials that are just as inaccessible, such as Buddhism or ancient Egyptian religion. Inaccessibility seems to be only part of the answer to the question of our blind spot when it comes to Islam.

To illustrate what I mean by our blind spot: When I looked in the library at the C. G. Jung Institute of Los Angeles, I found numerous books by Jungian authors who focus on Christianity, Judaism, Buddhism, Taoism, ancient Greek and Egyptian religions. Compared to this vast output, I found only three books that focused on Islam. These are *Sufism, Islam and Jungian Psychology*, edited by J. Marvin Spiegelman (1991); *Jung and the Monotheisms*, edited by J. Ryce-Menuhin (1994); and the fascinating private printing of *Muhammad ibn Umail's Hall ar-Rumuz* (von Franz 1999), an historical introduction and psychological commentary on an Arabic alchemical text, which is the last publication of Marie-Louise von Franz. Recently, I received notice of three books by the French psychoanalyst (and individual member of the International Association for Analytical

Psychology [IAAP]) Dr. H. Dhaoui, which address Islam, Jung, and psychological materials. (Dhaoui 1998, 2000, 2001) The mystery of our relegating Islam to the shadow still invites further exploration.

Jung himself was interested in and knowledgeable about Islamic culture. His acquaintance with Islam went back to early times in his life. In *Memories, Dreams, Reflections*, he reported that his father had studied Oriental Languages in Göttingen and had written his dissertation on the Arabic version of the Song of Songs. (Jung 1961/1965)

In Jung's writings and personal communications, there are references to Islamic culture and Islamic materials that show knowledge about the culture, and on occasion an opinionated approach. We are familiar with Jung's detailed psychological analysis of Sura 18 of the Qur'an as an example of a rebirth mystery in "Concerning Rebirth." (Jung 1950/1968) A detailed review of Jung's references to Islam would be a worthwhile undertaking, but must be left to a separate paper. I would like, however, to address one such reference here.

In *Memories, Dreams, Reflections*, (Jung 1961/1965) Jung described his reactions to meeting with Islam while traveling in North Africa, and related a dream he had on the night before he left Tunis for Marseilles. Jung felt that this dream summarized his experience in a better way than he could put into words, because on the conscious level he could not understand the meaning of the meeting with Islam. It was an important dream for him, as can be seen from the detail he gave to its description. I feel it is a crucial dream for us today, inasmuch as it indicates the psychological position of Westerners when we relate to and deal with Islam.

Jung wrote:

> I dreamt that I was in an Arab city, and as in most such cities there was a citadel, a casbah. The city was situated in a broad plain, and

had a wall all around it. The shape of the wall was square, and there were four gates.

The casbah in the interior of the city was surrounded by a wide moat (which is not the way it really is in Arab countries). I stood before a wooden bridge leading over the water to a dark, horse-shoe-shaped portal, which was open. Eager to see the citadel from the inside also, I stepped out on the bridge. When I was about halfway across it, a handsome, dark Arab of aristocratic, almost royal bearing came toward me from the gate. I knew that this youth in the white burnoose was the resident prince of the citadel. When he came up to me, he attacked me and tried to knock me down. We wrestled. In the struggle we crashed against the railing; it gave way and both of us fell into the moat, where he tried to push my head under water to drown me. No, I thought, this is going too far. And in my turn I pushed his head underwater. I did so although I felt a great admiration for him; but I did not want to let myself be killed. I had no intention of killing him; I wanted only to make him unconscious and incapable of fighting.

Then the scene of the dream changed, and he was with me in a large vaulted octagonal room in the center of the citadel. The room was all white, very plain and beautiful. Along the light-colored marble walls stood low divans, and before me on the floor lay an open book with black letters written in magnificent calligraphy on milky-white parchment. It was not Arabic script; rather, it looked to me like the Uigurian script of West Turkestan, which was familiar to me from the Manichaean fragments from Turfan. I did not know the contents, but nevertheless I had the feeling that this was 'my book,' that I had written it. The young prince with whom I had just been wrestling sat to the right of me on the floor. I explained to him that now that I had overcome him he must read the book. But he resisted. I placed my arm around his shoulders and forced him, with a sort of paternal kindness and patience, to read the book. I knew that this was absolutely essential, and at last he yielded. (Jung 1961/1965, p. 242-243)

Jung's reflections about this dream are instructive, for he understood the powerful impact of the confrontation with Islam on the psyche of the Westerner, and how threatening to the Western psyche such a confrontation might be. He also defines here the position of the Arab as a shadow for the Westerner, but places him not as a personal shadow, but as an ethnic-cultural shadow, which for Jung signifies the shadow of the Self. He writes,

> As an inhabitant of the casbah he [the Arab youth] was a figuration of the self, or rather, a messenger or emissary of the self. For the casbah from which he came was a perfect mandala: a citadel surrounded by a square wall with four gates. His attempt to kill me was an echo of the motif of Jacob's struggle with the angel; he was – to use the language of the Bible – like an angel of the Lord, a messenger of God who wished to kill men because he did not know them.
>
> Actually, the angel ought to have had his dwelling in me. But he knew only angelic truth and understood nothing about man. Therefore he first came forward as my enemy; however, I held my own against him. In the second part of the dream I was the master of the citadel; he sat at my feet and had to learn to understand my thoughts, or rather, learn to know man.
>
> Obviously, my encounter with Arab culture had struck me with overwhelming force. The emotional nature of these unreflective people who are so much closer to life than we are exerts a strong suggestive influence upon those historical layers in ourselves which we have just overcome and left behind, or which we think we have overcome. It is like the paradise of childhood from which we imagine we have emerged, but which at the slightest provocation imposes fresh defeats upon us … (Jung 1961/1965, p. 243-244)
>
> In traveling to Africa to find a psychic observation post outside the sphere of the European, *I unconsciously wanted to find than part of my personality which had become invisible under the influence and the pressure of being European. This part stands in unconscious oppo-*

*sition to myself, and indeed I attempt to suppress it.* In keeping with its nature, it wishes to make me unconscious (force me under water) so as to kill me; but my aim is, through insight, to make it more conscious, so that we can find a common modus vivendi. The Arab's dusky complexion marks him as a "shadow," but *not the personal shadow, rather, an ethnic one associated not with my persona but with the totality of my personality, that is, with the self. As master of the casbah, he must be regarded as a kind of shadow of the self* [emphases are mine – J H]. The predominantly rationalistic European finds much that is human alien to him, and he prides himself on this without realizing that his rationality is won at the expense of his vitality, and that the primitive part of his personality is consequently condemned to a more or less underground existence. (Jung 1961/1965, p. 244-245)

In Jung's opinion, the dream revealed how his encounter with North Africa affected him. He was not conscious of it during his stay, but later concluded that there was a danger that his European consciousness would be overwhelmed by an unexpectedly violent assault of the unconscious psyche. He wrote that consciously he was feeling rather superior about being European, but that he was unprepared for the existence of unconscious forces within himself "which would take the part of these strangers with such intensity, so that a violent conflict ensued. The dream expressed this conflict in the symbol of an attempted murder." (Jung 1961/1965, p. 245)

Clearly, Jung had given careful attention to the problem of the European's relationship with the Arab, and, through reflecting on his dreams, was aware of the psychological meaning Islam – in the figure of the young Arab prince – carried for the Westerner. The monotheisms are princes, in the sense of being entitled heirs to the dispensation of the royal Father. Just as Islam is the youngest of the three major monotheisms, Islam is the young prince in Jung's dream. Perhaps it is inevitable that its elder siblings would feel that it has had less time to learn how to carry its revelation in a human way.

Another of our Jungian ancestors, M.-L. von Franz, showed remarkable familiarity with Islamic materials, especially with texts about Muslim alchemists. In her introductory lectures on the symbolism of alchemy, von Franz devoted about seventy pages (nearly three chapters) to Arabic alchemy. (von Franz 1980) In her edition and commentary to the alchemical treatise *Aurora Consurgens,* (2000) von Franz reviewed the works of many Muslim alchemists, and includes references to the following Muslim alchemists and philosophers: Senior, Calid, Avicenna, Rhazes, Geber, Alphidius, Averroes, and Al-Farabi. Al-Ghazali, too, was mentioned in the *Aurora* in a note.

Perhaps our Jungian community's relationship to Islam could be best characterized as going through surge and decline. C.G. Jung himself was interested in Islamic culture, as was Marie-Louise von Franz. Famous Orientalists (as scholars of Islam used to be called) such as Henri Corbin and Louis Massignon were regular participants at the Eranos conferences (Cheetham 2003). Yet the interest of Jung and early Jungians has not galvanized the creative output of members of the Jungian community, and at present only a few analysts are attentive to the Islamic side. Although it appears that several Jungian analysts see Muslims in their clinical practices, there is only one Muslim among the members of the IAAP. That fact, too, may be an indicator of our community's openness to Islam.

## Psychological Difficulties of Taking in the View

Jung's dream expressed some of the unconscious underpinnings of our reactions to the meeting with Islam. Our psyche's fear of being overwhelmed, our dread of and fascination with Islam, the death-and-life violence of the meeting, and our view of Islam as our cultural shadow. In this last section I would like to consider what happens, psychologically speaking, when we in the West undertake to meet with Islam. I propose that two kinds of difficulties are involved: general difficulties of intercultural observation, and difficulties that are particular to our relationship with Islam.

For people raised and living in Western culture, attempting a view from the Islamic side presents an inherent psychological difficulty. C.G. Jung might describe our endeavor as trying to find and maintain a psychic observation post outside the sphere of the European (which Jung attempted by traveling to Africa). The difficulty lies in the fact that we are trying to register two completely different images of the nature of reality simultaneously. This task seems more suitable for whales, which have eyes on opposite sides of the head, than for humans. Perhaps, though, it is a fitting task for Jungians, accustomed as we are to considering different views of the nature of reality as they emerge in our patients' lives as well as in our dreams and active imaginations.

Closely related, is the problem of intercultural translation. A story titled "Averroes' Search" by Jorge Luis Borges (1998) illustrates the pitfalls of undertaking to translate the experiences of another culture. This time, the pitfalls plague a medieval Muslim who attempts to translate from Western culture. Borges tells of the Muslim philosopher Averroes, who is engaged in translating Aristotle's *Poetics* into Arabic. As the story begins Averroes cannot proceed with the translation, because he does not know the meaning of the words 'tragedy' and 'comedy.'

Since pre-Islamic times, Arabs have held poetry and individual poets in great esteem. They were accustomed to poetry gatherings, where individuals read poems to the rulers and the public, and occasionally vied for the title 'Best Poet of the Arabs.' Arabs were in awe of the power of poetry to glorify or vilify, bring about victory or defeat, honor or disgrace. But there was no theatre in the Arab world at the time. Arabs could thus relate to the experience of attending a poetry reading and being moved by it, but not to a performance by a group of actors. In our story, Averroes is stumped, because, never having experienced a play, he has no concept of words that describe different categories of plays.

As the story continues, Averroes attends a dinner party. Among the guests is a famous Muslim traveler, who is asked to tell about a marvel he witnessed in his travels. The traveler responds by describing what any one of us would recognize as a theatrical performance. When he traveled in China, he tells the guests, he was taken to a house where many people were assembled. They were seated in small balconies, one atop the other, and some people sat on the floor. On a raised terrace, some people played music, and some fifteen or twenty people wore masks and sang and conversed among themselves. The traveler says, "These masked ones suffered imprisonment, but no one could see the jail; they rode upon horses, but the horse was not to be seen; they waged battle, but the swords were of bamboo; they died, and then they walked again." (Borges 1998, p. 238-239) The traveler adds, that it looked like the masked people were trying to present a story by showing it, instead of telling it.

The traveler's narration is followed by a heated discussion in which the guests, who have never been to a theater, try to understand the traveler's tale. All of them agree that it makes no sense for twenty people to be presenting a story, when a single person (that is, a skillful poet) could tell it. For surely a poet can tell an audience anything, no matter how complex the subject may be. What, then, could be the meaning of what the traveler saw? After some discussion, the guests conclude that the masked people in the house were mad. Averroes is present at the discussion and listens carefully.

After the party, Averroes goes back to his library and resumes the translation. He decides that the word 'tragedy' means panegyrics and 'comedy' means satire. Panegyrics and Satire were well-known traditional forms of poetry in the Arab world.

To the Western reader, it is evident that Averroes had all the facts before him, but failed to put them together. He could not understand that the traveler's tale provided the key to the meaning of the words that eluded him. It appears that this famous philosopher was defeated by an unseen intercultural barrier.

Those of us who see patients from diverse ethnic backgrounds sometimes experience this psychological process of defeat in our interactions. At some point in the session, what makes perfectly good sense to one person seems like sheer madness to the other, because each views the situation from a different cultural angle and is unable to surmount the intercultural barrier. This may be accompanied by feelings of extreme frustration, helplessness and irritation by the clinician, and may lead to an impasse in therapy.

Borges concludes the story as follows, "In the preceding tale, I have tried to narrate the process of failure, the process of defeat ... I felt that the work mocked me, foiled me, thwarted me. I felt that Averroes, trying to imagine what a play is without ever having suspected what a theater is, was no more absurd than I, trying to imagine Averroes, yet with no more material than a few snatches ..." (Borges 1998, p. 241) As we try to imagine al-Ghazali with the help of the few snatches that I have presented, we need to be aware of the barriers and difficulties that at times turn the task into a process of failure.

The above difficulties are present whenever we attempt to understand the view from another culture, no matter which culture is involved. Other difficulties, I believe, are particular to our culture's relationship with Islam. Islam is the third mono-theism, and regards the teachings of Judaism and Christianity as revelations that have been superseded by it. For Judeo-Christian culture, thus, Islam does not occupy the position of a stranger, but rather of a troublesome brother-rival. Psychologically speaking, trying to relate to a complete stranger involves different feelings and experiences than interacting with a sibling with whom one has a history of destructive rivalry and violence.

This leads us to a consideration of the archetypal images that are constellated in the relationship between the West and Islam. In my opinion, these are images of the relationship of murderous brothers, whose myths form the cornerstone of our culture. (Consider Osiris and Set, Romulus and Remus, Cain and Abel, Jacob and Esau). These images prescribe an attitude of wary, sometimes hostile, interest in Islam. Consequently, undertaking to learn about Islam has often been motivated by a wish to gather intelligence about an enemy, or by an ethnocentric desire to affirm our culture's superiority, rather than by a genuine interest in another culture. The focus on and interest in Islam would thus increase in proportion to a perceived threat from it or to our wish to colonize it. (A fuller exploration of the archetypal images of "Murderous Brothers" is outside the scope of this paper, but is the subject of a paper I presented at the North/South Conference of California Jungian Analysts. (Hecker 2003)

These archetypal images may underlie the fluctuations that characterize our interest in Islam, where times of apathy alternate with sudden renewed focus.

As well, these images may account for our leaders' aggressiveness, impulsivity, emotionality, and inclination to act out when dealing with Islamic societies. It behooves us therefore to approach a view from the Islamic side with caution, keeping in mind the difficulties and pitfalls inherent in this undertaking – Borges' "process of failure" and "defeat."

Throughout the writing of this paper, I have had to struggle with feelings of frustration and failure. Each section of the paper feels incomplete and deserving of a fuller discussion. Each section presents only a few snatches of material. It feels absurd and grandiose to claim to present a view from Islam based on these materials alone. I am well aware that if we were to stop at these, we would come away with a very limited picture. Yet I believe we must resume our focus on Islam and devote efforts to learning about it. In this context, I propose several areas that are worthy of our attention as analytical psychologists: we need to educate ourselves about Islam in itself; we need to review the history of our own Jungian community's relationship to Islam; and finally, we need to reflect about what Islam carries for us as Jungian interpreters of culture and psyche, what we can learn from Islam, and what our relationship to it teaches us about ourselves.

Looking beyond the confines of our own discipline, it seems impossible these days for anyone in North America to have a discussion of destructiveness, terror, and violence without thinking about Islam. But whether the wish to include Islam and relate to what it teaches us will disappear or not remains a mystery. Speaking as someone living and working in the United

States, I know that only time will tell whether this disagreeable piece of our national shadow and the demons it conjures up for us will sink back into the unconscious, or whether there will be a continued, sustained effort to learn about Islam and about what it carries for us. My personal hope is that the conversations with Islam begun by our psychological ancestors will be resumed with renewed vigor, and that our minds and hearts will remain open to this old-new topic.

## References

Borges, J.L. (1998). "Averroes' Search," *Collected Fictions*. New York: Viking Penguin Books, p. 235-241.

Cheetham, T. (2003). *The World Turned Inside Out: Henry Corbin and Islamic Mysticism*. Woodstock, CT: Spring Journal Books.

Dhaoui, H. (1998). *The Travels of Carl Gustav Jung in Africa*. Tunis: Afanine.

Dhaoui, H. (2000). *For a Maghrebin Psychoanalysis*. Paris: L'Harmattan.

Dhaoui, H. (2001). *Love in Islam* Paris: L'Harmattan.

Franz, M.-L. von. (1980). *Alchemy: An Introduction to the Symbolism and the Psychology*. Toronto: Inner City Books.

Franz, M.-L. von. (1999). *Muhammad ibn Umail's Hall ar-Rumuz: Historical Introduction and Psychological Comment*. Egg, Switzerland: private printing.

Franz, M.-L. von. (2000). Aurora Consurgens: *A Document Attributed to Thomas Aquinas on the Problem of Opposites in Alchemy*. Toronto: Inner City Books.

Gibb, H.A.R., and J.H. Kramers (eds.) (1961). "Assassins," *Shorter Encyclopaedia of Islam*. New York: Cornell University Press, p. 48-49.

Hecker, J. (2003). "Murderous Brothers: Archetypal Images of the West and Islam" (conference paper).

Jung, C.G. (1961/1965). *Memories, Dreams, Reflections*. New York: Vintage Books.

Jung, C.G. (1950/1968). "Concerning Rebirth," *Collected Works*, Vol. 9i, p. 113-147.

Lapidus, I.M. (2002). *A History of Islamic Societies*. Cambridge, UK: Cambridge University Press.

Lewis, B. (1967). *The Assassins: A Radical Sect in Islam.* New York: Oxford University Press.

McCarthy, R.J. (tr.) (1980). *Deliverance from Error.* Louisville, KY: Fons Vitae.

McCarthy, R.J. (tr.) (2000). *Al-Ghazali's Path to Sufism.* Louisville, KY: Fons Vitae.

Ryce-Menuhin, J. (ed.) (1994). *Jung and the Monotheisms: Judaism, Christianity and Islam.* London & New York: Routledge.

Schimmel, A. (1975). *Mystical Dimensions of Islam.* Chapel Hill: University of North Carolina Press.

Spiegelman, J.M. (ed.) (1991). *Sufism, Islam and Jungian Psychology.* Scottsdale, AZ: Falcon Press.

# Archetypal Hatred as Social Bond: Strategies for its Dissolution

*John Dourley*

## The Paradox

Contrary to frequently heard criticism, Jungian psychology is not without profound social implication. It is, in fact, subtly anarchic because it is thoroughly subversive to all claims by every collectivity and individual to the possession of a political, religious, ethnic or cultural absolute truth within the confines of history. The corrosive nature of the archetypal psyche toward all such absolute claims is based on the inability of any archetypal expression to exhaust its source. This truth extends to all significant cultures and civilizations since all are expressions of archetypal foundations.

The inability of civilizations to give exhaustive expression to their creator, the archetypal unconscious, coupled with their too often heard claims that, in fact, they do, points to a dark, possibly insoluble paradox, at the heart of Jung's social psychology. The paradox is this. All civilizations, past and present, owe their existence and endurance to social processes of archetypal bonding that are expressed formally in their lasting cultural achievements. This bonding works a double effect. It at once legitimates the society's supremacy among societies and in so doing grounds that society's latent hatred of differently bonded societies.

Deepening his recognition of the social ambivalence of archetypal bonding is Jung's clear conviction that such bonding lowers the consciousness of those bonded in direct proportion to its bonding power. The greater the commitment such bonding forges the lesser the individual consciousness of the bonded. With the lowering of collective consciousness comes an inevitable lowering of the moral responsibility of the group and so of the individuals in the group. The psychodynamic Jung here describes leads to a grim psychosocial law: effective social cohesion is based on archetypal energies which breed an immoral unconsciousness in direct proportion to the strength of the social cohesion they provide. This cohesion is the ultimate basis of the potential hatred that then necessarily exists between archetypally bonded communities. Jung writes of such group possession, "This ghastly power is mostly explained as fear of the neighboring nation, which is supposed to be possessed by a malevolent fiend." (Jung 1937/1958, par. 85, p. 48) The victims of such societal faith are left with little ultimate choice in their interface than the options to convert or kill, as in the ideological warfare of the twentieth century, or sometimes to convert and kill, as in the European attack on first peoples in the invasion of the Americas following their discovery.

The foregoing is a general sketch of the paradox at the core of Jung's social psychology. Let us now turn to the specific elements that contribute to the paradox. Jung identifies at least four intersecting or synergistic elements that together identify the role of the archetypal in the creation of civilizations and cultures and so contribute to the potential hatred and destruction that attaches to that role.

*Jung's Appropriation of Levy-Bruhl*

The first two elements in Jung's social psychology are heavily indebted to Levy-Bruhl's original sociology and ethnography. From those sources Jung appropriated the ideas of the *partici-pation mystique* and the *représentations collectives*. Bruhl and the ethnological community were eventually to disown the concep-tion of *participation mystique* much to Jung's dismay. (Jung, 1956/1963, p. 250, n. 662; 1948/1960, p. 265, n. 12; 1939/1958, p. 504, n. 28) In spite of his reluctance to abandon the formulation entirely, Jung's reception of the idea and the psychology behind it is ambivalent and ultimately deeply critical, hedged about with caution and warnings of its questionable morality. On the one hand, Jung will occasionally express an almost wistful regret that contemporary Western consciousness has lost the animistic possibility of the experience the *participation mystique* describes. The lost experience, for Jung, is that of the continu-ity, if not identity, of the individual with the surrounding world of nature and of a human community, formed in consciousness by the dynamic "All-oneness" of the underlying unconscious. (Jung, 1921/1971, par. 430, p. 255) In this side of its meaning, the phrase "*participation mystique*" insinuates a theophany, the total transparency of one's environment to its matrix, familiar to nature mystics and to romantics and also to be found in many variations of microcosmic/macrocosmic interpenetration that could currently contribute to an ecological psychology.

Jung, however, both appreciates and criticizes the sense of community as communion such an experience generates. On the point central to the concern of this paper, he identifies the primary characteristic of the *participation mystique* to be the creation of that tight cohesiveness that is characteristic of "archaic" societies. (Jung 1921/1971, par. 12, p. 10; 1948a/1960, par. 127, p. 65; 1931/1960, par. 329, p. 153, 154; 1948/1960, par. 507, p. 264, 265)

At the same time, Jung sees the *participation mystique* as operative in a wide range of human activities, relationships, and conceptions. It is behind, for instance, Rousseau's influential, though possibly romantic, conception of universal relatedness (Jung 1921/1971, par. 123, p. 82); as such it may have entered into French Enlightenment theory of the collective will. In analytic work today, *participation mystique* can create the intersubjective unities, often unconscious and so questionable, between analyst and client in transference. (Jung 1921/1971, par. 146, p. 93; 1946/1966, par. 376, p. 182, 183, n. 27) It is operative in any form of projection in which an archetypal reality is identified with an object, which can then be divinized as mana (Jung 1948a/1960, par. 127, p. 65) or vilified as the hostile other, now perceived as a denier of one's own archetypal reality and so as a threat to one's own sacred truth. (Jung 1931/1970, par. 130, 131, p. 64, 65)

Jung's ambivalence about the *participation mystique* lies in his appreciation of the power of such experience to unite the individual with community and nature, even as he deplores the "... *state of identity in mutual unconsciousness ...*" that such an identification so easily breeds. (Jung 1931a/1970, par. 69, p. 37, author's italics; 1952/1967, par. 504, p. 327; 1935/1966, par. 329, p. 206) *Participation mystique* can foster the most intense sense of mystical communion with all that is as well as the "mass intoxication" and the "psychic epidemics" of archetypally generated group possession. (Jung 1950/1959, par. 225-227, p. 125-127) The ethical ambiguity of the phenomenon forces Jung to wonder, in the end, if critical consciousness and morality are compatible with it. (Jung 1939/1958, par. 817, p. 504, n. 28)

Closer to our contemporary situation, Jung extends the operation of the *participation mystique* to post-Enlightenment or modern political ideological communities. (Jung 1929/1967, par. 66, 67, p. 45) In certain ways these communities are much more highly developed consciously and technologically. However, their one-sided imprisonment in consciousness renders them dangerously vulnerable to manipulation by archetypal powers still operative in the collective unconscious, whose existence and power these communities ignore, vilify or suppress. As a consequence of this denial modern societies are victimized by the lethal ideological possession of collective reason severed from its depths by archetypal powers in those very depths. The effect is a devastating uprootedness that turned Jung's twentieth century and the beginning of our own into the epoch of genocide.

Such common cultural ideas as the holy soil of the father or motherland, the home of the ancestral spirits, the preferred religion, political system or movement remained for Jung but thinly disguised forms of the *participation mystique* in contemporary dress. (Jung 1931/1966, par. 128, p. 82) Jung is profoundly sensitive to the power of such archetypal attractions but in the end his psychology starkly exposes their dangerous shadow of group unconsciousness. His critique effectively identifies contemporary political, religious, nationalist, and ethnic bonding and their various combinations as little more than remnants of tribalism with the ever-present danger of tribal warfare.

*Jung and the* Représentations Collectives

As he develops Levy-Bruhl's related idea of the *representations collectives*, Jung's thought becomes more explicitly societal. He identifies these symbols shaping social cohesion as grounded in archetypal energies and bearing the psychic equivalent of a magical salvation to modern societies under the guise of "...religions and political ideologies ..." (Jung 1952/1967, par. 221, p. 156) Again there is the same ambiguity in Jung's evaluation of these bonding symbols and their mythologies which so readily become ideologies. Jung admits that such *représentations collectives* can be "therapeutic" (*Ibid.,* par. 683, p. 442) because they arise to consciousness from that dimension of the unconscious common to "mankind in general." (Jung 1921/1971, par. 692, p. 417) Imbedded in humanity they appeared in the distant past in more primordial images. In the present day they create the societal absolutes held by contemporary cultures, and there are none without them. (Jung 1921/1971, par. 692, p. 418; 1951/1966, par 247, p. 120) Moreover, where collective representations appear currently – for instance, in the form of a national flag, or the face of a leader – they carry with them an emotional power making them irresistible to individuals and societies, whose lives they can permanently possess and transform for better or worse. (Jung 1936/1960, par. 254, p. 122)

In the insane the *représentations collectives* are heard as the voice of God, (Jung 1946/1954, par. 207, p. 116) sometimes commanding irrational and destructive things, sometimes a hyper-ethical mission. Elsewhere they create as wide a range of phenomena as the religions themselves, (Jung 1954/1967, par. 478, p. 347) personal religious figures such as messiahs, prophets and shamans, (Jung 1936/1960, par. 254, p. 122) good poetry, and the lowly slogan. (Jung 1935/1966, par. 231, p. 145, 146) In the deeper, archetypal sense that Jung gives to them they connect the individual throughout human history with the unconscious and its vitalities. (Jung 1951/1966, par. 247, p. 120) They are the basis of the living substance of whatever truth is transmitted through esoteric teaching. (Jung 1954/1959, par. 6, p. 5) Though Jung is speaking, in this context, of such transmission among primordial peoples, he implies that Christian dogma, and by extension all dogma, once carried the possessive energies of the *représentations collectives*. (Jung 1961/1980, par. 551, p. 240; par 579, p. 253)

Possessive and dangerous though they may be, where the *représentations collectives* fail responsibly to reconnect or reroot individual and society with the unconscious in a conscious way, the mind is cut adrift and "… in practice is susceptible to psychic epidemics." (Jung 1950/1959, par. 227, p. 127; 1939/1959, par. 496, p. 278) This statement again addresses the full paradox of the *représentations collectives* in Jung's thought. Without them the individual is cut off from the stability they afford in grounding the individual, usually through a community, in the unconscious. But with them, and under their spell, the individual can easily be led into an unconscious conformity with unexamined archetypal ideas, divested of responsible moral judgment.

While the impact of the *représentations collectives* create historical epochs with their successive revelations and are, for Jung, the deepest of healing resources when consciously assimilated (Jung 1935/1970, par. 1043, p. 549) they are, like the *participation mystique* they foster, capable of reducing societies to the level of a mob possessed. Writes Jung in 1936:

> There is no lunacy people under the domination of an archetype will not fall a prey to. If thirty years ago anyone had dared to predict that our psychological development was tending towards a revival of the mediaeval persecutions of the Jews, that Europe would again tremble before the Roman fasces and the tramp of legions, that people would once more give the Roman salute, as two thousand years ago, and that instead of the Christian Cross an archaic swastika would lure onward millions of warriors ready for death – why that man would have been hooted at as a mystical fool. And today? Surprising as it may seem, all this absurdity is a horrible reality … The man of the past who lived in a world of archaic "représentations collectives" has risen again into very visible and painfully real life, and this not only in a few unbalanced

individuals but in many millions of people. (Jung 1936/1959, par. 98, p. 48)

What might Jung write today about the current reappearance of archaic humanity possessed by conflicting *représentations collectives* under whose power national/tribal leaders can call each other and their opposing empires "evil" or "satanic" and go for the most part unchallenged and even cheered on by many in their nations? The need for "mystical fools" and their prophetic insight did not end in the period preceding the 1930s.

Jung's ambivalence toward the collective representation as the agent of archetypal bonding is even more dramatically evident when he attributes to it the origins of such movements as Hitler's regime in the twentieth century and the witch hunts in fifteenth and sixteenth century Germany, on the one hand, as well as the rise and spread of Christianity in the second and third centuries and Islam in the seventh, on the other. (Jung 1948/1980, par. 1389, p. 607; 1952/1967, par 221, p. 156) Though morally of contradictory nature, these movements proceed from the same source and are charged with identical archetypal impulses and energies.

In their capacity to deprive their victims of conscious discrimination and moral autonomy, a connection exists between Jung's understanding of Levy-Bruhl's *représentations collectives* and his use of Pierre Janet's *abaissement du niveau mental*. Both describe states of loss or deliberate surrender of conscious control to unconscious forces. (Jung 1921/1971, par. 199, p. 123; par. 765, p. 451) Jung's own practice of active imagination involved a deliberate lowering of the threshold of consciousness with the purpose of a more immediate dialogue with unconscious elements in the interests of their conscious assimilation. Unfortunately such loss can also be wrought involuntarily by the power of archetypal attraction itself. (Jung 1952/1960, par. 841, p. 436) Under such a spell the total personality, possessed by one dimension of archetypal energy, is reduced to the status of fanatic single-mindedness. (Jung 1950/1959, par. 214, p. 120) The same psychology can apply to competing cultures themselves.

In linking the *collective representation* to the *abaissement du niveau mental*, the profile of archetypally informed cultural faith as a diminishment of the individual and as a danger to a wider world community becomes much clearer. Wherever humanity has lost sight of the true origins of faith in the psyche, (and here Jung usually has Enlightenment rationalism in mind), religion becomes insidiously transformed into secular ideologies. Archetypally inspired slaughter continues, now under the auspices of reason, which is itself under the suasion of archetypal possession.

## Jung and the "Isms"

Jung's critique of the archetypal cohesiveness afforded to culture and civilization at the cost of individual consciousness and morality continues with his attack on the "isms." The "isms" are but a variation on the more specific archetypal powers that bond society. Jung refers to such collective unconsciousness as "… the demons and gods of primitives or the 'isms' so fanatically believed in by modern man." (Jung 1954/1960, par. 366, p. 175) The "isms," he notes, can produce a "mass psychosis" in their victims. (Jung 1948/1980, par. 1389, p. 607)

They constitute a "magic word," effectively a new religion (Jung 1954/1960, par. 405, p. 206) which possesses those uprooted from their deeper humanity and wholly immerses them in mass collective unconsciousness. (Jung 1946/1970, par. 469, p. 234)

Not infrequently, notes Jung, religious leaders themselves extol such loss of consciousness as a commendable faith commitment to what is from his perspective a parochial revelation seeking universal acceptance. (Jung 1954/1960, par. 425, p. 219) As such the modern political "isms" are but "... a variant of the denominational religions...." (Jung 1954/1959, par. 125, p. 62) Yet no one, for Jung, is exempt from the influence of a dominant "ism" in the individual psyche. (*Idem*) It is to this personal "ism", the inner capacity (and near necessity) to commit to archetypal suasion, that the political and cultural "isms" appeal, even as such ideologies dull individual autonomous consciousness and moral responsibility in doing so. (Jung 1950a/1959, par. 617, p. 349) Jung would here align himself with thinkers like Paul Tillich in identifying a dimension of faith in the very constitution of human consciousness. Tillich would agree with Jung's position that no one can lay aside a faith without assuming another one. (1954/1959, par. 129, p. 62, 63) The paradox at the heart of Jung's thought on these matters can now be restated. Humanity cannot be without faith, whether in explicitly religious or more disguised secular and cultural form, even as it becomes increasingly aware that specific faiths in their collective concretions now threaten humanity's common future.

## The Collective Shadow

Jung's understanding of the collective shadow adds a final dimension to what has been said about archetypal bonding. For an archetypally bonded community, *any* differently bonded society becomes that community's shadow, a threat to the "truth" of its bonding power, and a residual and living insult to its God, culture and values. In the wider context of his thought on shadow, Jung locates "absolute evil" in the collective unconscious and so, effectively, in God or, more precisely, in those agencies which universally give rise to the experience of the divine. (Jung 1951/1959, par. 19, p. 10) Communities bonded in archetypally induced faith "know" themselves to be in possession of a saving truth, religious or secular, which confers a privileged position on them as the chosen with the right and duty to spread the good news. In fact, they are possessed by their truth. The archetypally conferred primacy and goodness of any group proceeds from the same unconscious source in which Jung locates absolute evil, which is why differently bonded communities are so readily identified as evil and quickly attain the status of the demonic. At this point the bonding archetype splits. Our absolute goodness demands their absolute evil. Our goodness can be criticized by our prophets who, in the end, remain faithful to the never-to-be-abandoned bonding tradition. Historically no punishing God has ever switched tribes. In processes of the projection of the collective shadow demonization becomes the first step to dehumanization and finally to elimination.

### The Huntington Paradigm

A specifically Jungian methodology seeks to find the meaning of any archetypal truth through variations of its expression. The variants support and expand each other, as, through such amplification, their underlying core is revealed by the contribution each partial expression makes to that core. Such a comparative methodology would generate the expectation that, if Jung's thought on the inescapability and dangers of archetypal bonding has any validity, variations on it would emerge independently of Jung's version. An impressive analogue does indeed lie readily at hand in Samuel P. Huntington's seminal essay, "The

*John Dourley*

Clash of Civilizations" (Huntington 1993, p. 22-49), widely
hailed as prophetic since September of 2001. Huntington is
Eaton Professor of the Science of Government and Director
of the John M. Olin Institute for Strategic Studies, Harvard
University. In that essay he argues that civilizations and their
cultures are based on religion as the most significant bonding
agency. (*Ibid.,* p. 25) Huntington contends further that future
wars will no longer be fought between princes, nation states
or, more recently, opposing ideologies, as were the twentieth
century so called World Wars and the Cold war, now more
accurately called European civil wars. (William Lind, quoted in
Huntington, p. 23) Rather, future wars will be between civilizations and their religiously based cultures. He names eight such
civilizations (*Ibid.,* p. 25); it is not necessary for the purposes of
this paper to identify them. It is relevant, however, to note that
Huntington fears the fundamentalism that can attach to each of
these civilizations in relation to the others and the possibility,
if not inevitability, of violence in their geographical interface or
what Huntington calls their "fault lines." (*Ibid.,* p. 29f) He makes
the point rather well that in ideological combat one could
change or modify sides or allegiances, say from communism to
capitalism or adopt a synthetic position. In the wars of civilization this is not possible. One cannot be half Catholic and half
Moslem. (*Ibid.,* p. 27)

In the end Huntington proposes the acceptance of the world
divided into these religiously based civilizations and recommends
strategic ploys for the maintenance of Western and American
power in the short and long run within this divided world, to
which he is apparently resigned. He does mention in passing
the value of identifying "elements of commonality" (*Ibid.,* p. 49)
between Western and non-Western civilizations. This remark
could point to a dawning recognition of the archetypal unconscious as the basic source and so common ground from which

competing cultures and their religious bases emerge. Huntington's own analysis, however, is starkly divested of what archetypal theory could add in identifying archetypal intransigence as the basis of the enmity that both Huntington and Jung would agree informs the clash of civilizations. For Huntington's grim realism uncovers few if any resources to offset a regression to a crusade mentality between civilizations and to what we have heard Jung describe as a return to archetypally based tribalism, each cultural tribe hypnotized by its *representations collectives*. There is little prospect in Huntington's realism of the nourishing of unity through cultural variety suggested, for instance, by Jung in his appropriation of the alchemical symbol of the *unus mundus*, the one world. (Jung 1956/1963, p. 533-553) In Jung's hands the symbol of the one world captures the consciousness toward which he would see the psyche moving in history, a consciousness that is aware that cultural differentiation has a common source in the unconscious, a vision that enables a deeper mutual sympathy among the differently bonded. Rather, Huntington evidences only an enlightened resignation to division and enmity and a concern for the maintenance of one's cultural supremacy within the international mayhem that results.

In the light of such a pessimistic analysis, psychology, the social sciences, the humanities and religious thought seem currently challenged to search for modes of communal affirmation that can move beyond the inevitability of the demonization of the different. This collective effort, to succeed, will necessarily entail a deeper examination of archetypal hatred as the shadow side of archetypal faith, currently the ever more obvious and still reigning agency in the generation of competing civilizations and the growing body count at their fault lines. Anything less will be ultimately evasive. The fact that no denial can cancel is that to date no significant civilization has achieved its self-affirmation without the cohesion provided by the hatred of an evil other. (Huntington 1993, p. 25) Jungians have contributed a great deal to the problem of the personal shadow, and this contribution has proved valuable to the therapy of the individual. Humanity's survival may now depend on extending this interest to the resolution of the collective shadow, where the murderous side of collective faith in bonding cultures would have to be faced without flinching.

*The Truth Shall Set You Free; the Doubt Freer*

In this collective psychological effort one ploy needs to be ruled out immediately. That is the option for a solution based exclusively on the powers of consciousness. Humanity may eventually be eliminated by its unconsciousness in a final *auto da fe* (act of faith) by archetypally generated competing civilizations, but humanity cannot free itself from this threat through solely conscious resources which are inevitably merely intellectual or willful. In reality, it is the denial of the unconscious basis of collective unconsciousness that is the first and surest step toward the next Holocaust. Jung's strategy would be different. Rather than a reliance on exclusively conscious strategies, his psychology works to persuade humanity of the power of the unconscious in matters societal. This is the first step in acknowledging humanity's fearsome role in ushering the unconscious into historical consciousness without destroying history in the process. Ever since Jung, late in life, wrote his *Answer to Job*, humanity has been challenged to accept consciously its role as the redeemer of divinity. In psychological language, this challenge means the endless ushering of the illimitable energies of the unconscious into the flow of historical consciousness toward that ideal point, never to be attained nor evaded, where consciousness would reflect the totality of its unconscious ground.

In this process, an attitude of that residual doubt which should accompany archetypal manifestation becomes a major resource that could free cultures from the devastation of archetypally induced collective unconsciousness. Archetypally grounded doubt is the skeptical side of wisdom that Jung affirms when he writes in reference to his debate with Martin Buber, "I 'abhor' the belief that I or anybody else could be in possession of an absolute truth." (Jung 1957/1975, p. 378) He confesses that he is grateful that his life has been enriched by "... the gift of doubt ..." (Jung 1944/1968, par. 8, p. 8) In a letter to the Dominican theologian, Victor White, in response to the latter's vocational insecurities, Jung confesses, "Doubt and insecurity are indispensable components of a complete life." (Jung 1954/1975, p. 171)

These remarks are not peripheral to the substance of archetypal theory but are, on the contrary, consistent with it, because archetypal theory would deny to any and every archetypal expression the possibility that it would or could exhaust the wealth of its source in its single formulation of it. Jung is explicit on this point when he describes the unconscious in terms that call up an infinite fecundity, one "... of indefinite extent with no assignable limits." (Jung 1941/1958, par. 390, p. 258) Any degree of realization of this fecundity in any individual and, by extension, in any culture or in history itself, is always surpassed by a remaining potential yet to be realized. This always unrealized potential is for Jung the only psychological, and so real, meaning of transcendence. Transcendence, so viewed, is the eternal difference between an intra-psychic unconscious plentitude demanding realization in consciousness and consciousness itself which can never resist nor fulfill this demand. This dialectic between aspiration and realization is the psychic substance of the meaning, the joy and the tragedy of human life, personal and collective.

In this dialectic, doubt and psychic transcendence coincide and the redemptive quality of both emerge. Archetypal doubt is aware that all archetypal expression, including that of the great civilizations and their supportive religious and cultural values, shares a common origin in the unconscious, whose creativity outstrips its expression in any and each of them. From this perspective, any claim by one cultural expression to being history's culmination becomes absurd. More, a keen understanding of their common origin should endow each civilization with a sense of its relativity enabling each to see the differently bonded not as threats to its uniqueness but as variants of a common matrix productive of all. The ongoing historical play between consciousness and the unconscious would come to be seen as the latter's drive to express the totality of its resources in humanity. The idea that any concrete expression would complete the process would be dismissed not only as dangerous but as immoral. The need to kill or convert would cede to a sense of awe at the art and genius of the unconscious expressing in other notes and keys the substance of one's own tradition.

The doubt that could make archetypal bonding relative and safe for the world is perhaps Jung's major contribution to a strategy for survival, because it identifies the source of the sense of the absolute and the doubt that should humanize it in the same psychological process. In this, Jung's psychology is one of the few modes of modern thought to combine the sacramental with the iconoclastic; the stability of the modern with the deconstruction of the post-modern periods. His sacramentalism, deeper than that offered by most religions, is grounded on his recognition of the proclivity of the unconscious itself to generate numinous experience. For Jung, the psyche itself is the ultimate sacrament. His iconoclasm is similarly based on the equally foundational psychic fact that the wealth of the uncon-scious cannot rest with any of its expressions. Moreover, his integration of the sacramental and the iconoclastic as the basis of both the sacred nature of all cultures, and of the doubt that renders them safe, is not the only resource his vision offers the contemporary world. There are others to which we now turn.

Very occasionally, Jung will speak of therapies or therapists as "intercepting" incipient mass movements and so offsetting their potential devastation. In these passages he seems to envi-sion therapies that would be able to discern the archetypal nature of incipient social psychoses and to aid in the legitimate integration, through the individual and into society, of whatever truth their archetypal allure might bear. (Jung 1946/1970, par. 461, p. 229; par. 473, p. 236, 237) No doubt, in these rare pas-sages, Jung was speaking of analytical psychology as contribut-ing to the early interception of that archetypal possession that funds psychic epidemics of every sort. It is not a theme that he develops widely in his work, possibly because such a process of interception would demand too much from any therapist. Therapists, in fact, must be assumed to be as deeply involved in their political and social milieu as their patients, and as suscepti-ble to being overcome by archetypal forces as was Jung himself in the period immediately before National Socialism revealed its true face to him. To ask a therapist to be immersed in and yet somehow to transcend such social forces in the interests of their more gracious personal and societal integration is to ask a lot, to say the least. Yet it cannot be denied that Jung, in his writings on social psychology, does, on occasion, point to the possibility.

Jung makes an equally great demand on the individual when he proposes as the ultimate resistance to mass epidemics the organization of one's personal psyche, in the form of an ego working in close collaboration with the self. The cultivation of the self in the individual would hopefully match and counter the self-organization of an archetypally possessed society. As Jung puts it, "Resistance to the organized mass can be effected only by the man who is as well organized in his individuality as the mass itself." (Jung 1957/1970, par. 540, p. 278) But how many individuals in Nazi Germany were psychologically as well organized as the Gestapo was politically? In this proposal Jung would seem to suggest that the next war, genocide, or ethnic cleansing can best be avoided through the birth of the self in a critical mass of conscious individuals who would then be in a position to act as a societal psychic prophylactic against unconscious, archetypal mass infection. This assumption is reinforced when Jung more than once affirms that only the grace of inner transformation or personal spiritual renewal would stand as the ultimate resource against the murderous proclivity of mass psychoses. (Jung 1945/1970, par. 441, p. 216; par. 443, p. 217; 1946/1970, par. 486, p. 243) In a letter to Bernhard Lang, amplifying the remarks cited above, he is explicit in locating personal political freedom and resistance to mass movements in those individuals who feel themselves to be "… 'anchored in God' …" (Jung 1957/1975, p. 371) In this context being anchored in God and in the self would, for Jung, mean the same thing.

Jung will describe this turn inward to the support of the self or of the divine as the culmination of what he terms "a millennial process." (Jung 1952/1958, par. 631, p. 402) This kind of interiorization amounts to the conscious recall of all Gods and all absolutes to their psychic origins. There, the conscious individual can converse with them in a psychic containment that is safer and promises more for the human future. But why is this so for Jung? It is so because as long as humanity continues to perceive the absolutes in any of their forms as imposed from beyond the individual, as opposed to identifying their origin in the depths of the psyche common to all individuals, the individual is relatively helpless to control their fragmenting divisiveness in one's psyche and in one's society. When these powers are realized to be externalizations of the depths of human interiority shared by all, commerce with them becomes safer though more painful because one must then squarely face the conflict within the containment of the psyche. One then has to deal with one's inner fascist, communist, democrat, capitalist, socialist, nationalist, or racist. All are part of our shadow, and shadow is always one's own potential. The same process must apply to the bevy of divinities that have escaped psychic containment for centuries and continue to deal arbitrarily with the human from their position of eternal self-sufficiency. Their return to source would modify, if not eliminate, their tyranny from beyond and the conflict between the communities that have sprung up in their name within history. If humanity does not kill over differences in bodily effluents, why does it do so over such equally natural psychic effluents as the divinities and their incarnations in religious or secular form? The rising consciousness of their origin within the human psyche should make it more difficult to take human life on their behalf.

## Jung's Myth as Ultimate Resource

In the end, and in conclusion, the greatest resource that Jung has to offer in the overcoming of archetypally based hatred between conflicting collectivities is the deeper dimension of his own myth, that is, in those dimensions of psyche that are specific to his myth and distinguish it from others. Jung's psychology is a myth in conscious continuity with precedents in Western culture that have heretofore been peripheral. In pointing to these often-excluded sides of the Western soul, his analytical psychology contributes to and fosters their current resurgence which is everywhere more evident. In continuity with certain streams of western mysticism, alchemy, and nearly every form of Platonic and neo-Platonic philosophy, especially in those forms it has assumed in and since the Renaissance, the core of Jung's vision would have it that the unconscious creates consciousness to become conscious in it. This means that each bearer of human consciousness necessarily shares a solidarity of origin with every human and that the common, though always unique, responsibility of each individual is to usher this origin into one's personal form of life-enhancing consciousness within one's allotted share of history.

Each of Jung's master images of the self and its dynamics; the mandala, the *anthropos*, the reality of synchronicity, alchemy, and alchemy's crowning symbol, the *unus mundus,* points to the natural inherence of each individual's consciousness in the source of all consciousness. This truth, for Jung, is the foundational possibility of an ever widening universal compassion. The life of the individual derives its greatest meaning in allowing itself to become the servant of the self in the emergence of a more "compendious personality" (Jung 1941/1958, par. 390, p. 258) whose sympathy would move to an embrace as extensive as the universal ground from which it emerges. This perpetually emerging consciousness would always be in some tension with the more constrictive collectivities out of which it is born and whose instinct it is always to supersede toward a more conscious and related human community.

Humanity's universal vocation, thus understood, is always fraught with danger, and now possibly with the danger that the process could be prematurely ended. The danger that so many of us sense today is ultimately based on the recognition that, so far, human solidarity and its oneness is only in the unconscious. As the archetypal unconscious creates consciousness and then seeks ever greater realization in it, it splits the conscious world into many compelling if not overwhelming manifestations, whose social incarnations divide humanity into warring factions. It remains humanity's task then to bring to its conscious differentiation an organic integration that is ever more consciously reflective of the total resources of the unconscious. Such integration would not only tolerate but revel in the variations of what seeks expression in it. Unless a sense of the common, deeply human origin of cultural archetypal differences becomes the centerpiece of a new myth, superseding currently competitive myths and the cultures they empower, Huntington's paradigm of an ongoing clash of civilizations would appear to carry the day and to define our future. The only real question about the future would then be profoundly discouraging. The question would be who will win and how to win the hopeless geopolitical struggles Huntington so well depicts.

Jung's myth has more to offer humanity than such collective despair. As already indicated, one image among his many that speaks to our current need for a transcending vision is that of the alchemical *unus mundus.* This consciousness comes as the crowning moment of an arduous and never ending ascetic process involving a life long integration of the shadow that most would recognize only in projection. At times this stage of the process is depicted as death and yet it always culminates in a full embodiment or incarnation in the finite world. However ephemeral or residual the culminating experience may have been, the consciousness the symbol describes is one that perceives the world from the vantage point of the "... eternal Ground of all empirical being ..." (Jung 1956/1963, par. 760, p. 534) Effectively, the image describes the perception of the other from the perspective of the common ground of individual and other. This vision describes nothing less than a theophany that makes personal or collective hate impossible to sustain because it is grounded in the experience that humanity and nature share a common origin beyond archetypal differentiation and visible in such differentiation. The consciousness alchemy describes as the *unus mundus* enables the embrace of the other as other, both individual and collective, through the experience that we and the other inhere in and emerge from a common source. Otherness as alienation or threat is thus overcome and an embrace of the different because different becomes possible.

To give such consciousness of the "One World" real significance in the face of realpolitik and contemporary fantasies of power appears romantic and vulnerable to cynical dismissal. Jung, however, saw the emergence of such vastly extended sympathy as the state to which the psyche moves in history, by its own nature and dynamic. Jung's social psychology, though so apparently fragile, is in a position to make a substantial contribution to any theory that would seek first principles for the survival of the species. His social psychology can also confront alternative solutions with many questions. For instance, it could ask "If such a universal compassion is not generated in historical consciousness by the source of consciousness itself, are not all other solutions to archetypal differentiation purely conscious? If so, are conscious solutions of no more hope for the future than they have been in the past, because they cannot touch the ground preceding conflicting historical differentiations and so are unable to foster a myth that would heal or unify them?"

Solutions contrived by a lesser psychological consciousness may lower the body count for a time, but they can never touch the enmity behind the count. In fact such well-meaning efforts, in the forms of treaties, cease-fires, economic packages, redrawing of borders and so forth, seem but to delay rather than undermine the next archetypal disaster. Nor does the learning curve seem to rise through the cycle of these catastrophes. The twentieth century began with the First World War through an assassination in the same culturally turbulent area where the century ended with attempted genocide. As this is written, another war to end wars rages in an all too familiar manner.

Jung himself was to die when the world was still immersed in the tensions of the archetypal divide and its competing "isms" known as the Cold War. Though the political divisions may have been as dangerous to human survival then as they are now, Jung did not leave us in despair. His confidence that the quality of mind he sought to describe in the image of the alchemical "one world" might itself attain the globalization it sought is evident in his late lines, "The afternoon of humanity, in a distant future, may yet evolve a different ideal. In time, even conquest will cease to be the dream." (Jung 1939/1958, par. 787, p. 493) The social implications of Jung's myth on the archetypal inevitability and dangers of social bonding may yet have an important role to play in humanity's reaching that distant afternoon if there is to be one.

## References

Huntington, S. P. (1993). "The Clash of Civilizations," *Foreign Affairs,* Summer.

Jung, C.G. (1921/1971). *Psychological Types,* CW 6.

Jung, C.G. (1929/1967). "Commentary on 'The Secret of the Golden Flower,'" CW 13.

Jung, C.G. (1931/1960). "The Structure of the Psyche," CW 8.

Jung, C.G. (1931/1966). "On the Relation of Analytical Psychology to Poetry,: CW 15.

Jung, C.G. (1931/1970). "Archaic Man," CW 10.

Jung, C.G. (1931a/1970). "Mind and Earth," CW 10.

Jung, C.G. (1935/1966). "The Assimilation of the Unconscious," CW 7.

Jung, C.G. (1935/1970). "Editorial" (*Zentralblatt für Psychotherapie*), CW 10.

Jung, C.G. (1936/1959). "The Concept of the Collective Unconscious," CW 9i.

Jung, C.G. (1936/1960). "Psychological Factors Determining Human Behaviour," CW 8.

Jung, C.G. (1937/1958) "Psychology and Religion," CW 11.

Jung, C.G. (1939/1958). "Psychological Commentary on 'The Tibetan Book of the Great Liberation,'" CW11.

Jung, C.G. (1939/1959). "Conscious, Unconscious, and Individuation," CW 9i.

Jung, C.G. (1941/1958). "Transformation Symbolism in the Mass," CW 11.

Jung, C.G. (1944/1968). *Psychology and Alchemy,* CW 12.

Jung, C.G. (1945/1970). "After the Catastrophe," CW 10.

Jung, C.G. (1946/1954). "Analytical Psychology and Education," CW 17.

Jung, C.G. (1946/1966). "The Psychology of the Transference," CW 16.

Jung, C.G. (1946/1970). "Epilogue to 'Essays on Contemporary Events,'" CW 10.

Jung, C.G. (1948/1960). "General Aspects of Dream Psychology," CW 8.

Jung, C.G. (1948a/1960). "On Psychic Energy," CW 8.

Jung, C.G. (1948/1980). "Techniques of Attitude Change Conducive to World Peace" (Memorandum to UNESCO), CW 18.

Jung, C.G. (1950/1959). "Concerning Rebirth," CW 9i.

Jung, C.G. (1950a/1959). "A Study in the Process of Individuation," CW 9i.

Jung, C.G. (1951/1959). *Aion,* CW 9ii.

Jung, C.G. (1951/1966). "Fundamental Questions of Psychotherapy," CW 16.

Jung, C.G. (1952/1958). "Answer to Job," CW 11.

Jung, C.G. (1952/1960). "Synchronicity: An Acausal Connecting Principle," CW 8.

Jung, C.G. (1952/1967). *Symbols of Transformation,* CW 5.

Jung, C.G. (1954/1959). "Archetypes of the Collective Unconscious," CW 9i.

Jung, C.G. (1954/1959). "Concerning the Archetypes, with Special Reference to the Anima Concept," CW 9i.

Jung, C.G. (1954/1960). "On the Nature of the Psyche," CW 8.

Jung, C.G. (1954/1967). "The Philosophical Tree," CW 13.

Jung, C.G. (1954/1975). "Letter to Father Victor White, 10 April, 1954" in *C.G. Jung, Letters,* Vol. 2, 1951-1961. G. Adler and A. Jaffe, eds. Princeton: Princeton University Press, p. 163 – 174.

Jung, C.G. (1956/1963). *Mysterium Coniunctionis,* CW 14.

Jung, C.G. (1957/1970). "The Undiscovered Self (Present and Future)," CW 10.

Jung, C.G. (1957/1975). "Letter to Bernhard Lang, 14 June, 1957" and "Letter to Bernhard Lang, later in June, 1957" in *C.G. Jung, Letters*, Vol. 2, 1951-1961. G. Adler and A. Jaffe, eds. Princeton: Princeton University Press, p. 370 – 372; p. 376 – 379.

Jung, C.G. (1961/1980). "Symbols and the Interpretation of Dreams," CW 18.

# Response to John Dourley

*Beverley Zabriskie*

On the morning of September 11, 2002, my friend, a poet, lay with other writers on the ground of New York City's Union Square. Wearing shirts with the logo "Not in My Name," they remained prone in silent protest, at the place where a year before, on September 11, 2001, a towering, spontaneous memorial had been created in the name of those killed in that day's attacks.

Their shirts declared that they refused to lend their names (some famous and some unknown) to political rationales for revenge. Their bodies were positioned against the appetite for retaliation through the body counts of war. They pressed against collective bonding too easily forged through enmity toward others. Many business men and women, en route to work, joined them, using briefcases for pillows. They added their names, rather than join with those who would misuse the ashes of September 11th's victims for "the creation of that tight cohesiveness that is characteristic of archaic societies." By lying down, they stood against what John Dourley, in his finely thought and felt argument, has termed archetypal hatred.

The next day, September 12, in Kabul, Afghanistan, a close relative, a young American journalist, and his colleague, a female photographer, were asked by a young Afghani surgeon, a devout Muslim, to join him at a Sufi meeting where he had been assured that his American guests would be welcome. When they arrived at a shabby apartment near Kabul's rug merchants and meat markets, the elder, "he who has left the world for a real love relationship with God," had not yet appeared, and the apartment was filled with Sufi men. The young man was immediately welcomed, but when an argument broke out about the woman's presence, she left. Later, the white-bearded Sufi elder arrived. After many songs and testimonies to the love of God, the old man rose to speak. He scolded the group saying, "Who are we to act as if we own this house? We are not the landlords of God's house, where all should be welcome." If this woman came, he went on, it is because "God brought her here to see our worship, and if we turned her away, we have turned away God." The Sufi men then spoke of their resistance to women as a Taliban holdover, remembering that women had taken part in other Sufi ceremonies, like the one held in the night at the graveyard. After some fighting over who would sing next, there were more songs. Then, one after the other, throughout the evening, the Sufis apologized to the surgeon.

The young journalist, who describes Afghanistan as "the massive convergence of all brands of opposing forces," was touched that these men offered him "their meager tea and sweets and biscuits" and, finally, their apologies, in "a show of the famed Afghan hospitality, so wonderful and so jarring in the context of twenty-three years of war and many more of ethnic, tribal, and sect hostilities."

Both these small stories, told by intimates from two geographical sides of our present cultural divide, speak to the possibility of standing against collectives shaped around hostilities toward the other experienced as a threat. In his excellent and profound paper, however, John Dourley, following Jung, posits what history and contemporary politics sadly show to be more often the rule: that it is the missing pieces in our beings, the lacunae in our sense of self, the most inhumane, alienated, frustrated, and dissociated parts of our personalities, that we attempt to fill by imagining, projecting, and connecting with them as if they were divine.

In some instances, as with the men in Kabul, who have lived in war, poverty, and the lack of potential to develop, we may perceive how exclusion of a questionable other might seem to seal over the wounds caused by external deprivation. But how, looking at the behavior of those on the other side of privilege, can one explain the presence of a similar syndrome among those who claim pride of place through family or abundant resources, or claim exemption from the norms through unquestioned opinions and unwavering beliefs? I would suggest that the enmity on the part of those who *have* against those who are *wanting* forms the needed scab over the narcissistic wound that is created by having too much – too much ease, too much rightness and righteousness, too much entitlement, and too much greed for even more. In such instances, the missing piece is that sense of self which emerges from an internal source. Such a self sense lends to character that depth and space necessary for interiority, reflectiveness, and a tolerance for encounter and ambiguity. As Dourley puts it, quoting Jung: "Doubt and insecurity are indispensable components of a complete life."

Dourley also asks, "If humanity does not kill over differences in bodily effluents, why does it do so over such equally natural psychic effluents as the divinities and their incarnations in religious and secular form?" Both absolute despair and absolute hubris may invent and invest in an image of a god to contain, carry, and supply the missing piece, and thus in a god who is used as a servant of compensation – sometimes for deprivation and hopelessness and sometimes for status and plenty. In such a covenant, God must be right, and then, in negotiation with a righteous God as both inspiration and servant, one is enabled to rise above both having been wronged and ever being wrong. One might say it this way: those who cannot bear to be an incarnated human imagine they may incorporate God so that they can disassociate from internal lacks and cement over internal splits.

We are accustomed to imagining that deprived people, "failures," hate those whose lives are plentiful and show accomplishment. But we need to recognize that the satisfied and successful also can detest those whose circumstances are other than theirs, in order to distance themselves from those who embody their own impoverishment of soul. The people who lay down in protest in New York's Union Square and who rose in apology at the Sufi meeting in Afghanistan moved through, and beyond, the shadow-projecting process that demands exclusiveness in the name of belonging. Dourley's paper helps us to face that an individual or collective system that is unable to tolerate the suffering of incompleteness is going to overfill itself with a divine right, which both drains its humanity and would take away the humanity of others. Those who cannot bear being relativized by a recognition that they are incomplete deliberately keep themselves far removed from Jung's "compendious personality" lest they have to experience a painful partialness in themselves and their beliefs. They cannot bear the comparison with the larger dimensions of the psyche and the truths that emerge from the fullness of psychic life.

Dourley's complex interpretation of Jung's insights about the defensive nature of most group bonding evokes questions about whether such archaic and historical layers of psychic structure are amenable to change. Jung saw that compassion for the diversity of the other could come through realization of oneself as "a multiplicity through a unity." This is akin to the perception of Robert Jay Lifton (1993), the psychiatrist of crisis and trauma, who speaks of internal interactions, and the shifts that these make possible, within a "protean self." Jung and Dourley hope for expansion of psychological range within persons and groups through fostering awareness of "a solidarity of origin with every human." Then the knowingly partial self may recognize itself as but a single and parochial expression of psychic potentials. Lifton, from his perspective, suggests that when post-traumatic consciousness is transformed through experience, understanding, and empathy, it creates species memory, species consciousness, and even a sense of species self.

Current neuroscience speaks of the same internal capacity for diversity in different language. Gerald Edelman, who won the 1972 Nobel Prize for Medicine, insists that talk of the brain as pre-determined and hard-wired is misleading: "Brains possess enormous individual structural variations at a variety of organizational levels. An examination of the means by which brains develop indicates that each brain is highly variable." (Edelman 1992, p. 223-224) Edelman's view underscores the need for broad and wide exposure and experience:

> We cannot individuate concepts and beliefs without reference to the environment. The brain and the nervous system cannot be considered in isolation from states of the world and social interactions. But such states, both environmental and social, are indeterminate and open ended. (Edelman 1992, p. 224)

Edelman further states:

> the patterns of nervous system response depend on the individual history of each system, because it is only *through interactions with the world* that appropriate response patterns are selected. This variation because of differences in experience occurs between dif-

ferent nervous systems and within a single nervous system across time. (Edelman 1992, p. 226)

Another eminent neuroscientist, Rodolfo Llinás, offers a model of the brain that gives hope to the possibilities of change and growth in our sense of species self. He puts it this way:

The brain, similarly to musical instruments, has great emergent properties. Remember that there used to be strings that one could not play in the old strings instruments, called "sympathetic chords," which were inside the instrument. I have suggested that this has happened inside the brain when it evolved. There is an enormous number of "sympathetic" chords that increase the cerebral capacity and that make our internal resonances more complex. This is the richness of the human brain, because the specific areas of the cerebral cortex are possibly the same in a monkey and in the human being, but the sympathetic chords are not. (Llinás, interviewed by Strejilevich 1998)

Dourley speaks of the lack of Jung's "compendious consciousness" as leading to an "inevitable lowering of the moral responsibility of the group and so of the individuals in the group." Yet in the human brain and psyche, sympathetic chords are waiting and ready to be played. In other words, individuals can continuously emerge through and into consciousness to declare like the New York poets "Not in our Name," and to say, like the Sufi elder in Kabul, not in God's Name.

*References*

Edelman, G. (1992). *Bright Air, Brilliant Fire: On the Matter of the Mind*. New York: Basic Books.
Lifton, R. J. (1993). *The Protean Self: Human Resilience in an Age of Fragmentation*. Chicago: University of Chicago Press.
Strejilevich, S. (1998). "Consciousness and the Brain: Interview with Rodolfo Llinás." www.epub.org.br/cm/n06/opiniao/llinas_i.html

# Escape/No Escape: The Persistence of Terror in the Lives of Two Women

*Mary Dougherty*

## Introduction

The images on the following page are of iron masks. Masks like these were used on women from 1600 to 1800, in villages throughout Europe. These so-called "bridles for shrews" were placed on women to punish them for speaking out against a domestic, religious – or otherwise male – authority. Some masks had internal spikes that mutilated the tongue, sometimes permanently. The women wearing them were put on display in the town square to receive insults and beatings. (Held 1986)

We can imagine that living under the threat of the imposition of an iron mask must have psychically terrorized all women; and yet women would also have had the sense that their fates were not completely outside their control. That is to say, if they kept their mouths shut, they could avoid torture. Never being sure, however, when they could speak, and always needing to be careful not to offend Authorities, could only have created a pervasive and deep-seated sense of powerlessness and hopelessness in women. (Novick and Novick 1999)

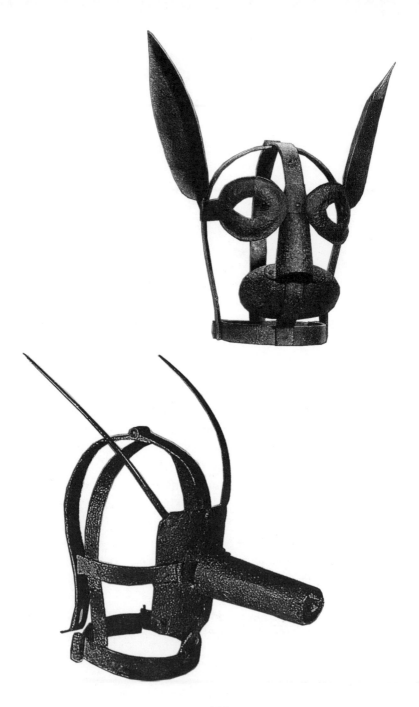

168

*The four images of masks,
reproduced here with the
permission of Lalli Editore, are
from Migliorini (2001).*

In what follows I will describe the analysis of two women who were similarly psychically terrorized by regimes that threatened the imposition of torture. In contrast to the women in the Reformation and Counter-Reformation European villages, these contemporary women had resources that allowed them to immigrate to a safer place. However, it is clear, both from their waking accounts and from their dreams, that they endured psychic trauma as a consequence of belonging to groups whose members were incarcerated, tortured or "disappeared."

## The Two Women

Shirin was in her early thirties when she immigrated to the United States from the Middle East, in response to the growing political and religious constraints within her native country. Because she was a woman with progressive values, she felt that her future was in jeopardy there.

Bianca was in her late twenties when she came to the United States from South America. She had been a teacher and political activist and had experienced the disappearance of a number of friends. She managed to escape the day before the regime came to arrest her.

My therapeutic stance with both Shirin and Bianca in the early phases of their treatments with me had elements in common with Renos Papadopoulos's work with patients who are survivors of torture. Papadopoulos expands the exclusive focus of psychoanalysis upon the intrapsychic to include the realities of the social, political, and historical organization of the culture. This expansion into cultural analysis is quite similar to the approach of feminist analysts, who have insisted on the inclusion of gender conditioning as a theme to be addressed in therapeutic treatment. (Benjamin 1988, Samuels 1993, Young-

Eisendrath and Wiedemann 1987). Papadopoulos has described his own stance as a "therapeutic witnessing" – a process of empowering people to develop their own new narratives, within which their experiences of torture can acquire different meanings. Rather than using such pathologizing terms as "dissociation" and "regression," Papadopoulos prefers the archetypal "narrative of frozenness." His stated therapeutic aim is to "thaw" the frozenness that originally developed as a healthy response to destructive experiences in order to minimize the disintegration of what he calls "the identity substratum" (Papadopoulos 1997, p. 14-15; 1998, p. 467) and what Donald Kalsched has been calling "the personal spirit." (Kalsched 1996) I would call this the true or core self of the client.

In my own case accounts, I will highlight the significant points in each woman's struggle to free her core self from the effects of regimes of terror. I will try to convey how my therapeutic stance shifted at different stages of each treatment, and I will place special emphasis upon the images from dreams and waking life that tended both to inform and to paralyze the treatment process of each woman. Each woman was in analysis with me for approximately thirteen years. Both women, I should mention, were competent artists and in the process of completing their graduate degrees when they entered treatment; they were thus unusually skilled at conveying the meaning of their experience to me in images.

## The Internalization of Cultural Confusion

Shirin (the woman from the Middle East) entered therapy at age thirty-seven, depressed and feeling unable to take action to change her life. Two early dreams showed her caught in situations that overwhelmed her capacities to respond:

Dream: A man is trying to get into my childhood house. I'm trying to light candles while someone is breaking into the walls. The other walls are collapsing. I try to telephone for help.

Dream: I have to go to court and a priest makes me swear, but the man I am with says I can't swear because I am not religious.

The despair expressed in the first dream, of having no protection against everything collapsing, had been with Shirin for as long as she could remember. The situation she faced recalled the turmoil of her childhood home: her father's rages and her mother's disobedience, his infidelities and her resignation. It also recalled the collapsing liberal structures of her native country.

The cultural confusion involved is conveyed in Shirin's second dream, in which she finds herself caught between two male authorities and is made to feel she will be wrong no matter which choice she makes. Associating to this dream, Shirin recalled that she had been religious as a girl, but upon reaching puberty found herself at odds with her religion's official prohibitions against women. She traced the beginning of her depression to that time. The disconnection from her native religious instinct, necessary for the survival of her individual spirit as a woman, was nevertheless a terrible blow to her psychic vitality, and she still longs for the peace that her spiritual life once gave her (see also Ulanov 2002).

Shirin was caught in a dilemma, from which there often seems to be no escape for many contemporary women who grow up within a society that is itself in conflict between tradition and modernity: the felt need to satisfy two conflicting cultural demands. On the one hand, Shirin felt the need to demonstrate her social worth by identifying herself as a traditional woman who would be obedient to male authority, both religious and secular, and on the other hand, she felt she had to honor her generation's insistence on women realizing their individual potentials, which for her meant functioning as an autonomous woman with intellectual and artistic accomplishments in the world, whatever men thought.

A third dream introduced a historical dimension to the way Shirin felt caught between these opposing demands.

> Dream: I am helping women from one hundred years ago dive into a swimming pool. They come out and are killed by men. I realized that I helped these men trap these women.

In terms of her personal history, Shirin associated her siding with the men against the women to her feelings of always wanting to be a boy; yet like other women of her generation she railed against the way women were made to suffer at the hands of men. She recalled her mother's account of her experience as a girl: of seeing her father hold her mother's head under water in the fish tank as punishment for an ill-prepared meal. Through her years with me, Shirin has recounted other stories of atrocities of a type no longer unfamiliar to people in the West, such as women having no claim to their children apart from the authority of their husbands, or being buried up to their necks and stoned to death for adultery or for having a child out of wedlock.

Shirin continually complained about her mother's relentless working to please her father and the masochistic selflessness this epitomized. "I would hate my mother and side with my father," she told me. At the same time, she would undermine her father's rages by trying to protect her mother from him. Later, her father's rages would be focused against Shirin, as when he broke through her bedroom door with his fists when she had closed it against him, or when he tore up her passport to retaliate against her growing independence.

Along with her dreams, such accounts of her past provided us with an empathic context to understand her more recent history of disturbed relationships with men. In her mid-twenties, Shirin had married a man who was both poetic and loving, but after several years she ended the marriage because there was no sexual passion. Now, she felt physical attraction for the men she was dating, but no emotional or intellectual connection. All the same, she expressed the fear of being abandoned by them: "As soon as I let myself love somebody, I fear I will lose them or that I will decide that he's not worthy of me."

From early childhood, Shirin sought refuge from relational difficulties in the felt sense of being an artist. Doing her creative work allowed her to escape the feeling of being like her mother. One of her recent endeavors has been a large project in which images from her dreams were key elements, which strongly suggests that her individuation is in her work. She and I have both felt positively about her making art through which she could create new narratives about her life and the lives of other women. At the same time, doing her work has generated anxiety in her from which she also cannot escape. It not only has brought her into open conflict with the part of her that needs to identify as a traditional religious woman, but it also has posed a threat, both real and imagined, to her safety if she speaks out too publicly against men.

As our work continued, Shirin has ever more strongly come up against the cultural prohibition forbidding her to speak in public about her private life. This prohibition has included even me, because I am an outsider, a Westerner. Any complaints to me could be heard as criticism of her culture. This has kept me on tenterhooks trying to decide what I could and could not say. I also have come under the influence of this cultural prohibition against speaking, not merely through an introjective identification with my patient's conflict, but also because it activated a similar prohibition in me against speaking up.

At the outset of our work together Shirin behaved as compliantly and submissively with me as with any authority figure.

Despite the tentativeness that characterized our early interactions, in which neither of us felt free to speak her mind, a fourth dream spoke to the feeling of a new quality of connection being born between us.

Dream: We are in bed together and are making love. We wash each other like newborns with placentas.

## The Denial of Vulnerability

Bianca (the woman from South America) entered therapy at age thirty-five, feeling anxious and depressed and some days wanting to hide in bed. She told me that she was not interested in exploring issues from her past; that she was here to deal with her "work," by which she meant her career as an artist. Right now there was "all this pressure": two exhibitions were opening in several weeks and an application for a full-time teaching job had to be completed. In this first session, she presented two dreams.

Dream: I'm flying in an air balloon with male teenagers. I'm on the ground looking up at myself.

Dream: None of the dead were buried. They had perfect hairdos. They were female – large Indian women who were dead but not rotten.

She had no particular associations to these dreams. I reflected that the first dream could be speaking about her work as an artist: that at one moment she feels as if she's flying high and at another as if she were being left behind. The second dream, of the unburied dead, seemed to bear witness to the dark feelings that sometimes inundated her. She had no affective reaction to this disturbing image, which seemed to hark back to the cultural history of her native country. Instead, she refocused our attention to her present concerns about the significance of her work, and its future. She feared being marginalized by the art world, and she particularly resented the aesthetic attitudes of those that she believed would discredit her work.

As I listened to her concerns, I kept in mind the dead but unburied Indian women in her psyche – perhaps an image of the killed-off elemental feminine (Meador 1992), or indigenous self (Gustafson 1997) in her psyche. Several months later she had a second dream of the dead.

> Dream: A handsome man in his forties is dead in a coffin. I see him move ... he is suffering. He is transforming back and forth from man into an iguana then back into a man. I call the university and they tell me to kill him and I do.

Bianca associated the call from the university as a call from the "art" authorities to squelch some of the magical irrationality of her own creative process: "I don't want to hear their voices ... their demand for the rational ... I'm losing my power of enchantment." We linked the iguana/man to this power of enchantment but noted that it was she who killed him in obedience to the university authorities.

Bianca, like Shirin, was caught in a persistent dilemma from which there was seemingly no escape: her own insistence on being a powerful artist was a compensation for the powerlessness she felt in the rest of her life, but this powerlessness seemed to be demanded by a cultural authority that still had power over her. Even her own demand for power and authority within the art world was in unconscious alignment with the internalized masculine authority that was insisting that she kill off the enchanted/transformative parts of herself – the elements within an artistic self that makes creative work possible.

As we continued to make sense of her conflict the frozen parts of her self began to thaw, and she became more willing to deal with her past. Like Shirin, Bianca associated "the authorities" in her dreams to her own distant, authoritarian father who had been extremely demanding, especially on her mother. Bianca recalled her mother as depressed, erratic, and sick. One day when Bianca was dancing to the "Ritual Dance of Fire," her mother broke the record over her head. It was shortly after this incident that Bianca's father lost all his money – quite possibly because of illegal activities – and had to move the family to a remote place. The family left everything behind, including Bianca's dancing lessons. "That is when I got fat," she told me.

From the beginning of her life, Bianca had felt burdened by her relationships with others. She had grown up with the sense of being responsible for her family – that it was up to her to save them. When she and her sisters played house, she was always the father. She married at twenty-five mainly to get out of her family home, and divorced shortly after. She then had a series of women lovers. She has complained that she is always falling in love with emotionally unavailable women and that she usually ends up feeling responsible for her lovers. We reflected on how this feeling of being responsible for the women she loved, and of carrying the energy for the relationships that developed between her and them might account for why the relationships felt burdensome. Privately, I had the sense that her being the "father" in charge of any relationship allowed her to feel self-sufficient but also kept people from seeing her immensely vulnerable core sense of self.

A year and a half into Bianca's treatment, images of "the dead" continued to press forward in her dreams:

Dream: There was a coup d'état; prisoners were being taken to a concentration camp. One man's tortured swollen body was put in the back of a truck and was being shown around the city as a warning to others. He wasn't dead but unconscious.

We worked to metabolize the feelings embedded in the images, to feel the turmoil of a life disrupted, the sensation of being taken away, and the anxiety occasioned by leaving everything familiar behind with no sense that you could count on things to continue as you had known them. Bianca was able to acknowledge that this complex of disintegration was a central experience for both her child self and later, for her adult self, which she felt as an identification with her friends who were "disappeared." We also reflected on how this dream might be warning her about repressed, defended-against feelings that, even though they are unconscious in her, were not dead, feelings associated with the vulnerability of her core self that had been terrorized.

Shortly after this dream, Bianca left therapy to spend more time on her creative work. I felt she was actually seeking to escape from her growing connection to me, which was beginning to melt the defenses she had erected against the terrified aspects of herself that were now starting to be imaged in her dreams. I did not confront her decision to interrupt the therapy directly but attempted to mediate it, by asking her to think of her departure as a kind of sabbatical, indicating that she could call me if and when she wished to continue.

As may already be clear, in working with victims of atrocities I resonate with Renos Papadopoulos's stated intent to de-pathologize the treatment as much as possible by keeping the therapeutic focus on their capacity for resilience. Like Papadopoulos, I try to normalize their experience of trauma as tragic and rooted in cultural history rather than seeking to identify their symptomatic responses as evidence of pathology. On the other hand, I do not believe it is possible to separate the frozenness in response to the particular cultural traumas suffered in adulthood from the frozenness in response to cumulative traumas suffered within the family in childhood. Beverley Zabriskie has used a term taken from quantum physics, 'frozen accidents,' to describe how events with significant others in early childhood can interact with archetypes to affect patterns of development. (Zabriskie 1997, p. 31) The frozenness that then embeds itself in psychic structures can certainly be characterized as a pathology. For example, both Shirin and Bianca demonstrated a high degree of resilience in managing to get on with their lives after their escapes from cultural repression. Their doing so, however, was in many ways in spite of their traumatic experiences rather than the result of a conscious working-through and empathic acceptance of what they had suffered, and resulted in defensive constriction of their personalities rather than individuation (see Covington 2002, p. 189).

My sense is that for both of these women the original psychological traumas experienced during childhood in relation to their parents' ways of interacting had become embedded as intrapsychic sadomasochistic complexes in their personalities. These original complexes were dug up and magnified by the bodily, sensory anxieties they experienced under the threat of literal torture as young adults coming of age in hostile political contexts. These political contexts reinforced the hold of the original complexes on my patients' psyches through repressive cultural practices that took on archetypal proportions because they were embedded in religious convictions. The repressive external authorities were internalized by each of my patients as part of a diabolical self-care system as defined by Kalsched (1996).

Despite the fact that both of my patients had been resourceful enough to escape their countries of origin, neither had been able to escape the emotional patterns of their response to their original cultures; in fact, their original cultural and religious contexts now were embedded in their psychic self-care systems. For each of them, the culturally overdetermined self-care system promised safety *only* if the woman continued to live within the constraints that affirmed her victim status. The persistence of the attachment of these patients to their victim status through the course of their treatments often left me feeling ineffective and at sea as an analyst.

When Bianca resumed therapy after a six month "sabbatical," I underscored the need for us to engage the negative experiences from her past that continued to interrupt her life in the present. The story of her mother breaking the record over her head resurfaced. This time, I asked her to draw how her nine-year-old self might have felt about this event. She made three drawings using red and black pastels, scrubbing the pastels into the surface of the paper with increasing intensity as she worked. She described the drawings as:

1. Anger getting out
2. Anger negating my mother
3. Trying to eradicate my depressed mother/self ... but it is not enough.

Making these drawings allowed Bianca to begin to see the intensity of her rage against her mother and herself. She hated being depressed like her mother, and she was furious that all her efforts to eradicate her own depression were *never* enough. With my help, she could see how a Junta-like energy, manifesting through the red and black pastels, was attacking and even "disappearing" the part of her self that felt depressed and powerless. She could also sense being the victim of the attack, just as she had been at the hands of her mother. Through the therapeutic relationship, she began to experience a different way of relating to her inner and outer material that allowed her to see how she treated vulnerable parts of herself and of others in the very ways that she had been treated. (Covington 2002, p. 194)

As therapy continued, Bianca's early defensiveness against being in treatment gave way to her making use of our relationship as a space where she could be herself. Simultaneously, she was making gains in her life: she was enjoying success as a college professor, her creative work was gaining some recogni-tion, and she was forming a close relationship with a woman who would become her life companion. Despite these gains, however, there was a core part of her that felt demoralized, impotent, and spiritually "tired." The realization that she was unconsciously holding at bay (and this took a great deal of psychic energy), was the terrifying possibility that the universe could actually provide what she needed. Like Shirin, Bianca was deeply ambivalent about the prospect of realizing the potential of the feminine self she appeared to embrace.

*The Grievance*

Jan Wiener's conceptualizations on *grievance* have been help-ful in clarifying some of the frustrations I experienced in my work with Shirin and Bianca. (Wiener 1998) Wiener posits that early trauma in some patients can lead to the development of a defensive structure in which hateful affects are split off and then become constellated in the form of a grievance. Holding onto this grievance serves to keep the core sense of self intact and out of the reach of further injury. The grievance functions to encapsulate the self against any selfobject relationship, includ-ing the analytic one. This distance from energizing selfobjects, however, leaves the self impoverished and eliminates the poten-tial for the mediation and metabolization of split-off affects by the warded-off other persons who otherwise would be used, as extensions of the self, to enhance self-experience. The rigid attitude associated with a grievance, when first contacted by the analyst in the countertransference, can be experienced as an all-embracing emotional straightjacket that can deaden the analyst's capacity to function, even as it enormously hampers the patient's psychic functioning. I believe that the images of the iron masks that I described at the beginning of this paper are palpable representations of such intrapsychic constriction.

My sense is that the ultimately self-destructive grievance functions in tandem with the archetypal self-care system that Kalsched has described as a pervasive defensive posture that both protects and punishes the true core self. The ego's energy is quite consumed in maintaining the grievance, which is the expression of hate serving to fend off fears of disintegration at the hands of the original, terrorizing trauma.

Both of the women whose treatments I have described were burdened with a self-destructive attachment to their griev-ance. I say this even though I felt then, and still feel now, that for each the grievance was an understandable response to the trauma she had suffered in childhood and was understandably reinforced by the threat of actual torture she had to endure later on. I well recall trying during these treatments to main-tain my empathic response to the real traumas my patients had endured but feeling stymied and frustrated by their responses to ordinary adult responsibilities, such as paying bills and grocery shopping. They seemed to be unable to muster the everyday assertiveness required to carry out these normal life tasks. Their aggression was entirely tied up in maintaining their grievance postures, leaving them to experience tasks that most of my patients experience more or less pleasurably as aspects of their autonomy, agency, and initiative as attacks against their artistic identities and pursuits. Their relationships with others would soon leave them feeling aggrieved, either because the other wanted too much from the relationship, or didn't want enough. These two women inevitably wound up disappointed in any relationship, including the one with me, because they unconsciously expected the persons who related to them to be taking care of their split off vulnerabilities without their own participation or even awareness. In relating to each of these women, I found myself in the position of trying to take care of a self they had disavowed in favor of a vague but pervasive agenda of disappointment with life.

Bianca's specific grievance, to the degree that she could verbalize it, was over never having had a competent mediating female presence to protect her against a terrorizing masculine authority. The only way Bianca had found to make it in the world was to appease that authority. She repeatedly stated, "I want acceptance by the Fathers – if I don't have their acceptance then I want my work to be great." Her grievance had led her into an unconscious collusion with the masculine authority, whose demand for greatness was unmediated, at the cost of her unprotected terrorized self. In taking up this demand as her own, she was also expressing retaliatory hatred, which she proceeded to direct against any external male authority – real or imagined – that she encountered. At a much more unconscious level of her identification with the aggressor, the hatred embedded in her grievance was directed against her own unconscious vulnerability which she lost touch with in her pursuit of "greatness."

> Dream: A little girl was running away from home with two other girls. There was a man's hand with a gun out a car window – it shoots them dead .... My father was dressed as a fascist wearing a black shirt and Vietnam glasses. I felt something dead inside me.

This dream overtly linked her father, as a fascist, to the killers in her dreams. She could then associate these covert killers to the Junta. We understood the images of the dead in her dreams as evidence that the Junta was still *here*. Analytically, we tracked the Junta down and discovered it at work in her self-criticism and impulsive attacks on others, in the ways she would kill off the good work of the previous session or deny that good things were happening in the present one. In the countertransference I discovered the Junta, subversively undermining our analytic process, in my feeling inadequate and in my impulses to retaliate. Nevertheless, we continued to confront the internal replication of her former external persecutors, an approach which gradually allowed her to access and finally redirect the hatefulness of her own aggression (see Ulanov 2001).

In accessing and using her aggression to support ego development and to protect her core sense of self, Bianca experienced both an increase in anxiety that made normally instinctive actions such as breathing difficult, and, at the same time, a greater capacity to take responsibility for her own self-care. This self-care included swimming. I actively supported physical exercise as part of her treatment, and this eventually included movement therapy as adjunct to our therapeutic process.

Shirin experienced a similar recovery of core vulnerability, and flexibility, in the course of our work. Throughout the analysis, she was haunted by an image of a woman buried alive in a cave. Sometimes she thought of this figure as the central image in a potential artwork. At other times it served as an embodiment of how she felt. Originally I thought the image was a dream figure, but it turned out to be taken from an ancient story about a beautiful woman who was loved by two men who happened to be father and son. In order for the father and the son to resolve their conflict, both finally had to relinquish the woman. Because neither could tolerate her being with the other, they sacrificed their love for the woman by burying her alive.

This story portrayed for Shirin the relentless struggle of the opposing demands that divided her psychic energy: the demand that she be a traditional religious woman, represented by the father, versus the demand that she be an accomplished artist, represented by the son. And just like the father and son in the story, neither side of this conflict of demands could tolerate Shirin's psyche belonging to the other. Practically, this meant that any achievement Shirin was able to make in the world as an artist would be destroyed by the accusations from her "carping traditional woman," and that everyday life tasks were also negated by the artist's "worldly cynicism" toward such bourgeois accomplishments. Consequently, Shirin could never give herself to any activity because that would mean choosing an identity not allowed by the other.

Shirin's grievance took the form of a refusal to choose sides, even a refusal to accept limitation or compromise between the material obligations and the creative aspirations facing all artists. This refusal was rationalized as an attempt to escape the proscribed boundaries of a woman's life. In actuality, however, it was an unconscious alliance with an internalized masculine authority as part of a well-organized archetypal self-care system that channeled her aggression against *any* choice she made. This particular form of "self-care" left her body invaded with anxiety, her ego incapable of assertion and her core self buried alive.

Shirin's grievance, in other words, inevitability hated the thing she was doing and longed for what she wasn't: when she was at work, she longed for the peace of her home; when she was at home, she longed for the freedom of her work. Any action she took was against this paralyzing force, and any enjoyment occasioned by taking action was fleeting.

Despite this bind at the core of her self, Shirin became a full time college professor and gained international recognition for her critical reviews of art. Her refusal to accept limitation made it impossible for her to say "no" to any demand, or even any request from another. To say "no" was to choose sides. She had become overly accommodating in her relationships with others, especially men, and at the same time resentful of their having taken advantage of her.

Shirin tended to be sexually attracted to men who were demanding, and disdainful of men who were more accommodating. Four years into her treatment, Shirin reconnected with a former lover who was an artist and poet living abroad. She had shared her doubts with me about his stability as a man, his suitability as a husband, and the workability of their relationship. I supported her efforts to question this relationship, but once the plans for marriage were in place there was an irrevocable quality to her decision that she was unable to escape and that I was unable to confront. They were married the following summer and divorced two months later.

A year later, Shirin began a similar relationship with a man in the United States. It ended the same way. But this time she was pregnant. This time, however, she said "no" to the man's insistence on her having an abortion and "yes" to her own wanting the baby. She was blissfully happy with the birth of her son; happy that is, until they came home from the hospital together. Shirin struggled to raise the child on her own and did not seek child support for fear that the father or his family would take the child from her. Overwhelmed by the demands of motherhood, she found herself unable to contain the affective states of her baby. If he bit her, she couldn't stop him; if he cried, she couldn't soothe him. Having refused limitations for herself, she could not set limits on her son.

Having to raise this child, however, was what would eventually drive a wedge between her and the grievance she harbored that refused limitation. I had continued to confront her inability to say "no" to her son by comparing her attitudinal stance to being a martyr like her mother. She accused me of not understanding her because I was a Westerner, and she was also furious with me because I was supposed to *fix* things. I, for my part, was furious because she was so stubborn. For some time, I fought the feeling that perhaps she was right, that perhaps there *was* an existential gap between us that we were unable to bridge. Then one day, I simply gave up: I told her that I didn't know how to help her, that she knew all the things I was going to say anyway, and that I didn't think anything I said would make a difference. There was a stunned pause. Then she looked at me, smiled wryly, and we both began to laugh.

I believe this was an instance, described by Ann Ulanov, when the hateful affects present in both of us allowed the destruction of the persona level of the analysis that had been maintaining the status quo. Ulanov quotes Jung:

> … at the climax of the illness, the destructive powers [are] con-verted into healing forces. This is brought about by the archetypes awaking to independent life and taking over the guidance of the psychic personality, thus supplanting the ego with its futile willing and striving. (Jung 1932/1969, para. 534, p. 345, cited in Ulanov 2001, p. 33)

The intervention that I had ended up making was something that came up from the depths and was beyond my personal will, or hers. It was, so to speak, the accidental spill of paint on the canvas that changed the direction of the painting.

We continued, of course, to struggle with Shirin's grievance within the analytic relationship as she continued to struggle with the demands of real life. When her son was with other kids at school, he was either too aggressive in his attachment to others (he hugged too hard) or he was alone on the play-ground. Seeing her son unable to negotiate relationships with peers forced Shirin to recognize her own dysfunctional rela-tional patterns being lived out in him. She got him into therapy with the encouragement of both the school counselor and me. His therapist turned out to be a man from India with a com-plexion similar to her son's. This therapist reinforced the need for Shirin to set limits for her boy and at the same time gave him some badly needed paternal holding.

Despite this additional support, her son continued to act out at home and to have difficulties in school. His recalcitrance gradually ground Shirin down into a real surrender. Now she needed to choose not to be victimized by her son's behavior so that he could have a non-masochistic mother. And finally she did. A year ago, she made a one-year contract with herself to concentrate all of her efforts on containing and attending to his needs. She would meet her obligations at work but say "no" to extra projects. Her saying "no" to some things allowed her to say "yes" to being with her son, and therefore, herself. Her saying "yes" released her self into trusting that she was doing what she needed to do to survive, no matter how imperfect.

*Conclusion*

The challenges I have described in my work with Bianca and Shirin required me to bear witness to the terrorizing realities they had experienced in life as well as to confront the internalized terrorizing forces that continued to paralyze their capacity to trust. The analytic work, to be valid, needed to acknowledge the tragedy of their suffering as well as their tenacity and courage that permitted their escape. But it also needed to confront the fact of their "no escape" – the persistence of the terror inflicted on them by their attachment to a 'grievance,' a complex attitude that insisted on their greatness and refused limitation.

The work also required them to initiate me into a world of terror beyond my own cultural innocence – even as the United States has been initiated into the world culture of violence in the months following 9/11/2001. I had to imagine myself into the terror of my patients' experiences even as you, reader, contemplating the images that begin this paper, may have imagined yourself into the terror of wearing an iron mask. At the same time I have had to challenge my patients' hereditary ties to a familial cultural lineage that has traditionally denied the possibility of female authority while idealizing female suffering across the generations of female oppression. The paradox of the work has required us to resist surrender to these forcefully imposed external expectations as well as to the destructive internal forces that live them on as psychic constriction. At the same time, it has been necessary to hold a space open, for each of my patients, to the potential surrender of ego intentions, so that a transcendent energy can emerge to enrich and to guide the analysis.

But finally, in this therapy of "no escape" from terror, we have had to endure the deconstruction of all our good intentions. My initial, heroic stance as analyst in charge of engineering my own professional assaults against the "internalized forces of terror" had finally to give way to a willing yet sometimes deflated endurance of my clients' ongoing suffering. Similarly, their persistent railing against their fate has had to give way to a less than heroic acceptance on their part of what is. In other words, both my patients and I have had to endure what we could not do and to be with who we were. In this deconstructive analytic field, we were both the *prima materia* being decomposed as well as the observers attending the process. And there we sat, doing the "humdrum work of analysis," enduring the stillness of *nothing* until a trickle of *something* could be felt. (Ulanov 2001, p. 36)

*References*

Benjamin, J. (1988). *The Bonds of Love*. New York: Pantheon Books.
Covington, C. (2002). "Response to Renos Papadopoulos," *The Journal of Analytical Psychology*, Vol. 47, no. 2, p. 189-194.

Gustafson, F. (1997). *Dancing Between Two Worlds: Jung and the Nature of the American Soul.* New Jersey: The Paulist Press.

Held, R. (1986). *Torture Instruments from the Middle Ages to the Industrial Era.* Florence: Qua d'Arno.

Kalsched, D. (1996). *The Inner World of Trauma: Archetypal Defenses of the Personal Spirit.* London and New York: Routledge.

Jung, C. G., (1932/1969). "Psychotherapists or the Clergy." *Collected Works,* Vol. 11. Princeton, Princeton University Press.

Meador, B. (1992). *Uncursing the Dark: Treasures from the Underworld.* Wilmette, IL: Chiron.

Migliorini, A. (2001). *Tortura Inquisizione Pena Di Morte.* Poggibonsi (Siena), Italia: Lalli Editore.

Novick, J. and Novick, K.K. (1999). "Dialogue: The Endurance of Impotence: The Dynamics of Persecutory Violence," *The IPA Newsletter,* Vol. 8, no. 1.

Papadopoulos, R. (1997). "Individual Identity and Collective Narratives of Conflict," *Harvest,* Vol. 43, no. 2.

Papadopoulos, R. (1998). "Destructiveness, Atrocities and Healing: Epistemological and Clinical Reflections," *The Journal of Analytical Psychology,* Vol. 43, no. 4.

Papadopoulos, R. (2002). "The Other Other: When the Exotic Other Subjugates the Familiar Other." *The Journal of Analytical Psychology,* Vol. 47, no. 2.

Samuels, A. (1993). *The Political Psyche.* London and New York: Routledge.

Ulanov, A. (2001). "Hate in the Analyst," *Journal of Jungian Theory and Practice,* no. 3.

Ulanov, A. (2002). "Religion's Role in the Psychology of Terrorism." Unpublished paper.

Wiener, J. (1998). "Under the Volcano: Varieties of Anger and Their Transformation," *The Journal of Analytical Psychology,* Vol. 43, no. 4.

Young-Eisendrath, P. and Wiedemann, F. (1987). *Female Authority: Empowering Women Through Psychotherapy.* New York and London: The Guilford Press.

Zabriskie, B. (1997). "Thawing the 'Frozen Accidents': The Archetypal View in Countertransference," *The Journal of Analytical Psychology,* Vol. 42, no. 1.

# Cultural Complexes and Archetypal Defenses
# of the Group Spirit

*Thomas Singer*

*Everybody stands on the shoulders of others who brought him or her along. Two whose shoulders have been especially broad for me are Joe Henderson and Tom Kirsch.*

## Credentials

The topic of "Terror, Violence and the Impulse to Destroy" is so hideous and daunting that I suspect most who consider writing about it have second thoughts, turn on their heels and leave the subject to those of us foolish enough to take it on.

I am not sure what qualifies one to write about this subject. Violence has touched us all in one way or another, but some lives are affected by it much more than others. I feel especially awkward giving expression to my reflections in front of colleagues from New York who have recently and directly experienced far more of collective violence than I have. I did, however, become one of those instantaneous terror/violence counselors the very day after 9/11/01, when I moderated a discussion in an auditorium filled with high school students, including my fifteen-year-old daughter Eliza. I had two messages I wanted to convey that day:

1. Don't let the media spin-doctors tell you what 9/11 means. It may or may not be another Pearl Harbor.
2. Don't let people tell you how to feel about yesterday's events.

Six weeks later, Eliza came to me with a nightmare, only one of a handful she has shared with me in her life:

> She was looking across the Bay to San Francisco from our home on Mt. Tamalpais in Marin County. Fiery blasts were exploding all over the city. A helicopter was flying directly towards our house and its propeller smashed through the dining room window. A tall bearded man, whom my daughter recognized as Bin Laden, got out of the helicopter. Terrified, she asked him: "Are you going to kill me?" Bin Laden smiled cruelly, responding to her question by saying simply, "You spoiled my surprise." Eliza ran from the house with Bin Laden's men in pursuit. She woke up in terror.

The kind of invasion and destruction of the home envisioned by my daughter has been lived by many people that Renos Papadopoulos has treated. With Hildebrand, he observed that:

> ... the destruction of homes [is akin to] a nuclear explosion when all the contained forces erupt creating widespread destruction.... [W]hat [victims] yearn for may not be just the specific [house] ... which they left behind but the restoration of the holding function which the home symbolized and actually performed.

These authors state that 'Home' is a "key construct which interconnects three overlapping realms – the intrapsychic, the interpersonal, and the socio-political." (Papadopoulos and Hildebrand 1997, quoted in Papadopoulos 2000, p. 130) Papadopoulos adds that

The State, like the home, has a certain protective membrane which enables opposites to coexist. In these circumstances, differences are tolerated and even provide enriching possibilities. However, once that membrane is damaged by violence, then according to the colloquial expression, "all hell breaks loose." (Papadopoulos 2000, p. 130)

Participating unconsciously in this collective experience, my daughter's dream psyche already knows this reality. She shared in what Daimon Publishers a year later entitled "The Global Nightmare." (Zoja and Williams 2002) Along with Eliza, we have all been newly sensitized to what happens when the protective membrane of home and state is ruptured by a violence that is psychologically "akin to a nuclear explosion." In the face of such monstrousness, it is the natural human tendency to want to make sense of the outbreak of these forces – to understand what is incomprehensible. Economic theories, sociological theories, theories of history and religion – even theories from analytical psychology – are put on parade to reassure us that we understand what is happening. In such a context, George Bush's "axis of evil" idea makes sense, in its very attempt to make sense to the American people of what, in fact, makes no sense. I suspect that most who will hear or read my lecture share my view that President Bush has misidentified "the axis of evil." But, in naming an "axis of evil" at all, I think he has come close to an archetypal truth about the kinds of situation we find ourselves in after 9/11/01. And, by the end of this paper, I hope you will have from me a clearer idea of what might actually constitute the "axis of evil," as distinct from George Bush's version.

As we all know, any theory – including our own Jungian theory – can be used defensively to immunize us against the very thing we are probing. But, theory at its best opens up new ways of seeing the world, prods us to ask good questions and, at times, allows us to help – even heal – because we have a sound, vital theory that informs our practice. As Dr. Joe Henderson has said to me on occasion, "Theory is the plow that turns over the earth." In that spirit, this paper will be unabashedly theoretical.

## Towards a Theory of Cultural Complexes

During his training at the C. G. Jung Institute of San Francisco, Sam Kimbles began to think about some of the collective, unconscious processes occurring in our own Jungian community around issues of race and the analytic training process. In the course of his reflections, Sam coined the phrase "cultural complex." Further exploring these themes, Sam contributed an essay, "The Cultural Complex and the Myth of Invisibility" to a volume I edited entitled *The Vision Thing*, which was the culmination of a decade-long study on the intersection of myth, politics and psyche that I had been coordinating. Our ongoing work together has led to a renewed consideration of Jung's original theory of complexes. We each focus on somewhat different aspects in this reconsideration of "complex theory" – while sharing a common ground and spirit as we work together to articulate the core concepts of a theory of cultural complexes. We view our work as an evolutionary extension of traditional complex theory. We also hope that as we circle around our theory of cultural complexes in our companion papers for this volume, our vision of "cultural complexes" will add a bit to the understanding of terror, violence and the impulse to destroy in the collective and individual psyche – whether the outbreak is occurring between the Israelis and the Palestinians or the post-Jungians and the archetypalists.

There are two essential threads of Jungian theory that get woven into our current thinking:

a. Jung's original theory of complexes
b. Joseph Henderson's theory of the cultural unconscious

By weaving these two distinct threads together and then mixing in the threads of our own particular perspectives and concerns, we have begun the work of extending complex theory into cultural life and conflicts. Several other colleagues are considering similar themes in the cultural arena – in this country Michael Vannoy Adams' fine work (Adams 1996) comes to mind. Let us very briefly review these two essential threads: Jung's complex theory and Henderson's theory of the cultural level of the psyche.

1. As you all know, Jung's earliest work with the word association test led to the development of his "complex theory." When a group of analysts formed around Jung and they were deciding what to call their new psychology, serious consideration was given to the name "complex psychology." For more than sixty years in San Francisco, succeeding generations of analysts, including Joseph Henderson, John Perry, Donald Sandner, John Beebe, Florence Irvine and others have made Jung's complex theory the foundation of training and how we go about thinking and practicing clinically.

I am not sure if the same emphasis is given to complex theory in other training programs around the world, but in all centers the individuation process with one of its primary tasks being the individual's differentiation out of his or her collective experience has been the goal. The "collective" has not been a particularly positive word in the Jungian lexicon, and adapting to the "collective" has not been at the heart of our work. It is not that Jung and his followers did not have a keen sense of the "collective." To the contrary, they were astute observers of the "collective" – mostly in its negative self-constricting aspect. It is safe to say that for the most part the "collective" falls into the Jungian shadow and rarely does one sense in our own collective an affirmation of the positive value of the group spirit. God knows that most of the twentieth century and the beginning of the twenty-first century have given us more than enough reason to tremble at the thought of an aroused group spirit and the collective emotion it generates. The point I want to make here, however, is that, although Jung and the analytical psychologists he trained spoke at length about the nature of the collective psyche, including discussions of different national, ethnic, and religious characteristics, Jung's theory of complexes was never systematically extended beyond its fundamental relevance in the development of individual psychology to include its application to group life or the study of how complexes shape collective experience. Complexes clustered around archetypal cores have been at the heart of our understanding of the individual psyche but only peripheral to our study of the collective psyche. A Jungian psychology of group complexes as distinct from, independent of, and yet interrelated with, personal complexes has not been elaborated. For this reason, our psychology has tended to collapse group experience between the archetypal and personal poles. This brings us to the second thread of the theoretical fabric that Sam Kimbles and I are trying to weave

2. Over a several-decade period of time, Joseph Henderson introduced the notion of a "cultural level" of the psyche that he called "the cultural unconscious." He posited this realm as existing between the personal and collective unconscious. He further elaborated this idea in his book *Cultural Attitudes in Psychological Perspective.* (Henderson 1984) To Jungians, Henderson's work opened the theoretical door on that vast realm of human experience that inhabits the psychic space between our most personal and our most archetypal levels

of being in the world. He also developed what can be thought of as a typology of this realm, through which he differentiated various primary cultural "attitudes" (or cultural orientations) that characterize different individuals: the social, the aesthetic, the philosophic, and the religious attitudes. Dr. Henderson's elaboration of the cultural level of the psyche has made greater space for the outer world of group life to find a home in the inner Jungian world and allowed those immersed in the Jungian inner world to recognize more fully the deep value the psyche actually accords to the outer world of collective cultural experience. He also emphasized the different ways each of us has of experiencing the importance of culture. One can think of Dr. Henderson's work as carrying over Jung's typological approach to individual differences into the cultural level of the psyche, but he did not elaborate Jung's complex theory into this same realm. Extending Jung's theory of complexes into the territory of the "cultural level of the psyche" as first described by Joseph Henderson is the work that Sam Kimbles and I have been addressing. It helps to specify how the cultural unconscious impinges on individuals and groups and has important implications for a Jungian perspective on collective violence.

Personal complexes and cultural complexes are not the same, although they can get all mixed up with one another. We suggest that personal and cultural complexes share the following characteristics: (one might try to identify one of one's own most "familiar" cultural complexes and see if this list fits)

a. They express themselves in powerful moods and repetitive behaviors.

b. They resist our most heroic efforts at consciousness and remain, for the most part, unconscious.

c. They accumulate experiences that validate their point of view and create a store house of self-affirming, ancestral memories.

d. Personal and cultural complexes function in an involuntary, autonomous fashion and tend to affirm a simplistic point of view that replaces more everyday ambiguity and uncertainty with fixed, often self-righteous attitudes to the world.

e. In addition, personal and cultural complexes both have archetypal cores; that is, they express typically human attitudes and are rooted in primordial ideas about what is important, making them very hard to resist, reflect upon, and discriminate.

Attending to the personal, cultural and archetypal levels of complexes requires respect for each of these realms without condensing or telescoping one into the other, as if one realm were more real, true, or fundamental than another. For instance, if at the cultural level the group experience of spirit is good-enough, then intense bonding in the group does not necessarily and automatically activate archetypal hatred, as asserted by John Dourley's trenchant reading of Jung's social psychology. (See Dourley 2003, in this volume.) On the other hand, cultural complexes are based on repetitive, historical experiences that have taken root in the collective psyche of a group and in the psyches of the individual members of a group, and they express archetypal values for the group. One can think of cultural complexes as the fundamental building blocks and contents of an inner sociology. One can even begin to imagine a cartography of this cultural level of the psyche and mapping out its various group complexes.

## A Specific Type of Cultural Complex: Archetypal Defenses of the Group Spirit

In reflecting on "cultural complexes," I have focused my attention on what I have come to think of as a specific type of cultural complex. When this type of cultural complex is triggered, it activates in group life and at the cultural level of the individual's psyche what I have termed "the archetypal defenses of the group spirit."

Let me describe a bit how this notion first began to crystallize for me. It comes from a peculiar brew of my passionate involvement in the record of early Greek life; a keen interest in the intersection of myth, politics, and psyche in contemporary culture; and a deep admiration for the kind of work Don Kalsched, Renos Papadopoulos, and others have fostered in their study of how trauma affects both the individual and the group. I would like to evoke for you how these separate concerns and passions of mine coalesced in the notion of "the archetypal defenses of the group spirit."

*Baby Zeus, surrounded by his shield-bearing protectors, the Kouretes (or Daimones). Archive for Research in Archetypal Symbolism (ARAS), San Francisco.*

Reflect for a moment on an image from Ancient Greece of Baby Zeus who is surrounded by his protecting youthful warriors, the *kouretes* – also known as the Daimones. Baby Zeus sits at the center of a group, and the hymn that is sung in his honor – the Hymn of the Kouretes – is of and for the life of the community. As explored in Jane Harrison's book *Themis*, which is a fabulous 1912 study of pre-Olympian, mostly matriarchal Greek religion, the earliest Greek spirit was a group spirit, a collective spirit. (Harrison 1974; see especially p. 45-49) Taken together, this image and its accompanying ritual "Hymn of the Kouretes" are among the oldest known poetic and lyrical representations of group life in Western civilization. They are a celebration of the spirit born of the group, symbolized by the infant Zeus and the Kouretes, which was later more fully realized in the earliest Olympic games. It is noteworthy that the subtitle of Harrison's *Themis* is "A Study of the Social Origins of Greek Religion."

My focus, today, however, is not on the positive aspect of this archetypal spirit, but on what happens when the spirit of the group is injured or thwarted in its development and its warrior protectors, such as those who guarded Baby Zeus, get over-stimulated. In a sense, I am focusing on the shadow of this glorious drama, or the cultural psychopathology of the traumatized group spirit and its protective guard.

A few years ago, Don Kalsched and I were presenting some material at a conference in Montana. My focus was on the outer-world expression of intrapsychic dynamics in groups in several contemporary conflicts. Dr. Kalsched was, of course, focused on his primary interest – the inner world of trauma in the individual. During a break in the conference, I showed Dr. Kalsched the image of Baby Zeus and the Kouretes, which he had never seen before. He told me later his hair literally stood on end when he first viewed this picture. He instantaneously recognized the Kouretes, and said, "Those are the daimons." He was right. In the Hymn of the Kouretes, the dancing warriors are called both Kouretes and Daimon(e)s. Dr. Kalsched recognized them as the very same daimons he has labored to understand and depotentiate in the contemporary psyches of the severely traumatized individuals he has worked with. These daimons are also what he calls "the archetypal defenses of the personal spirit." Don Kalsched, in other words, saw this image in terms of the inner life or psyche of the traumatized individual. I was seeing the image in terms of the collective psyche of the traumatized group, that is, as a representation not of the individual psyche alone but of a central experience in the life of the group. So, we each identified a vulnerable spirit – personal on the one hand, collective on the other – sitting in the middle of the protective circle of defenses. Don perceives the daimons or protective warriors as the "archetypal defenses of the personal spirit," and I have come to identify them as "the archetypal defenses of the group spirit." To jump ahead and let you see where I am going: Can you imagine these same daimonic warriors becoming Palestinian suicide bombers, impersonal (and would-be immortal) incarnations of an archetypal, defensive, violent impulse to protect a wounded, group spirit?

This notion assumes that there is a collective spirit at the core of a group, which can be thought of as expressing something of the Self, but as it manifests itself at the cultural level. When healthy and well nourished, this collective spirit – expressed in ritual song and dance and games and commerce – sustains and orients home, city, state and nation. But when the spirit of the group is injured, the daimons or archetypal defenses of the group spirit can easily become militants or terrorists of any persuasion. They take on all of the ferocity and energy of warriors or *mujahedeen,* protecting the sacred but endangered value of the group. In the collective, cultural version of this complex then, there are three essential components:

1. traumatic injury to a vulnerable person, group of people, place, or value that carries or stands for the group spirit – like the World Trade Center and the Pentagon.
2. fear of annihilation of both the personal and group spirit by a "foreign other," as in my daughter's dream of an attack on San Francisco and our home.
3. emergence of avenging protector/persecutor defenses of the group spirit, e.g., figures like John Ashcroft and Donald Rumsfeld.

Building, then, on Don Kalsched's insights, I have constructed a model of a specific type of cultural complex which, when activated, almost inevitably and inexorably results in terror, violence and the impulse to destroy in threatened groups. In Dr. Kalsched's formulation of the so-called archetypal defenses of the *personal* spirit, the daimonic defenses direct most of their savage aggression against the development through object-relations of the personal spirit or Self, by encircling and encasing it in a monstrously defended isolation chamber that permits no further exposure to the light of day. In the name of guarding the personal spirit against any further injury at the hands of the outside world, the archetypal defenses simply obstruct all further development or maturation of the personal spirit through engagement with others. Kalsched likens this defensive self-care system of the daimonic defenses to the functioning of the body's immune system when it goes haywire in autoimmune diseases and turns its most formidable defensive aggression back on its own tissues.

In my formulation of the so-called archetypal defenses of the group spirit, as activated in some cultural complexes, the daimons can certainly direct their savage aggression back onto the wounded spirit of the group. The self-mockery and self-denigration entrenched in the humor and self-perception of any number of oppressed, minority groups attests to this phenomenon. But these same daimonic archetypal defenses of the group spirit can just as easily turn their savage aggression out onto whomever or whatever appears to be a threat to the spirit, basic value, or identity of the group. I see this response as automatic, reflexive, impersonal, and in some ways the most natural way for the group psyche in the grips of a cultural complex to react.

Let's consider the rise of radical Islamism in terms of the model I am proposing. The terrorist agenda of Radical Islamism can be understood as an expression of archetypal defenses of this group's spirit, triggered by a cultural complex with more than a thousand years of accumulated historical experiences. In the case of Bin Laden and al Qaeda, their radical Islamist dream of creating a new "caliphate" can be interpreted as the geographic projection of a wish to restore a wounded, collective Muslim spirit through the creation of an empire that transcends national boundaries. The traumatized collective spirit of the Muslim world has suffered centuries of humiliation at the hands of a rapidly expanding Western civilization that captured the scientific, technological and materialistic initiative that once belonged to the Muslim world. By the most ironic of historical twists, however, the Muslim world – deeply wounded in its collective self image – ended up with the richest share of the world's oil that is the current fuel for the materialistic advances of Western civilization. This is a perfect example of how cultural complexes beget cultural complexes.

If the collective spirit of the Muslim world has been traumatized repetitively for centuries, bin Laden, Al Qaeda and the *mujahedeen* are in a sense its daimons – human but terrifyingly impersonal embodiments of the archetypal defenses of the collective spirit. Certainly they conceive themselves to be the avenging angels of the long and deeply traumatized spirit of the Muslim world. As daimons, they may well end up further wounding and torturing the very traumatized Muslim Self that they have set out to defend. I was reminded of the self-destructive aspect of this process by a quote I read not long ago in the paper: "'Islam has been the victim of September 11,' said Ahmad Turkistani, a Saudi living in Virginia who made the pilgrimage to Mecca."

In addition to the awful tragedy of inflicting further injury to the Muslim spirit that its modern self-appointed daimons seek to protect is the psychological fact that possession by a cultural complex automatically triggers its bipolar, reciprocal opposite, namely the response of the Western world. George Bush made a slip of the cultural unconscious when at first he spoke of a "crusade" in outlining how he thought the West should best respond to the World Trade Center and Pentagon bombings. His slip, reflexive and automatic, was no accident; it was backed up by a centuries-year-old memory. A Crusade is our cultural complex's answer to a holy *jihad.*

Of course, for much of the Muslim world and perhaps many who read this essay, George Bush, also self-appointed in his role, is the arch daimon. And, it is precisely at this intersection – where the daimons or archetypal defenses of the spirit of one group's cultural complex trigger the daimons of another group's cultural complex – that I think we can most accurately locate "the axis of evil," be it the daimonic forces of Sharon aligned against the daimonic forces of Arafat, or the daimonic forces of Bush aligned against the daimonic forces of Saddam Hussein. These negative alignments truly form an "axis" in the sense that a direct line or connection is drawn between the daimons of one group, protecting their sacred center, and the daimons of a rival group, protecting their sacred center. Such negative alignments create the conditions for the eruption of incomprehensible violence, destruction, and the impulse to destroy. By making the link between the demonic defenses in one group and the demonic defenses of another, they form, most potently, the conditions in the cultural unconscious for the wholesale emergence of evil, and that, in the cultural unconscious, is the true "axis of evil."

As we see from the radical Islamist movement and the response of the West to it, cultural complexes that trigger archetypal defenses of the group spirit tend to have long, repetitive histories. In terms of inter-group conflict, Christians, Jews, and Moslems have been at it for two thousand years. Blacks and Whites in America have been at it for over three hundred years. Freudians and Jungians have been at it for almost one hundred years. What makes the complexes that drive these conflicts so potent is that they take on a life of their own, not only in the group's response to attacks on its collective spirit, but also in the way that they seem to take up permanent residence at the cultural level of the psyche in the individual.

Thinking about these intractable, recurring conflicts in terms of cultural complexes enables us to avail ourselves of the discoveries of complex theory more generally, and that can bear the fruit of insight, with the potential for greater consciousness. More modestly, it prepares us for the difficulty of finding quick or easy resolution to such complexes; for the familiar accumulation of stereotypical memory and behavior that accrues around any complex; and for the seemingly endless autonomy and perplexing unconsciousness of the phenomena involved. In speaking of the resolution of personal complexes, Jung warned,

> A complex can be really overcome only if it is lived out to the full. In other words, if we are to develop further we have to draw to us and drink down to the very dregs what, because of our complexes, we have held at a distance. (Jung 1954/1959, par. 184, p. 98-99)

205

Applying that same wisdom to cultural complexes, we certainly have had recent experience of the need to drink "down to the very dregs" our cultural complexes. For almost a quarter century, the Balkans and the Middle East have been reminding us almost daily of the impossibility of easily treating or resolving cultural complexes. Formulating these phenomena in terms of cultural complexes is thus a heavy prescription, rather than a panacea, but it allows us to appreciate and make more room for a level in the individual's psyche that belongs neither to personal experience nor to the archetypal depths and permits us a way to work toward deeper understanding of the role of cultural complexes in structuring the psychological responses of the individuals and the group in the face of particular conflicts.

Even more importantly in my mind, the theory of cultural complexes and defenses suggests that Jung was not entirely correct when he said "… nowadays particularly, the world hangs by a thin thread, and that thread is the psyche of man." (Jung 1957, p. 303) An important piece was left out of that otherwise remarkable and one might even say primal insight. The fate of the world does not in fact hinge on the thread of the individual psyche. Rather, the emergence of a theory of cultural complexes suggests that an understanding of the individual psyche through its consciousness will not be enough. The group itself will need to develop a consciousness of its cultural complexes. Perhaps each injured culture – be it Balkan, American, Black, White, Palestinian, Israeli, Iraqi, Catholic, Jewish, Jungian, Freudian, Men, Women (the list is endless once you begin to think in terms of cultural complexes) needs to learn how to drink to the dregs its own complexes, as well as those of its neighbors, allies, and enemies. To settle down the archetypal defenses of the group spirit, the collective psyche itself, and its often traumatized, sometimes immature or stunted, spirit needs to individuate – and this is not the work of an individual analysis alone.

These reflections on cultural complexes lead to the obvious conclusion that there is not a ready antidote to my daughter's nightmare of terror and violence or to the will to destroy that many of us understandably feel at one level or another of our superheated collective psyche. I do think we all sense the need to quell the vengeful daimons or archetypal defenses of the group spirit inside of us, lest they lead us beyond ourselves willy-nilly into more violence, terror, and destruction. At a minimum, we can try to limit their destructive potential to spark any number of "axis of evil" conflicts that are ready to flare. It is hard to imagine drinking the dregs of all the hair-trigger cultural complexes that are waiting to fire off at a given moment anywhere in the world. They litter the global psychic landscape like so many land mines – tribal, racial, ethnic, gender, religious, political, economic bombs left undetonated, but ready to explode. These land mines are the residue, reminder, and carrier of past unresolved conflicts that have accumulated in the collective memory and emotion of generations of so many people that carry deep wounds to their collective spirits – almost as if they have become part of the group's genome.

Such a world geography, history, and collective psychology of explosive and exploding cultural complexes makes one long for a more positive relationship to the group spirit – a time and place when one might join in the singing of "The Hymn of the Kouretes" that I mentioned earlier in this paper. This was a song that, some three thousand years ago, joyously celebrated the Kouros Most Great, the baby Zeus accompanied by his Daimones, a well-defended Divine Child embodying the most generative spirit of the group:

207

*Io, Kouros most Great, I give thee hail, Kronian, Lord of all that is wet and gleaming, thou art come at the head of thy Daimones. To Dikte for the Year, Oh, march, and rejoice in the dance and song*

*That we make to thee with harps and pipes mingled together, and sing as we come to a stand at thy well-fenced altar.*

*For here the shielded Nurturers took thee, a child immortal, from Rhea, and with noise of beating feet hid thee away.*

*And the Horai began to be fruitful year by year and Dike to possess mankind, and all wild living things were held about by wealth-loving Peace.*

*To us also leap for full jars, and leap for fleecy flocks, and leap for fields of fruit, and for hives to bring increase.*

*Leap for our Cities, and leap for our sea-borne ships, and leap for our young citizens and for godly Themis.*

(Harrison 1912/1974, p. 7-8)

## References

Adams, M. V. (1996). *The Multicultural Imagination: "Race," Color and the Unconscious.* London and New York: Routledge.

Dourley, J. (2003). "Archetypal Hatred as Social Bond and Strategies for its Dissolution," (in this book).

Harrison, J. E. (1912/1974). *Themis: A Study of the Social Origins of Greek Religion.* Gloucester, MA: Peter Smith.

Henderson, J. (1984). *Cultural Attitudes in Psychological Perspective.* Toronto: Inner City Books.

Henderson, J. (1990). "The Cultural Unconscious," in *Shadow and Self,* Wilmette, IL: Chiron Publications, p. 103-113.

Jung, C. G. (1954/1959). "Psychological Aspects of the Mother Archetype," *Collected Works,* Vol. 9, pt. i.

Jung, C. G. (1977). In William McGuire and R. F. C. Hull (eds.), *C. G. Jung Speaking.* Princeton: Princeton University Press.

Kalsched, D. (1996). *The Inner World of Trauma: Archetypal Defenses of the Personal Spirit.* London and New York: Routledge.

Kimbles, S. L. (2000). "The Cultural Complex and the Myth of Invisibility," in Singer 2000, p. 157-169.

Papadopoulos, R. K. (2000). "Factionalism and Interethnic Conflict: Narratives in Myth and Politics," in Singer 2000, p. 122-140.

Papadopoulos, R.K. and Hildebrand, J. (1997). "Is Home Where the Heart Is? Narrative of Oppositional Discourses in Refugee Families," in Renos K. Papadopoulos and John Byng-Hall (eds.), *Multiple Voices: Narrative in Systemic Family Psychotherapy*. London: Duckworth.

Singer, T. (2000). (ed.) *The Vision Thing*. London and New York: Routledge.

Singer, T. (2002). "The Cultural Complex and Archetypal Defenses of the Collective Spirit: Baby Zeus, Elian Gonzales, Constantine's Sword, and Other Holy Wars," *The San Francisco Jung Institute Library Journal* Vol. 20, 4, p. 4-28.

Zoja, L. and Williams, D. (2002). (eds.) *The Global Nightmare*. Einsiedeln: Daimon Publishers.

# Cultural Complexes and Collective Shadow Processes

*Samuel L. Kimbles*

Soil of annihilation, soil of hate
No word will purify it ever.
No such poet will be born.
> — Czeslaw Milosz, from "The Spirit of History"

In the sand we saw
The ashes of centuries mixed with fresh blood,
Pride then left us and we rendered homage
To men and women who once lived and ever since
We have our home founded in history.
> — Czeslaw Milosz, from "A Legend"

*Introduction*

Though I have come to know both cultural complexes and collective shadow processes through my own lived experience, my clinical practice, and my analytic studies, the very pervasiveness of their hold on psychological life makes them hard to write about objectively. This is an area that engages me as a psychologist with mad, agonizing contradictions at a feeling level – for example, between my faith in what we can do as humans to make a better world and my pained recognition of the horrendous destructiveness we wreak on each other. Mostly I have been moved between outrage and silence when confronted with the primal irrationalities of our world today, and yet it is these irrationalities that I propose to attempt to explicate here with the help of the theory of cultural complexes and their relation to the collective shadow.

My paper will be in three parts. The first part is entitled, "The ashes of centuries mixed with fresh blood," a line that comes from Czeslaw Milosz's poem "A Legend." The ninety-four year old Polish poet, a Nobel Laureate in Literature, has spent seventy years writing and speaking out about the destructive tumult of our times, all the while arguing for the transcendent worth of every human being's life. A prime example of someone who is a strong witness for engagement with the world, Milosz has placed his own high standards for human decency and dignity into a world that seems intent upon destroying itself. He has used poetry as resistance, as affirmation, and as a mode of remembering. His inspiration gives me the courage to present some of the events that have expressed collective shadow processes in the twentieth century.

The second part of my paper is entitled "If you can't see my mirrors I can't see you." In this section, I present some more personal examples of cultural complexes and collective shadow processes, including a dream I had a couple of months after the cataclysm that was 9/11.

Part three will be devoted to my current thoughts about the dynamics of these complexes followed by some concluding remarks about the prospects for their therapeutic analysis.

*The Ashes of Centuries Mixed with Fresh Blood*

Against fashion, some of my favorite essays in Jung's *Collected Works*, are in Volume 10: his "Preface" to *Essays on Contemporary Events*, "Wotan," "After the Catastrophe," "The Fight with the Shadow," and the "Epilogue" to the *Essays on Contemporary Events*. I realize that these writings have been the source of much criticism of Jung, having been seen as containing his alleged anti-Semitic ideology, his identification with the Teutonic god Wotan, his interest in the "Aryan" unconscious, his insensitivity to Jews, and a notable lack of expression of regret for the misunderstandings caused by the points of view expressed in many of these essays. I feel, however, that the strength of these essays is that they offer an attitude toward the larger dimension of culture that has largely been absent from depth psychology. Jung's pioneering work remains of value in helping us to get a better understanding of the psychological power of collective events and is a primer in the nature of collective complexes, even if Jung himself was not immune to their negative effects. In the second paragraph of the preface, Jung starts out by saying, "We are living in times of great disruption." In the middle of that paragraph he states, "Were he [the analyst] to remain aloof from the tumult, the calamity of his time would reach him only from afar, and his patient's suffering would find neither ear nor understanding." (Jung 1946/1970, p. 177) In this line, as in many of those in the entire series of essays, we find Jung speaking with the passion and emotion that comes not only from engaging the collective world with his analytic understanding but also from allowing his own psyche to be affected by the cultural complexes and shadow issues that he was exploring. Even now, in our time, these essays provide an archetypal foundation to the exploration of group, or, as Jung preferred to say, collective, shadow processes.

To create a scaffold from which to reflect on these regular features of what Joseph Henderson has called "the cultural unconscious," I turn to Jung's essay, "After the Catastrophe." The 'Catastrophe' Jung referred to embraced the Holocaust and the destruction of most of the political and cultural structure of Central Europe, including much of German culture, as the consequence of Hitler's policies before and during World War II. The Cataclysm of 9/11 that we are trying now to understand "after" is an event very different in scope, with particularities Jung could not have foreseen, but in my mind there is a resonance between the catastrophe Jung was confronting in 1945 and the cataclysm we are trying to take stock of now.

As his starting point, Jung takes the psyche in its archaic, universal form. Following his lead, I will be starting with archetypal aspects of the group as the *prima materia* out of which a theory of cultural complexes must be distilled. My view is that the individual psyche, with its appetites, instincts, images, fantasies, and irrationalities, grows out of and in relation to the world of human others founded on kinship libido. As humans, we lean on and are symbiotically tied to the need to feel that we belong, are held, and are respected by our reference group of related others within which we develop our individual identities. Although as we grow we may become aware in individual ways of both an archetypal and a personal unconscious, the medium through which the psyche comes into existence as a psychological reality is mediated through interpersonal experiences. Our cultural awareness is based on the way groups interpret both individual and archetypal experiences.

Jung's approach to the subject of the collective shadow in his *Essays on Contemporary Events* proceeds through his noticing disturbances in the unconscious of his German patients that he says are not reducible to personal complexes. He notices specific mythological motifs (Wotan, Dionysus) and an overall increase in mythological symbols, both emerging out of (and possibly helping to propagate) an affective field characterized by emotional primitivity, cruelty and upheaval. He identifies a "German" psyche, exceptionally vulnerable to possession by archetypal ideas, organized around a charismatic leader (Hitler), who himself personifies these forces, embodying the dream of a new order. Jung diagnoses this psyche as suffering from upheaval of mass instincts, which he feels as a doctor is symptomatic of a severe unconscious compensation for a conscious attitude that is estranged from the instincts. Collective shadow processes are therefore rife, expressed in violent, cruel and destructive acts, which, though triggered by ideological, political situations are more deeply rooted in archetypal disturbances in the unconscious due to a lack of psychological balance. Jung uses the term "collective" to refer to any and all psychic contents that belong, not to one individual, but to the many, i.e., to a society, a people, or mankind in general.

The advantage of this approach is that it addresses collective phenomena in a psychological way, giving us a strong starting point in approaching the cultural life of the psyche analytically. Collective shadow processes, from Jung's point of view, would be generated just as are individual shadow processes, through the return of repressed elements in the ethnic, racial, religious, and/or national group that have not been consistent with the collective ideals of the group. Specifically, for Jung, looking at the German psyche, the repressed elements would be the instinctive aspects that the spiritual ideals of the German people have ignored. In the case of the German psyche, he saw this repressed part as violent and pagan, generated through unconscious identification with what he had earlier called the "blond beast," the ruthless shadow side of a solar, patriarchal, heroic ideal.

As an African-American, my own starting point is my unavoidable experience in and of the collective shadow of what we can call the American psyche, even though none of us in it can tell each other exactly what that is. Experiencing nonetheless the force of the shadow of that psyche, I needed a framework that grew out of collective group dynamics. I grew up highly aware of the forms of collective shadow processes that emerge as group dynamics when an excluded group is forced to carry the neglected, repressed group characteristics of the main body politic as its part of an ongoing socio-political reality.

I first became consciously aware of collective shadow forces when, as an eleven-year-old boy growing up in Jackson, Mississippi, I read that a black man had been murdered by some white men, apparently for whistling at a white woman. This frightening event awakened me like a flashbulb to the reality of race as a psychological reality that triggers the group psyche to make collective shadow-projections. Though I could not know it then in thinking terms, the seed of the concept of the cultural complex was planted in my first jarring reactions to the madness of the collective around me as a child, reacting to what for me was still the new idea of race, and this gave rise to my drive to understand the darkness that moves in group life in relation to collective ideas. A statement of Jung's has mirrored my own doubts, ever since, about our collective humanity: "It has filled us with horror to realize all the evil that man is capable of and of which, therefore, we too are capable. Since then a terrible doubt about humanity, and about ourselves gnaws at our hearts." (Jung 1945/1970, par 412, p. 200) Jung was referring to the events leading up to and including the Holocaust, a scant fourteen years before my own discovery of the same anxiety.

When I reflect on the intergenerational black holocaust in my history, I am faced with: 244 years of Chattel slavery, eighty-one years of Jim Crow laws, the fact that for over fifty years running some black person was found hanging from a tree every week, and a fifty-year history of *de facto* Apartheid laws to preserve racial "integrity." Currently, I am confronted by a criminal justice system population that is over-represented by young men of color under the age of thirty, and by the continued disparities in access to education, health care, housing that characterize the experience of the races in America. Looking at and holding what many have called this "mess" has led me at times to a kind of world-weariness. "If you gaze into an abyss," as Nietzsche said, "the abyss will gaze back into you." (Nietzsche 1886 /1955, Chapter 4, Aphorism no. 146)

In our common collective histories as Americans there are many examples of the collective shadow at work that are easy enough to recognize, if we dare to look beyond what James Baldwin, echoing Blake, called our "willed innocence." If we look around unflinchingly, then we can step toward our larger darkness as human beings. The seemingly unlimited atrocities, barbarities, bestialities and cruelties of the twentieth century and beyond are there for us all to see. Samantha Power, in her (2002) book *A Problem from Hell: America and the Age of Genocide*, documents that there have been at least six major cases of genocide in the twentieth century: these are the unimaginably systematic killings of Armenians by Turks in 1915; of Jews by Hitler in the 1940s; of Cambodians by the Khmer Rouge in the 1970s; of Kurds in northern Iraq by Saddam Hussein in the 1990s; of the Tutsi of Rwanda by the Hutu, also in the 1990s; and of Croats, Muslims, and the Albanians in Kosovo by the Serbs in the 1980s and 1990s. In 1948 the United Nations General Assembly approved the Genocide Convention, which essentially outlawed the destruction, in whole or in part, by any government of a national, ethnic, religious group. It took the United States forty more years to ratify this convention. One

217

asks, "Why?" Isn't there a moral imperative at the foundation of American democracy, based in the minds of our Founding Fathers on human dignity and decency, that constitutes the basis for at least this rhetorical level of action against other governments on behalf of our humanity? Is our ambivalence about responding to these atrocities even with condemnation (something we saw in our country during the Holocaust with Franklin Roosevelt, who understood perfectly the need for all peoples' freedom from this form of persecution and yet did not feel, politically, that he could afford to speak out) not a form of denial of the shadow that gets reflected in the abyss we are sometimes forced to look into when we contemplate the moral record of our culture? Puzzling over a similar inaction in relationship to the rising Nazi threat, Jung said,

> The sight of evil kindles evil in the soul .... The victim is not the only sufferer; everybody in the vicinity of the crime, including the murderer, suffers with him. Something of the abysmal darkness of the world has broken in on us, poisoning the very air we breathe and befouling the pure water with the stale, nauseating taste of blood.... When evil breaks at any point into the order of things, our whole circle of psychic protection is disrupted. (Jung 1945/ 1970, par. 410, p. 199-200)

If we add to the above mentioned genocidal atrocities our awareness of scores of sanctioned massacres – two World Wars, followed by the Korean and Vietnam wars and a myriad of other "smaller" ones, including those in Palestine, the former Yugoslavia, and Iraq; the history of Europe's colonialization of Africa and Asia; Japan's imperialism in China and Korea; the ugly story of Apartheid in South Africa; and the current push, called "globalization," for a ruthless control of the world's economic resources by multinational corporations based in the West; the maiming, raping and degradation of women in all parts of the world; the vicious homophobia that pervades both Christian and Muslim societies, we begin to get the feeling of the pervasiveness of the collective shadow.

Though it is beyond the scope of this paper to examine in any detail particular instances of genocide, colonization, or domination that have been the result of the activation of collective shadow processes, I would point out that all these atrocity-ridden situations stem from two dynamics that I have postulated for the destructive emergence of cultural complexes: (1) the constellation of repressed aspects of group identity and (2) the projection onto some group of reviled "others" of disowned aspects of the group's identity. Both of these dynamics are operative whenever collective shadow processes shape cultural history.

Each of us privileged enough to attend a conference like this has benefited, at least economically, from Western domination through globalization. The mention of the collective shadow processes operative in producing that benefit therefore brings up for us all, in a way we can easily feel, the issue of collective guilt, which is a cultural complex of its own. This complex involves us in guilt not, or not usually, or not so much, in a moral or legal sense, though many have suggested that we in the West should pursue that implication, but in guilt as sense of our "tragic fate, or what Jung calls "magical uncleanness." This is the kind of guilt that inevitably comes by virtue of being related to one another in various relations of power that are unfair; and we know that is the "Family of Man," the group, that has made us do the sort of things we cannot feel entirely good about as individuals.

Jung speaks to us again, this time on the issue of collective complicity:

> True, we are innocent, we are the victims, robbed, betrayed, outraged; and yet for all that, or precisely because of it, the flame of evil glowers in our moral indignation. It must be so, for it is nec-

essary that someone should feel indignant, that someone should let himself be the sword of judgment wielded by fate. Evil calls for expiation, otherwise the wicked will destroy the world utterly, or the good suffocate in their rage which they cannot vent, and in either case no good will come of it. (Jung 1945/1970, par. 410, p. 199-200)

Psychologically, the inner relationship between the collective shadow and the personal shadow is clearly the issue here. Jung is describing a *psychic* milieu organized around group and collective unconscious forces that are charged with affect. If we think of the words that filled our language following 9/11 we can experience these forces actively galvanizing cultural complexes which we had forgotten we had: "Axis of evil," "the enemy," "holy war," "innocence," "global terrorism," "sacrifice," "victim," "suicidal bombers," "retaliation," "vengeance," "collateral damage," "weapons of mass destruction." These words have rapidly constructed a collective emotional sign language, one that induces us to act in this time in accord with our cultural complexes rather than with reasoned insight into the forces actually at work in the world. This emotional sign language has reduced the world in which we have always lived into a battle between us and them, good and bad. Blinded by our righteousness, we degrade the humanity of the "them" (and our own humanity in the process).

Bion's "beta elements," those sensory-experience dominated, emotional, undigested expressions of the infantile psyche come into play here, signaling catastrophe of an unnamable kind. In such a pre-mind state of mind, everything becomes solid, emotional/symbolic space is lost, and raw affective states fusing image, sensation, perception and behavior coalesce into a potential for action with one purpose only, to relieve the intolerable anxiety. In this territory we find ourselves at Jung's infrared end of the psychic spectrum, where boundaries and people are violated and destroyed. As an analyst, when I read about or hear of examples of crimes against humanity, I think of the states of mind in which such atrocities must have been committed, and I find myself wondering how the violent, intrusive actions that were chosen to relieve distress in particular moments of crisis have continued to influence our conscious and unconscious ideals, our object relations, our view of ourselves as humans, and our hopes for the future.

Over fifty years after Jung's *Essays on Contemporary Events*, it is quite possible to see the group, historical processes that he described having a current effect upon our analytic work with descendants of victims and perpetrators of the Holocaust. We can see how historical complexes function – autonomously and intergenerationally, organizing affect and mediating feelings around belonging and identity. Work with Holocaust survivors shows the interplay of cultural complexes and collective shadow processes that inevitably follows collective traumatization. I do not believe it is possible to separate a description of the effect of a collective shadow process that does not also involve a description of the effect of a cultural complex.

We know, for example, that many descendants of both Jewish victims and German perpetrators of the Holocaust feel themselves to be typically joined in a silent, guilt-ridden, non-narrated sense of an absence-presence in relation to their shared family history. One clinical approach to these two groups has been to help the individuals wounded by the same cultural complex find and give psychic representation to what has wounded them. In individual work, the analytic effort has been directed at the splitting the ego utilizes to defend against fragmentation while simultaneously dealing with another part of the ego that registers what is happening while attempting to preserve a connection to life. But the following examples go beyond splitting and involve other kinds of psychological processes that seem to go beyond individual defenses and shadow processes.

Exploring the dynamic consequences of being descended from the perpetrators, Anne Springer, a German Jungian analyst, has written a paper entitled "The Return of the Repressed in the Mask of the Victim," in which she describes actual cases in which Jewish symbols were used by descendants of German perpetrators as a way to identify themselves as victims. To quote Springer,

> Not infrequently, these children seem to present their fate in a form in which they identify themselves as Jewish victims. Their identification fulfils several functions: it brings out into the open the historical role of persecution denied by their parents and points not only to the victims who receive no mention from the parents but also to the magical resurrection of the victims by the unconscious displacement of the victim imago towards their own children. (Springer 1990, p. 243)

This is the opposite of the typical process we are familiar with of identification with the aggressor.

Another example comes from the work of two French psychoanalysts, Nicolas Abraham and Maria Torok, who described an intrapsychic structure they called the "phantom." They focused on the kinds of psychopathology that are produced through the phantoms of events that have been concealed but for that very reason go on being experienced, in a shadowy way, as presences too shameful even to be spoken about by previous generations. Significantly the symptoms that result from such phantoms of an earlier generation's traumatic complexes are not the result of the usual processes of repression. Abraham and Torok concluded that

> The phantom is a formation of the unconscious that has never been conscious ... It passes – in a way yet to be determined – from the parent's unconscious into the child's. Clearly, the phantom

222

has a function different from dynamic repression. The phantom's periodic and compulsive return lies beyond the scope of symptom-formation in the sense of a return of the repressed; it works like a ventriloquist, like a stranger within the subject's own mental topography." (Abraham and Torok 1994, p. 173)

... it is reasonable to maintain that the "phantom effect" progressively fades during its transmission from one generation to the next and that, finally, it disappears. Yet, this is not at all the case when shared or complementary phantoms find a way of being established by social practices...." (*Ibid.*, p. 176)

The French analysts call the processes involved in the continuity of transgenerational phantoms 'preservative repression.' They feel that the phantom can infiltrate and haunt family lines and skip generations as it is passed down through successive generations. Hence, the affective field of the initial traumatic cultural complex is preserved across generations by an unconscious-to-unconscious communication dynamic that continues to structure both collective and personal events. I see the phenomenon of the 'phantom' as a powerful illustration of the autonomy of a specific cultural complex. That such complexes operate intergenerationally in individuals relates to the way group trauma can generate phantomatic processes as well: think of the Palestinian and Israeli youths, as well as the drive among contemporary American blacks to seek reparation for slavery, a group traumatization that ended in the United States well over a century ago. The cultural complex continues to operate in such situations as if the psyche's need for survival and continuity is at stake at the level of the group. Through such examples, we become aware of the defensive and reparative functions of the cultural complex.

To convey the way a cultural complex invades the personal realm, I would like to share a dream that I had following the 9/11 cataclysm:

I have been called to be a psychological consultant in a small mid-western town. I arrive and am greeted by someone who leads me to the meeting place. I notice that we are walking outside along side a hill and that I am barefoot. We walk past a pond in which the water is clear, and I can see that the pond has only one very large fish in it. We arrive at the meeting place where I meet with several of the townspeople. As they describe their concerns, I realize that they are mostly talking about how they are upset with a member of their community, whom I recognize as Harold Searles. Apparently, he says strange things and is considered inappropriate. I realize instantly the problem: they are taking and thinking literally about what he is saying, whereas he speaks in a primary process language. It's a problem of communication level or modality. Then, I am walking along a street in this town. Every house has a yard with fenced-in dogs. I suddenly find myself in front of a particular house that has two large, black dogs tied onto an oblong structure, so that they can only run in an oblong way. When I look closer at these dogs, I see that they have human faces and dog bodies. Their eyes are a cold gray and stare into nothingness.

Though there are certainly aspects of this dream that relate to my personal complexes, I would like to approach each of its main elements from the viewpoint of the cultural complex.

Let me start with the figure of Harold Searles. Searles, a seminal figure in psychotherapeutic circles, is best known for his pioneering psychoanalytic work with schizophrenic patients. In the 1950s and '60s he was outspoken in disputing the notion of the incurability of schizophrenic people and other severely disturbed patients, which gave healthy neurotics hegemony in analytic practices. By contrast, he presented the analysis of schizophrenic analysands with whom he had worked for more than thirty years. In an interview, given a few years ago, he reflected on some of this work, which had begun at Chestnut Lodge, a private psychiatric hospital that had specialized in the psychotherapeutic treatment of schizophrenic patients pioneered in this country by Harry Stack Sullivan and Frieda Fromm-Reichmann:

> I realized after I had left there [Chestnut Lodge] that I had not been able to keep the negative mother transference on their [the schizophrenic patients'] part sufficiently in perspective and I had come to accept that I was in fact a totally ineffectual mother to them, that is that my own sense of self-worth had become swallowed up in this collective negative mother transference to me. (Searles 1992, p. 325)

Searles felt, in other words, that having tried too hard to hold and work with the negativity of his patients, once the institution was no longer there to accept some of this transference, had actually resulted in the kind of injury to his own self-image that a personal negative mother complex would have caused.

Searles also wrote a paper thirty years ago entitled "Unconscious Processes in Relation to the Environmental Crisis," in which he examined some of the unconscious anxieties and fears that have kept us, and continue to keep us, from responding to the crisis of our environment with our full energy. I find it interesting that this is the cultural analyst my dream selected to comment on the complexes bedeviling our response to contemporary times. Reflecting upon his presence in my dream, I found myself asking, "Why is it Searles and not Jung that's so hard to understand? What does Searles say that's so hard for Jungian analysts to hear (for it is they who live in a model of the psyche, perhaps the small Midwestern town in my dream, that focuses on only one cultural complex, the Self, symbolized by the fish in these townspeople's pond, or image of the unconscious)? And I wondered if Searles, as my cultural consultant, was saying that it's not as pure and simple as that, and that in fact the negativity of the world is too much, and is threatening to swallow us all up? Certainly, Searles would argue that it is too much for any one individual to hold and contain the world's

225

negativity, and that (contra Jung) individual consciousness is not enough.

I next would like to call attention to the fenced-in areas of my dream. These, I felt, were symbols of an acute or chronic, defensive, paranoid, encapsulated collective space. Such structures are often erected in response to the feeling of threat, insecurity, and vulnerability. We can certainly see this instinctive response at the center of the collective debate over the necessity of America to give up certain civil liberties in order to achieve national security. Both collectively and intrapsychically, archetypal defenses of the collective spirit can be very rigid containers.

When I turn to the most haunting image in the dream, the two large half-human black dogs, I realize that I was witnessing presences that are unusual in my inner world. These dogs, in stark contrast to my usual calm receptivity, suggested an animal aspect of the psyche that seems to be on high alert, although to a vague, ill-defined danger that is dreaded in a vacant, soulless way that is only half-human. These dogs seemed to embody nature stripped of psyche, the animating force drained from its being. The eyes of the dogs are cold and blank, with no capacity for comprehension or compassion. (We sometimes see the same look in the eyes of our leaders.) The dogs seem to bark through the emptiness of their souls. They are not, I think, simply complexes of my personal anxiety, as a contemporary American fearing an uncertain threat. Rather, I have come to think of these dogs' eyes as the archaic, infantile aspects of a frightened collective peering through repressive, paranoid encapsulation. They are the very image of our contemporary cultural complex about terror and violence, and this is a collective shadow problem, which to some degree affects all Americans, leading among other things to their apathy in the face of serious political decisions about how the actual problem of terrorism is to be handled.

I am reminded of a statement from Jung in "After the Catastrophe":

> For the first time since the dawn of history we have succeeded in swallowing the whole of primitive animism into ourselves, and with it the spirit that animated nature.... Now, for the first time, we are living in a lifeless nature bereft of gods.... The mere act of enlightenment may have destroyed the spirits of nature, but not the psychic factors that correspond to them, such as suggestibility, lack of criticism, fearfulness, propensity to superstition and prejudice – in short all those factors that make possession possible. Even though nature is depsychized, the psychic conditions which breed demons are as actively at work as ever. The demons have not really disappeared but have merely taken on another form: they have become unconscious psychic forces. (Jung 1945/1970, par. 431, p. 211)

The dogs in my dream are demonic, unthinking beasts, and they symbolize a chthonic aspect of the psyche that experiences the world, not through reflective consciousness but through projective identification, that is, by means of automatic, reflexive evacuation of psychic contents into external objects, whether individuals or groups.

The townsfolk have little tolerance for differences; yet there is a difference within their midst in the form of the dogs. These strange dogs are chained to an oblong structure. Is that the narrowing of options that comes as the price of fear? When fear becomes the primary affect that organizes their world, it leads to scapegoating. Collective shadow projections become then a kind of contagion, and totem signs of group identification such as slogans collapse cultural space and discourse into a collective sign language indicating only threat. Under such circumstances the creative relationship between conscious and unconscious that characterizes moral imagination and consideration of a range of complex options is replaced by marked splitting and a tendency to black-and-white thinking, again fueled by an unexamined fear of differences.

Such a process within a culture generates a continuous need to project and externalize blame, organizing a destructive certainty as a bulwark against new attacks and annihilation at the hands of the plural psyche of tolerated differences. It is these hateful and destructive processes that Searles would like to engage the townsfolk in recognizing. Of all analysts, he would be the one most likely to understand these as paranoid/schizoid defenses, affecting in this case the middle American people's mutuality, personal relating and even their very humanity.

America has long seen itself as a city on the hill with its manifest destiny. We have felt invulnerable, exceptional; God was on our side. But like the big fish in my dream, our identification with the Self may have caused us to become alone and isolated on the world stage.

There is little doubt that the attack of 9/11 constituted a narcissistic blow to our collective sense of self, and this has proceeded into our experiencing on a continuing basis a threat of annihilation to both self and world. It would seem to be the hope of my dream, however, that recognizing this dull anxiety in the background of our lives as the feeling-tone of a cultural complex can help us from acting it out in a collectively shadowy way.

## If You Don't See my Mirrors I Can't See You

Cultural complexes are dynamic energic fields that distort consciousness, which is always a dialogue between the self and the other that is the world, by generating automatic, reflexive responses to the other, making the reality of the other invisible even as it renders unconscious to ourselves the process by which we are seeing. This point was brought home to me recently on my morning drive to my office when I was slowed down by a large truck in front of me, which had printed in bold letters "If you don't see my mirrors I can't see you." I thought to myself "What a statement about the invisibility of our process of projections! When we don't see the other, the other cannot see us. And even when we do see and are seen, it is never a direct encounter, it is always by way of a mirror, the lenses of our own and the other's subjectivity." This a tragic reality, for the mutuality of seeing and being seen is the process by which observer and observed, self and other, create an intersubjective context for psychic life. The wisdom on the back of the moving van was ominous, and perhaps reflective of the present difficulty with face-to-face seeing and I-thou encounter, expressing less an eternal verity than the cynical ideology of the current cultural complex.

I would name five defining aspects of my conception of cultural complexes:

1. They are complexes that operate at the group level of the cultural unconscious
2. that function autonomously within each individual or group
3. to organize the attitudes, emotions, and behaviors that make up group life
4. by facilitating the individual's affective relationship to the group's cultural patterns,

5. thus providing both individual and group a sense of belonging and identity within an historical continuity of shared emotional assumptions.

Let us look more closely at each part of this definition of the concept:

1. Complexes that operate at the group level of the cultural unconscious organize deeply held collective beliefs and emotions in such a way as to organize much of group life as well as fantasies within the individual psyche. Cultural complexes mediate an individual's relationship to a specific reference group, nation, or culture by linking personal experiences to group expectations. We have seen such linkages in the commonality of contemporary German and Jewish responses to the Holocaust and in the community's collective denial of its actual relation to threat, symbolized in various ways in my dream.

2. That cultural complexes function autonomously within each individual or group beneath our awareness means that they either impose constraints on the perception of differences or else accentuate them into caricatures. Cultural complexes, that is, emphasize *either* identification with the group *or* differentiation from the group, and thus they allow both for feelings of intense belonging or painful alienation.

3. In order to organize the attitudes, emotions, and behaviors that make up group life, cultural complexes have to function as energic emotional fields, but the dynamics are impersonal – cultural complexes are no respecter of persons, care for no one but the group's survival and continuity, and don't serve individual reflection. They simply propel people toward feelings and action. They function through psychic induction, a morphic resonance that produces in widely disparate individuals a feeling of commonality, mediated by language used as what Lacan has called a symbolic register, and by a logos

that is grounded in the semiotic of specific environmental settings whose biases go unrecognized.

4. That cultural complexes facilitate the individual's affective relationship to the group's cultural patterns means that when these complexes are functioning positively, they structure the individual's sense of belonging. Identity is then achieved through identification with one's cultural, racial, ethnic or social group. On the basis of this very belongingness, however, the negative function of the cultural complex is released, in its generation of stereotypes, prejudices and an attitude that sees otherness as essentially threatening.

5. That cultural complexes provide both individual and groups a sense of belonging and identity within an historical continuity or shared emotional assumptions means that the archetype of the Self is evoked by cultural complexes, which then have available to them all the energy of the archetypal and personal levels of the psyche. Needless to say, this can make cultural complexes very dangerous (the lynch mob) even as it enables them at other times to inspire the collective spirit in more positive ways (patriotism).

## Conclusion

Collective traumas of the kind stirred up by terror, violence, and the impulse to destroy are organized by, and kept alive in an unresolved form, by cultural complexes. These complexes carry the historical memory of the group built on an "archaic form of justice," an eye for an eye. (Hersh 1985) When we use the concept of cultural complexes to organize the psychological history of a culture, we can readily see that cultural memory belongs not just to the individuals residing in the culture but also to the culture itself, which generates its own emotional fields. These fields of course operate through the psyches of individuals to achieve their effects. Cultural memory uses the psyches of individuals to channel libido, propagate affect, and constellate ideologies, thus shaping a group's values, expectations, prescriptions, proscriptions, rituals, and history. Particularly the way cultures imagine their debt to the past and the reparative processes they will exact from the future are almost entirely shaped by cultural complexes.

Like all complexes, however, cultural complexes are susceptible to insight. Psychological work, whether done individually or by the collective, may transform what had been experienced as pure fact into thoughts, feelings and beliefs that can be reflected upon and altered. Individual awareness that some of one's complexes are cultural, symbolic processes derived from the group and operating at the collective level allows for the creation of a narrating third, a space for symbolization, and the possibility of reflection. This is the conscious road that analysis has charted to our human potential for reparation and reconstruction.

Finally, the existence of cultural complexes opens the possibility that as a collective we might be able to do a therapeutic type of cultural analysis. Is it too much to ask that, given the multinational world we live in, with its multiple psychic realities, we begin to work collectively with the negative processes that function within and between groups? At the very least we could begin by recognizing that a sense of specialness, omnipotence, entitlement, innocence, and righteousness can spring up in groups no less than in individuals, and that these processes are fostered at the group level by cultural complexes that we can analyze. We need look no further than our government's sense of entitlement to impose its views by force on nations that are perceived as dangerous to see the kind of work that needs to be done.

The questions that depth psychologists who would like to begin the therapeutic analysis of cultural complexes must ask are these: Can we find ways of working through the processes that generate unconscious fears, which lead groups to view each other as negative, parasitic containers that threaten to engulf one another? Can we develop ways of getting people to recognize the encapsulated containers that are created by nationalism, ethnocentrism, and reference groups of all sorts? And can we collectively grow in the individuals of our culture the emotional capacity to hold in creative, generative tension our national survival needs and the integrity of the world as a whole, so that this pair of seeming opposites can become what the cultural complex insists it anyway is – a single, united, inter-dependent system?

## References

Abraham, N., and Torok, M. (1994). *The Shell and the Kernel*. Chicago, University of Chicago Press.

Hersh, J. (1985). *From Ethnos to Polis*. Dallas, Spring Publications

Jung, C.G. (1945/1970). "After the Catastrophe," *CW 10*.

Jung, C. G. (1946/1970). "Preface" to *Essays on Contemporary Events. CW 10*.

Milosz, C, (2001). *New and Collected Poems*. New York, HarperCollins.

Nietzsche, F. (1886/1955). *Beyond Good and Evil*. Marianne Cowan (trans). Chicago: Henry Regnery Co.

Power, S. (2002). *A Problem from Hell: America and the Age of Genocide*. New York, Basic Books.

Searles, H. (1972). "Unconscious Processes in Relation to the Environmental Crisis," *The Psychoanalytic Review*, 59:361-374.

Searles, H. (1992). "Harold Searles talks to Martin Stanton," *Free Associations*, 3/3 No. 27.

Springer, A. (1990). "The Return of the Repressed in the Mask of the Victim," *The Journal of Psychohistory*, 17(3), Winter.

# Blood Payments

*Sherry Salman*

## Introduction

Unceasing, relentless, implacable, ever-grudging, the archetypal affects of the Furies avenge all betrayals and sins against
primal relationships with a pitiless, ruthless intensity. We find
them at the interstices of all kinship conflicts: in those initiated
by willful disregard of others' humanity, through envy or greed;
in unintentional insufficiencies of love; and in the genuine struggles between relationship and independence. As the ancient
Greeks understood, the darker octaves of the "play" of opposites usually draw blood. And as depth psychology has had to
re-discover, this libidinal blood *must* be paid for in kind, by the
dramas of guilt and retribution, sacrifice, or ritual transformation. At this level of psychological process, that is, at the level of
archetypal affect, *concrete embodiment is all.* The fury of wounding and betrayal cannot be denied, but rather must be suffered
through to its meaning and embodied conclusion. Drinking the
dregs of fury's rage, our own and that of others, is part of the
psyche's move toward wholeness, leading us into an initiation
below, in the underworld, whose dark fruit is the blood-bond

of communion. As mythology and world events repeatedly illustrate, the Furies, if not given their due, will always have the last word in vengeance, even if it brings the whole house down.

*I.*

In her book *The Fragility of Goodness,* philosopher Martha Nussbaum notes that Orestes is not mad, but is at his most sane, at the moment that he recognizes that his mother's Furies are in pursuit. What would it mean in the treatment situation, and in collective processes of conflict resolution, to achieve and work prospectively with such a moment, at this bald level of archetypal process, in the midst of such dismemberment and coagulation? In treatment, analytic technique must be capable of making evident the body of this dramatic process, which takes place beyond the margins of ego awareness. In our patients, pockets of identification with the Furies don't speak the same language, have the same morality, or engage in the same analysis as the rest of the psyche; yet for treatment to be complete they must at least be integrated into the overall economy of the psyche, and at best, the Furies provide *prima materia* for what William Blake envisioned as 'the marriage of heaven and hell.'

Many patients, often termed 'borderline,' relentlessly cry out with the voice of the Almighty for validation of their early wounds and betrayals. They furiously insist on our vindication of their self-representations and identifications, striking moral fear in our hearts should we try to deny them their due. In this timeless tragic place, transference or reductive interpretation is almost always experienced intrapsychically as co-incident with destructive defenses and pointless re-wounding, and in the transference as a counter-attack by the analyst that renders the patient more, rather than less symptomatic. In the *Orestia,*

the Furies lash out against such "gods of the younger generation":

> That they could treat me so!
> I, the mind of the past, to be driven under the ground, outcast
> like dirt!
> The wind I breathe is fury and utter hate. (Eumenides, 837-40)

If such a dissonance in process occurs between patient and
therapist, analysis screeches to a halt. In order to achieve a
truly functional rather than a merely technical, neutrality, blood
payment of some sort must be made for the violation of the
integrity and natural order of the early world of the analysand.
This blood is often exacted from the analyst in such sacrificial
dramas as projective identification. Without this retributive
justice, there can be no willing freedom on the patient's part
to descend into the symbolic dialogue of interpretation; there
is only relentless fury, acted-out or introjected in a psychological *jihad*. The teleological perspective which moves archetypal
affect toward meaningful incarnation is essential to treatment.
Our discovery in analytic work of the need to give the vengeful
affects the dignity they deserve could perhaps help us understand and better impact the blood payments and sacrifices currently being extracted in the collective psyche as well. In both
individual and collective situations, the question is, how do we
stay related to this level of psyche in ways that are not just
destructive, palliative, or propitiatory?

On Sept. 11th 2001, in an explosion of violence that made
borderline rage appear benign, the archetypal affects of the
Furies burst into flame. By this terrible wound our eyes were
opened to the blind faith with which we have pursued the modern vision, to the fiction in the seemingly bloodless, shadowless
expansion of the free-market, and to the rising tide of western-
ization threatening to flood the world. We were even forced
to see that our faith in our beloved secular democracy has in

many ways been a blind one. Our bewilderment bore witness to our collective resistance to seeing the blind hate, envy, and fury in what culturally had been deemed "the other." Our blind faith and its shadow, the western hegemony, had led us, through broken bonds of relatedness, to the deepest, darkest levels of psyche. Then, for a moment on 9/11, we became one with the wounded soul of the world.

But since, as the archetypal shadow of "the evil other" is cast back and forth in the vehemence of public discourse, the Furies have struck again and again, revealing in these very splits and betrayals of humanity, that we are still paying for the betrayals of the world's body and soul. "All life repays its debt to nature, that is, to matter," wrote Bachofen. Or else, fury curses the land.

> The easiest way to escape the Furies, we think, is to deny that they exist … The conspiracy to forget them, or to deny them, thus turns out to be only one more contrivance in that vast and organized effort by modern society to flee from the self. (Barrett 1958, p. 279-80)

So commented William Barrett in his existential treatise *Irrational Man.*

In an effort not to flee, I turn now to give the Furies their psychological due. The Furies have been portrayed in tragic drama, from Aeschylus to Albee, as heavy hitters in the great web of human destiny. This may be because they embody an archetypal reality that belongs not only to affective experience in its individual and collective manifestations, but to the fundaments of earthly existence itself. The Furies emerge out of the unifying ground between psyche and the world, like fate, growth, and death. (Sanford 1955) Their origins are placed very close to the beginning of time: The Greeks imagined them as daughters of simply, "the Night" … or as the daughters of Uranos and Gaia, sky and earth. Hesiod tells that when Cronos flung the severed phallus of his father Uranos toward the sea, the Furies were born from the blood that fell onto the earth, as the phallus received by the sea was fathering Aphrodite, who would mother Eros. The Furies speak of the dark, bitter side of the binding power of eros. And it is to blood betrayed that the Furies always return. They came to be imagined as three winged, whip-wielding sisters, beastly predators when enraged, with serpent-filled hair and deadly claws, who lived in dreadful Tartarus or Dis, the region just before the Gates of Hades, the region reserved for those souls who committed terrible offenses. They appear in Dante's *Inferno,* guarding and hovering over these Gates (Fig. 1), fettering impure souls with unbreakable bonds, leaping on the guilty with avenging fury. The Furies emerge from their underground lair to punish the most heinous crimes, particularly murder, particularly blood-guilt within a family, and especially matricide. Their names, Allecto, Tisiphone, and Megaira, mean "unceasing," "vengeance," and "strange dark memory." They are not, archetypally, compassionate or mournful. Only Orpheus with his music was able to bring tears to their eyes, but only temporarily.

The Furies were also conceived as the unpurified spirits of the dead, particularly the ghosts of the murdered, and they appeared as dark-colored doves, in tune with all the goddesses of fate and death who appear as black birds: crows, vultures, ravens; the Morrigan, Nekhbet, and the wrathful Valkyries. Many of us from New York remember being terribly unnerved by the appearance of black birds in patients' dreams before 9/11 and by the stories and dreams of so many burning birds crashing to earth at the scene of the World Trade Center attack. (See accounts by Zabriskie and Gosling in Steinberg 2001, p. 59, 61.)

The Furies frightful wailing was called a "binding hymn," and, like the Sirens song, it had the power to grip its victims, to cast a spell which reached all the way into the blood, chilling it, drying it up, and driving its victims mad. Like Nemesis and the Fates, the Furies weave a curse, through the maddening rage and guilt they invoke, which bind us by, and to, what is most basic and elemental in our natures: the body, the non-rational psyche, and to our deep instinctive drive towards integrity and individuation, at whatever cost. The way the Furies bind us to ourselves, 'primitive' though it may be, is nevertheless, like all unspoken vows, the expression of a religious function of psyche. The gods of Olympus, and later, the heroes of psychoanalysis, would try to break these bonds established by the Furies, imagining that by severing us from this single-minded devotion to blood-order, they could free us from it. But there have been unsettling and ambiguous consequences to this civilizing 'progress.'

Our present understanding of the Furies' place in psychological history derives primarily from the *Orestia* trilogy by Aeschylus, which concerns the resolution of the curse on the house of Atreus for the sin of hubris. In brief: when Agamemnon returned home after the Trojan war, he was murdered by his wife Clytemnestra, who, angered by his sacrifice of their daughter Iphigenia to curry Apollo's favor in the war, had assumed rulership of Mycenae in his absence and taken a new husband. Apollo commands Orestes, son of Agamemnon and Clytemnestra to avenge the murder of his father by killing his mother. Orestes protests, but afraid of Apollo's curse and his father's Furies, he reluctantly murders his mother to avenge his father, knowing full well that the Furies will drive him mad for such a deed. And they do, immediately rising up to begin their pursuit and persecution of what for them is the most repulsive human crime: matricide. They insist that blood payment must be paid for this blood-crime, deemed by the Furies infinitely worse than killing a king or husband.

Your mother's blood is on the ground. The moist liquid is gone. But you in return must give to me to drain from you alive the red fluid from your limbs. From you would I take nurture … and having dried you up alive I will lead you below. Over our victim consecrate, this is our song-fraught with madness, fraught with frenzy, crazing the brain, the Furies' hymn, spell to bind the soul, untuned to the lyre, withering the life of mortal man. (*Eumenides*, p. 341-6)

Orestes tries in vain to escape. After a year of torture, he attempts to take refuge at Delphi. Apollo orders him to Athens instead, to appeal to Athena to protect him. The play climaxes in the trial of Orestes on the hill of the Acropolis, before a tribunal of Athenian citizens. This is the first human jury. Apollo defends Orestes, insisting on the ultimate primacy of paternity and citing the oracle of Zeus against 'mother-right.' The Furies defend themselves.

When we were born such lots were assigned for our own keeping. So the immortals must hold hands off. Is there a man who does not fear this, does not shrink to hear how my place has been ordained, granted and given by destiny and god, absolute? Privilege primeval yet is mine, nor am I without place, though it be underneath the ground and in no sunlight and in gloom that I must stand. (*Eumenides*, p. 389-96)

The vote by the Athenian citizenry is an uneasy tie, which is broken by Athena on the side of Orestes. He is thus freed from the Furies' curse.

But upon his acquittal, the Furies become completely enraged and threaten to destroy everything, including the fertility of the earth, and every infant in the womb.

Gods of the younger generation, you have ridden down the laws of the elder time, torn them out of my hands. I, disinherited, suffering, heavy with anger shall let loose on the land the vindictive

241

poison dripping deadly out of my heart upon the ground. (*Eumen-ides*, p. 778-83)

Athena again intervenes, acknowledging that although the Furies should not be "allowed to descend without limits into future generations" and must be tempered by reason, that there is a primal honor and wisdom in their claims. The goddess declares, "These women have a work we cannot slight," and agrees that the moral fear they inspire is sometimes a good thing. She gives the Furies a sanctuary near the Acropolis and places the newborn children they threatened under *their* protection. The spirits of violent revenge are thus persuaded to accept a new dwelling in Athens, the place of reason, and, reformed and honored, they become known as "the Eumen-ides," the "kindly or gentle ones" who bless the land and its people. At the end of the *Oresteia* they are led off the stage in dignified procession to their new abode. Their transforma-tion is impressive: at the beginning of the play, the Furies were presented as beasts, crouching dog-like creatures enthralled by the smell of blood. At the drama's end, they stand erect, clothed in robes given to them by the citizens of Athens; now they appear to the audience as human women. So began a trend toward their elimination: in later Greek tragedy their role becomes less and less deadly, until in Sophocles' *Electra* there are no Furies at all to pursue Orestes and his sister. The curse of the house of Atreus was, seemingly, over.

## II.

There is an abundance of literary and philosophical com-mentary on the *Orestia,* and it is strikingly impassioned, ambigu-ous, and split. Some, like William Barrett (1958), see the play as expressing the paragon of the redeemed relationship with primitive affect and the true beginning of Western civilization, a utopia where justice of the jury, reason, and a measure of mercy all supercedes the compulsive blood-payment justice of the Furies, however 'right' the claims for this retribution may feel. It would seem to be enough that the new order of human justice pays a price to the old archetypal system of justice in the form of honor and recognition, which hopefully means integrating the latter instead of repressing it. The pact Athena makes with the Furies is seen by Barrett and others as suggesting meaningful contact with the archaic life of the unconscious, and not just the alienating triumph of reason over the darkness of our deeper selves.

Another group of critics, led by Nietzsche, has found another meaning in what they read as Aeschylus' ironic, ominous ending. Suspicious of the cool barter that is depicted, they wonder why the Furies 'accept' the deal at all, and at how quickly they seem to succumb to the song of reason and respect. Such critics cite the immense difficulty, even the futility and hubris, of 'making nice' with the mystery of such daemonic forces. Nietzsche, challenging the optimistic Greek solution, asked: can goodness exist without the coercion of God or civilization? Will goodness flow from the unfettered, and tragic experience of strength and destruction? Or is suffering daimonic affect "the essence of all the prophylactic healing forces?" (Nietzsche 1927, p. 77) Depth psychology is still struggling with this insight. Nietzsche's questions might be framed psychologically as follows: Has archetypal possession actually been contained and humanized? Has there been a 'marriage of heaven and hell' in Blake's sense, and in the Jungian one of a *coincidentia oppositorum,* or merely one of superego coercion and ego convenience? Has fury been 'converted,' changing its essential nature to become well-disposed, or has it been silenced and appeased? Does the final act of the Oresteia record a process of genuine transformation that trust in human and psychic relatedness makes possible, or merely a "cover-up" which will not hold? These questions have been answered in one way by Freud, in his call for 'sublimation of the instincts,' and in quite another by Jung through the image of the *mysterium coniunctionis*, which implies an actual transformation of darkness. These questions move us toward the heart of darkness in our analytical work, where we so often find that only the deep experience of dangerous but numinous depths has real transformative effects.

The Greeks certainly recognized he fragility of Aeschylus's solution. They knew it to be too easily reversible. Euripides, coming after Aeschylus, makes a dramatic point of inverting the process: in his plays, such as *The Trojan Women,* noble women with kindly intentions become dog-like furies, thirsty for blood; reason is exposed as a defense within the inevitable dynamics of revenge. The robes of humanity, Athena's stock in trade, are easily removed. Says Nussbaum

> Suspended between beast and god ... the human being is defined against both of these self-sufficient creatures by its open and vulnerable nature, and the relational character of its concerns. But if being human is a matter of the character of one's trust and commitment, not just a natural fact, then the human being is also the being that can most easily cease to be itself – either by moving upwards towards the self-sufficiency of the divine, or slipping downwards into the self-sufficiency of doggishness. And the difference between the two is not altogether obvious ... both involve a closing off of human things. (Nussbaum 1986, p. 417)

In the original 'mother-tongue' of analytical psychology, the Furies are one face of the Terrible Mother, a devouring dynamism of the death-mysteries: regression, sickness, fixation, madness, death, dismemberment. Belonging to the psychology of the Great Round of the Goddess, it is no mere conceit to say that when it comes to the Furies, 'what goes around always comes around.' And the ego, in its heroic phase, is heroic precisely because it halts, at least temporarily, the Terrible Mother of compulsive repetition. While our analytic forbears acknowledged the "suffering" of the vanquished unconscious, and knew this had to be suffered in turn by the ego, usually in the form of guilt, this suffering had to be "overcome" or put aside, in order to fully realize the ego's individuality and value.

We have not often enough heeded Jung's warning that this is a merely partial solution at best, even a trick of the mind, and at worst leads to unconscious apotropaic defense-magic. One consequence of this defense is that we personalize transpersonal reality (usually by reduction to family dynamics, to an 'anatomical-unconscious,' or even to internal objects). Another is that we engage in denial or even exorcism of archetypal affect in an effort to "handle it." We are at our most touchingly optimistic, in our cautious and propitiatory re-naming of archetypal fury, i.e., as "intense self assertion," following in the footsteps of Aeschylus's Athenian, who euphemistically renamed the Furies the Kindly Ones. For example, Bachofen claimed

> as the Eumenides the Furies *yearn* to cast off their bloody office, to change from avenging earth goddesses to mothers of all blessing, ... taking under their protection him whom they have so long persecuted and make him one of their own. (1967, p. 183)

The implication here is that rather than the gods hounding us, they yearn to be 'on our side.' We hear something similar in much of the current political rhetoric. Jung early on pointed out that when we deny the autonomy of any complex, much less of archetypal affect, trying to "assimilate" it, eat it and make it 'one of our own,' we are engaging in essentially the same kind of apotropaic activity (Jung 1934/1960 para. 206, p. 99), a magical solution that is doomed eventually to fail. It is unsettling to observe how easily in our analytic practice and training, what we often find left behind after a therapeutic meal of such ego-satisfying interpretations, are still the Furies. They live on in their Athenian disguise, as child-protectors, patron goddesses of the 'cult of the inner child,' to which so many contemporary therapists and patients have fallen prey, identifying with the Furies or their victims, through a relentless, reductive pursuit of the never-ending, unfinished business of childhood.

This kind of apotropaic identification with the Furies is a solution that blocks a deeper process: the pursuit of Orestes by his mother's Furies enacts a deep ethical response in the psyche to take ownership and responsibility for one's totality. Thus, "Orestes is not mad, but at his most sane, when he recognizes that the Furies are in pursuit." (Nussbaum 1986, p. 41) They bring him face-to-face with death, guilt, fear, despair, pain, and all that appears hostile. Madness dismembers, and that, in traditional fertility magic, is the first step: dissolution provides the seeds of rebirth. The Furies' demand for blood payment stimulates an alchemy of dissolution and coagulation, which they relentlessly exact. Once Orestes has broken the original matriarchal container (and this, clearly, is his fate), the Furies call him to coagulate at a more inclusive level of psyche. Only then can he claim himself in his totality. The more he is dismembered and bound by their hostile rage, the more firm and solid he is challenged to become. They aim, in some way, to purify.

*III.*

I turn now to the specific questions of the psychological process involved. Identification with the Furies expresses deep primal affect, symbolized as the 'old order' of "mother-right," expressing the cry of betrayal of one's very substance and identity, unmitigated by any other psychological functions. This is archetypal compensation for lack of personal mediation in its most elemental form. On a collective level, John Sanford put it this way:

> The Furies, in their function as guardians of the world of the Mother, were represented in Greek mythology as capable of

afflicting the land itself with pestilence in reaction to a wanton disregard by human beings of the rights of nature as our Mother....
In nature everything is related to everything else. When this interlocking web of relationships prevails and is not disrupted, nature
preserves a creative balance that favors life, but when disrupted
or violated, nature produces ruin. All this is "the Furies." (Sanford
1995, p. 93-94)

At this level of experience, the tension of opposites remains
just that: a tense balance, an eye for an eye, a crime for a crime,
blood pays for blood. This is the world of borderline psychology that analytic clinicians know well: the coincidence of interpretation and wounding; killing envy; terrorizing inferiority;
splitting; scapegoating; lack of space between the opposites
with a resulting inability to hold ambiguity; and, above all, lack
of tolerance for "the underworld initiation." This level of therapeutic process is always characterized by its lack of resolution
into "a third," into a reconciling symbol, or activation of the
transcendent function.

Aeschylus' play demonstrates the psychological accomplishment of separating the opposites, while hinting at the perils
of this paranoid-schizoid resolution. The classical psyche
envisioned its own development in the imagery of matriarchal
consciousness developing into patriarchal consciousness, as the
lower and darker evolving into the higher and more temper-
ate, placing the attendant clash of opposites, with its spilling of
blood, guilt, and retribution, in the context of civilizing progress.
This classic developmental view stops short of pressing forward
into the *mysterium coniunctionis*, which would be a real transformation of the furious libido into a 'third.' Instead we find as
the solution Athena, whose motherless paternity replaces the
ancient fatherless maternity and whose blend of logos and eros
bespeaks the embodiment of the androgynous soul-anima of
the classical psyche. It is no coincidence that she is a goddess of

warfare, particularly rationally justified war, whose roots grow deep in the underworld of the Furies. Although Athena represents a particular order of psychological achievement, this level of psychological process does not seem to adequately hold the Furies' rage.

Instead, the 'classical' solution to the archaic affect of the Furies appears to split this aspect of the 'feminine' in two: Athena represents on the one hand a sublimation into a new ethos, but on the other the primal rage of the feminine driven further underground where it festers and breaks out in violent crises. That such outbreaks repeatedly occur suggests that the catabolic, destructive processes necessary to life and psychological development have been stripped of their essential character and function in an effort to control them. The Furies as we knew them appear to 'pass into' the figure of Athena, much as Medusa's head appears on her shield; they are transmogrified into a blessing through their subordination to the 'solar' law. But is this their integration or an ominous attempt to deny their power by possessing it, a by-passing of the internal underworld initiation that would submit to such trans-human power and only then be less likely to be possessed by what we have sought to control? Without such an initiation, we are left without collective containment for the suffering of anxiety, dismemberment, disintegration, raw need and aggression, for madness and hate, and a space in which catabolic and 'recessive' processes can do their work as part of the natural cycle of creation and destruction.

And without this contained suffering there is no real alchemical transformation of primal, threatening, and demonic affective states. For although identification with the Furies may seem to bring its own level of meaning through Dionysian ecstasy and all that that implies about the expression of rage and healing, in the end, in an effort to avenge their wounds, the Furies also merely wound in turn. But if stripped *entirely* of their catabolic function, hidden in Athena's logos, their deeper claims become more, rather than less, unconscious. They eventually erupt.

This modern predicament, familiar in Western history, is also enacted in various practices of psychotherapy, where it may be expressed psychologically as the attempt to move the angry patient's psyche toward sublimation into higher-order ego functions, vs. the acceptance of the violence as a natural move toward transformation. I mean transformation here in Jung's later sense, a conjoining of the 'lower' with the 'higher' which forms the psychological third, not a sublimation or canalization of one 'upto' or 'into' the other, as in matriarchy to patriarchy. 'Transformation into the third' is the basic perspective of a discipline that accepts dangerous affective states as an initiation, with its roots in the alchemical and Mystery traditions where body and spirit are one at the psychoid layer of process, and later conjoined in the alchemical *mysterium coniunctionis*. The therapeutic question becomes, are we to enlist the Furies in the service of collective and individual ego development, a perhaps 'damned if we do, damned if we don't' proposition, or trust in their corrective potential as dynamisms of the Self?

*IV.*

I turn now to some case material, and the way in which what I have been calling suffering the underworld initiation brought about a pact with the Furies more lasting than that achieved by Orestes under Athena's protection. For my patient, a middle-aged woman, fury almost destroyed everything, but it also acted as a coagulant. The psychological dismemberment which it finally brought served as its own kind of fertility magic: a dissolution in the service of change. When she first came for treatment, a beautiful woman with a strong, fiery look and temperament, she presented herself as "stuck" and in need of a "mentor," identified with her role as caregiver. Eventually she spoke about 'fits of rage' at work, and with the man she lived with in painful animosity and dependence. She had a violent, terrifying, severely disturbed mother whom she had to serve as a kind of abused Cinderella, and an alcoholic father who colluded in denying his wife's illness.

The initial work provided insight and catharsis, but, lucky for her, I would say, little real symptom relief. It served more deeply to take the lid off the cauldron, and what emerged from underneath was an identification with the Furies, the intensity of which I had never seen before, and put the diagnosis "borderline" to shame. She seethed with resentment at the inadequacy of her early world, lashing out at herself and those who had wounded her with ruthless intensity. Both hounded by, and identified with the Furies, her system of persecution was so complete at times as to be delusional, coming out of an alternative universe, projected into current slights and hurts distorting them almost beyond recognition with a righteous hate which knew no bounds. It took my breath away, and I was often aware of feeling frightened by what seemed like a smell of poison in the air and the sound of serpents hissing. It seemed imperative, however, that I suffer this, that the Furies be given their due. As therapist I had to tow the line without being dragged under, either into collusion with the Furies, or with the Athena-mentor who seemed to offer a way out. Eventually I just worked to keep myself and the space open for her, surrendering all interpretation, in awe of an identification with the dark so complete that conventional shadow work was almost impossible. I watched in horror as she tore herself and everything to pieces, feeling that she was well on the way to destroying what life she had made for herself, which was, given her background, a considerable one. I also witnessed an intractability of pathology which bespoke a dynamism of the Self.

The fury served initially as a powerful archetypal defense, a self-care system guarding her against further wounding, whether on an objective level or through a meeting with her shadow. (Kalsched 1996) For every wound inflicted on her she took vengeance in kind, and that was quite enough to restore her damaged honor and identity. This ethic of revenge was basically ego-syntonic, for although I think she registered my distress and empathy with the suffering she endured and inflicted, she felt no sorrow for herself, or anyone else. Her experience had been that voicing distress brought no relief; fearing being overcome by her own suffering, or my compassion, she simply killed it off. The daimonic Furies themselves were what protected her regressing ego-persona from further trauma, from her own failures in life, and above all, from a descent into an underworld initiation. Guardian angels they were not; avenging angels with access to the powers of Hell, most definitely. The internal and external cycles of terror and fury seemed endless. Unable to confront these furious witches, I felt in my more despondent moments that the whole process was Macbeth-like, "a tale told by an idiot, full of sound and fury, signifying nothing." (*Macbeth,* V, v, 26-28) At other times, I had the peculiar feeling that only the appearance of a god would save my patient (this is not unlike what I sometimes feel now in the face of the world situation) and I found myself hoping against hope, for the compensatory constellation of benign archetypal processes which would preserve life. This constellation is depicted in Blake's drawing of the righteous angel, powerful enough to stand against the Furies (Fig. 1). But unconscious archetypal compensation didn't work exactly that way in this case.

Her early dreams were as follows:

> I'm running and hiding because I've committed a crime, I don't know what it is but it's serious, and I'm trying to escape and hide my face, running through the woods, without shoes, sometimes

*Figure 1: William Blake,* The Angel at the Gate of Dis *(1824-27), pen and watercolor over pencil and black chalk. National Gallery of Victoria, Melbourne, Australia.*

alone, sometimes with others, looking out for myself, hiding in basements and attics. Sometimes I'm running from my mother's house, trying to find a new apartment, but someone has been killed, and I end up back there.

Although at one level my patient seemed perversely to persist in evading what the analysis might offer in terms of nourishment, and to remain in perpetual flight from shadow confrontation, it was at a deeper level to her immense credit that she resisted any attempt to break with the Furies until their deeper purpose had been realized. Finally, therapy, the most important and thus the last link, was all there was left standing intact. Many times, of course, I had fantasized about terminating the treatment, and many more I had heard the siren-song of enlisting the Furies in the service of her ego. But the dynamics of projective identification, through which I was being made to suffer with her, insisted that I sit with the blood-bath of her rage and endure it. These dynamics ensured that our unconsciouses were in dialogue, and although she also felt the treatment wasn't really helping much, she held on because I was, as she explained in a poignant slip: "a very patient with her." I did, however, about three years into the treatment, go on maternity leave, and on returning had to change her standing appointment time to accommodate my schedule. Previously, although she complained about the therapy, she had also kept me, and the work, conspicuously out of the deeper whirlwind of her cycles of rage and retribution. But now I had presented her with a concrete wound and re-enactment which had to be met: cut-off, abandoned, and then asked to serve my needs, the ancient Furies were called up. But the stakes were very, very high for her, and this, mingled with a bit of faith and trust in our human and psychic relatedness, shifted the way in which the wound was met, opening a chink in the defensive system, creating a window into an actual negative transference with both reductive and prospective dimensions that we could explore together. She had the following dream:

> Sherry and I are opposite each other, like in session. Then I realize I'm in a hospital gown, and Sherry says I have to stay in the hospital for a while, over my birthday, and also says 'it's about *time*' (or 'it's *about time*'). I am furious and think 'well, if she thinks I'm that depressed and suicidal I'll show her, by killing myself.' I then get very upset that I would really think of threatening Sherry.

This dream signaled the beginning of her sanity. It showed a beginning disidentification from her furious remorseless form of self-pity which blocked any access to the shadow, and the appearance of a 'third,' *the suffering soul* capable of concern for another and herself. Through their pursuit of me, she recognized the Furies in pursuit of her, and began her descent into the underworld, rather than her possession by it. The idea introduced by her dream of being in the hospital meant suffering one of the worst indignities imaginable to her, and confinement there evoked all the attendant archetypal motifs of a healing incubation: imprisonment in her own afflicted body; suffering her karma; submission; and the 'deliverance' from self-preservation into genuine descent. She began to feel "upset" at her desire for vengeance. Realizing that she didn't want to hurt me, she recognized her self-pity and lust for revenge as psychological killers. Previously, I had suffered in her stead, and this blood-bond between us was also the 'Sherry' in the dream, the archetypal piece in the transference that held her psyche through its fragmentation, into descent into her own depths. This time, the Furies sent her through the Gates of Dis, and with their catabolic function freed from its defensive aspect, she was able for the first time to turn inward, falling, now Hamlet-like, into doubt and conflict. She was drained dry, mortified and deflated, but 'taken below' as the Furies ordained, and put in touch with profound abandonment and its attendant suffering.

A year and a half later came 9/11, which enacted in a synchronistic way the persecutory dynamics of her early world that she was now confronting. A month after the attack she dreamt:

> There is something very important I have to figure out. I see on a computer or TV screen a video of Princess Di and Dodi Fayed. They are holding hands. Suddenly they are made to disappear. Just absolutely gone. There is an implication that they had something to do with it, with 9/11.

She considered Princess Di a "closet borderline living in a fairy tale," a fiction she envied, resented, and longed for. This fantasy was now lost forever, blasted by the fury of the 9/11 attackers. In the unerring logic of the dream world, she 'knew' that the 'fairy tale' had instigated the attacks. The catastrophic

*Figure 2:* The Tower. *The King and Queen topple to earth, signifying complete and sudden change. Smith-Waite Tarot Deck, published by Rider in 1909.*

death of this inner couple, whom the Furies had at first protected and then destroyed, symbolized the next step: the death of the regressed and idealized King and Queen (Schwartz-Salant 1986), a substitute for the healthy internal dynamic she had never known. This death allowed 'how it should have been' to be replaced with 'how it is' in this woman's psyche. (Fig. 2 depicts the death of the inner couple and the radical change accompanying this event.) Now neither righteous nor wicked avenger, and no longer bound by the Furies' curse, she was released to take up her own life. The shift occurred once again by fury's rupture, but this time into the death of a malignant archetypal identification. Subsequent to this, the Furies never arose in the same way again.

Analysis, for this patient, provided for the ritual embodiment of fury and rage, allowing the affect to be 'drunk to the dregs,' and thus metabolized.

My patient's association of the injury to her inner world with the suicide bombing of the world Trade Center is an important amplification. The dynamics of this woman's early inner life, displacement, revenge, and fury, are not unlike that of the fury of terrorism, or nationalism, which are also outgrowths of afflicted archetypal attachments to earth, family, and clan. My furious patient and the furious terrorist, concrete and limited as their inner worlds may be, definitely have their "hearts in their work", acting from the primordial depths to protect and defend their birthright. William Pfaff, wrote in *The Wrath of Nations:*

> Islamic fundamentalism is a form of "national" resistance, an assertion of political autonomy and independence vis-à-vis the western powers, and an attempt to reclaim a jeopardized cultural independence and wholeness. (p. 128)

This archetypal fantasy, of reclaiming a golden age which has been lost, is quite pertinent to the individual dynamics of fury and rage encountered in analysis, where what is often at issue is the lost, and concretely irreclaimable 'golden age' of Childhood. The Furies protect this Golden Age, whether it be collective and literal like the lost Ottoman Empire, or an internal archetypal fantasy projected backwards, onto the fiction of idealized inner Parents. And for a long time they do so with fierce resistance to any encroachment. But they also, if allowed to fulfill their potential, destroy it.

Fury, revenge, and the madness it brings seem built into the fabric of our cultural unconscious. The collective psyche is also a plural psyche, and it is premature to imagine that our cultural complex with the archetypal image of the Furies at its core has been transformed in any essential way. At this point we merely seem to turn up, or down, the volume. We still need to ask, in what way may this level of archetypal affect be transformed? What does it serve beyond compensatory omnipotence and destructive grandiosity? Is its periodic eruption characteristic of moments of rupture and re(foundation), as the history of revolution and my patient's process would suggest? Do the Furies fuel, and in turn become fueled-by, the winds of change? I feel that they speak for essential and evolving issues of iden-tity, connection, and dissolution within the psyche. Perhaps the ultimate service the madness of fury brings is to drop us back into the unifying ground of the primordial psyche, into the underworld initiation, a communion with the darkest and universal corners of human experience. Whether we are truly transformed by that experience may depend, in large part, on how we are held when we are there.

But there is a terrific press not to hold this experience at all, to adjudicate the Furies, send them to court, or turn them in service to a collective ego-ideal. As historian Arno Mayer has noted:

> There are certain affinities between the Furies of [Greek tragedy], religious crusades, revolutionary terrors, overseas civilizing mis-sions, and the Furies of the killing fields, firebombing, and atomic discharges of the two world wars. The ultimate genius of these ordeals of 20th c. war was less the deadliness of modern weapons than their *sacralization* along with the causes they were made to serve." (Mayer 2000, p. 72)

However, this sacred aspect of the Furies instinct is usually hidden until it erupts with great collective force. On an individual level, analysis may provide for the ritual expression of fury, where the affect can be 'drunk to the dregs,' its poison received, its suffering revealed. But collectively we lack such explicit rituals. The lumbering trinity of bureaucracy, technology, and information is powerful enough to mask the Furies' archaic-spirit. And so, from out of the shadows comes the weird and terrifying appearance of errant and furious individuals, terrorists, whose archaic and 'spiritual' identifications allows them to be the very agents of vengeful justice. The Furies' archaic spirit seems to have entered the cracked vessel of terrorism, and a fearsome 'God' may be found on everyone's side, behind both the terrorists' acts and the wars we conduct in response.

The bomb-laden, airplane-flying terrorist, empowered by the eternal undertow of evil, is indeed a frightful postmodern apparition, destabilizing the dominant culture, bloodying our collective idealization, and releasing our own fury. From a cultural perspective, we may have reached a nightmarish crisis of consciousness. Archaic fury has always disrupted the collective ideal by embodying various forms of "other": the feminine upsets the masculine, the body upsets the ego, but now, terrorists take down the Twin Towers and evoke a President's anger. Archaic shadows, imbued with undertones of the demonic, are once again forcing their way into collective consciousness (Rushing and Frentz 1995), demanding blood payments. How is the creative aspect of this destabilization to occur in the collective psyche, so that our culture isn't just crushed and swept away in this undertow, but recentered within a larger matrix? What, at a collective level, would a real pact with the Furies look like?

*Conclusion*

The 'mother tongue' of our own discipline reminds us that all culture of any kind actually originates in incursions of the unconscious … The etymological relationships between fury, frenzy, passion, song, storms, possession, oracles, and rage, characterize the *creative aspect of the unconscious* [italics mine], whose activity sets man in motion, overpowers him, and makes him its instrument … This possession causes higher, supraconscious powers to appear, and so is sought after in cult and ritual. (Neumann 1955, p. 297-8)

Two of these *destructive* cults and rituals are terrorism and war which come together in a 'war on terrorism.' But if we try and apply the dynamics of the case material more consciously to our collective situation, where might we look for, and foster, the 'creative aspect of the unconscious'?

Identification with the Furies' destructive blood-lust for revenge has always served as an archetypal defense against creative descent. This identification has to be transformed, not for the sake of the ego's individuality or for collective values, but in order to face the shadow. In the madness that the Furies bring, that is, in the mad dynamics of projective identification and so-called primitive affect states in which there is a collapse of boundaries and a powerful communion between souls, there is also fertile ground for the activation of creative archetypal images. One of these is the 'suffering soul,' which I think is the creative face of fury's impulse to destruction.

Jung speculated in *Job* (1952/1969) that the archetypal elements of God are "tamed" or humanized, by being 'passed through,' suffered by, the human psyche. If this needs to be so, now more than ever, we have to look for, or create containers in our collective and culture capable of withstanding the concrete suffering of the underworld initiation the Furies press for. At this level of process, a place where uncontained violence is chaos, concrete embodiment *is* all; sublimation or seeming assimilation of violence will not suffice. Consciously suffering the numinous archaic spirit in the Furies instinct moves us into connection with the suffering soul of the world, a face of the *anima mundi* not seen in Athena, or Apollo or Dionysus, or even a redemptive Christ. Our culture is being called to find not just a tragic vision, but a tragic embodiment of fury's madness in our movement toward psychological wholeness. This means among many things, granting others the 'right of rage.' Granting this creates a common ground for the experience of communion. If allowed to do their inner work of dismemberment and 'de-linking,' the Furies break down defensive structures, until only the bones of the archetype remain upon which a new body may be created. As dynamisms of the Self they aim to 'correct,' both in their defensive, protective aspect and in their prospective dismemberment towards wholeness.

In analysis and collectively, we face into the process of trans-forming the rage and ecstasy of mutual cannibalism that the Furies unleash. But both archetypal amplification and clinical experience suggests that this cannibalism has as its telos *communion,* a shared blood-bond that releases compassion. The Furies, as highly ambivalent mana-figures may both abase and transform, just as cannibalism enacts a regressive fall into undif-ferentiation, *and* a communion of shared-blood. The difference seems to lie in a recognition of this ambivalence, but also in a willingness to take a chance and let the archetype unfold and fulfill its potential to 'lead us below and set things right.' To do this is to choose communion over apotropaic assimilation, to risk losing all by drinking our own and others' fury down to the very dregs, imbibing this dark, transformative brew in pursuit of the suffering, violent, 'other' within and without. To keep the Furies' wound open.

## References

Aeschylus (1953-56). *Complete Greek Tragedies*, Vol. I, *Orestia: Agamemnon, The Libation Bearers, The Eumenides*. Tr. Richard Lattimore. Chicago: University of Chicago Press.

Bachofen, J. J. (1967). *Myth, Religion, & Mother Right*, Vol. X. Bollingen Series XXXIV. New York: Princeton University Press.

Barrett, W. (1958). *Irrational Man*. Garden City, NJ: Doubleday.

Jung, C. G. (1934/1960). "A Review of the Complex Theory" in *Collected Works*, Vol. 8. Princeton, NJ: Princeton University Press.

Jung, C. G. (1952/1969). "Answer to Job," *Psychology and Religion, Collected Works*, Vol. II. Princeton, NJ: Princeton University Press.

Kalsched, D. (1996). *The Inner World of Trauma*. London: Routledge.

Mayer, A. (2000). *The Furies: Violence and Terror in the French and Russian Revolutions*. Princeton, NJ: Princeton University Press.

Morford, M. and Lenardon, R. (1999). *Classical Mythology*. Sixth Edition. New York: Oxford University Press.

Neumann, E. (1955). *The Great Mother*. New York: Princeton University Press.

Nietzsche, F. (1927/1995). *The Birth of Tragedy*. New York: Dover Publications.

Nussbaum, Martha (1986). *The Fragility of Goodness*. Cambridge, MA: Cambridge University Press.

Onians, R. B. (1951). *The Origins of European Thought: About the Body, the Mind, the Souls, the World, Time and Fate*. Cambridge, MA: Cambridge University Press.

Pfaff, W. (1993). *The Wrath of Nations: Civilization and the Furies of Nationalism*. New York: Touchstone, Simon & Schuster.

Rushing, J. H. and Frentz, T. (1995). *Projecting the Shadow: The Cyborg Hero in American Film*. Chicago: University of Chicago Press.

Sanford, J. (1995). *Fate, Love, and Ecstasy: Wisdom from the Lesser-Known Goddesses of the Greeks*. Wilmette, IL: Chiron Publications.

Schwartz-Salant, N. (1986). "On the Subtle-Body Concept in Clinical Practice," *The Body in Analysis*. Wilmette, IL: Chiron Publications.

Steinberg, W., (ed.) (2001). "Reactions to September 11, 2001," *Journal of Jungian Theory and Practice*, Vol. 3, Fall, p. 55 - 62.

Wakefield, H. and Underwager, R. (1994). *Return of the Furies: An Investigation into Recovered Memory Therapy*. Chicago, IL: Open Court.

# Music and the Psychology of Pacifism:
# Benjamin Britten's *War Requiem*

*Arthur D. Colman*

Benjamin Britten is one of the great composers of the twentieth century. He is also one of those rare individuals who was able to live fully and creatively the life he fervently wished for as a child. Musical composition was his desired life throughout his life; in the spirit of Puccini's great aria from Tosca, "*Visi d'Arte,*" his was a life in art, and art in life.

A child may be filled with desire to express objectively the music that is in his mind, and because music is so demanding an art form it may take years to master even the technical and aesthetic requirements. Finally, though, a composer will be judged on something more than his skill and the beauty of what is created. For Britten to become a great composer, which was his conscious desire, his music would need, in the words of Indian musicologist Anupam Mahajan, to be "a realization of the essence of existence beyond the routine life of man." (Mahajan 1989, p. 13)

I believe that Britten achieved something of that essence in much of his music. Britten was a composer whose music communicated his deepest moral convictions, his fundamental truths in life. Because these were not consonant with the world around him, his music became the language of a prophet who lived, as prophets often do, on a fragile boundary between the Wilderness and the Ruler's Court. The compelling beauty of his music made it possible for Britten to navigate this line and be heard by many people who preemptively disagreed with his message. His subjects, so relevant to his own and today's world, were the subjects of many prophets before him: Violence, Injustice, Innocence Betrayed, the Scapegoat, and most of all, War.

This paper is primarily a contribution to Jung's psychology of individuation. As we shall see, Britten was an individual whose powerful sexual and political preferences were overwhelmingly antagonistic to the consciousness of the collective in which he lived and worked. Britten's individuation was inextricably bound with changing that consciousness, and musical composition was the transformative element that he used as a "third thing" (Montero and Colman 2000, p. 218) to simultaneously change world and self – the work of individuation. Britten's *War Requiem* is a work of great beauty and power; it is also the ripe fruit of his individuation process – an interpretation, offering, and challenge to institutions and nations committed to violence.

What first connected me to Britten's music was my own work in awakening the consciousness of the collective to the problem of scapegoating. (Colman 1995) Great art must reflect the culture with a mirror whose image unsettles, inspires, and ultimately transforms. Britten's musical *oeuvre*, especially his *War Requiem,* is a potent communication to his species about the great scourge of War. It is probably easier to see such an interpretative praxis in those whose work is political or ideological. I hope, however, to show how Britten's personal and creative development led to music that could evoke a collective emotional and intellectual response strong enough to manifest his desire to transform the world around him. The *War Requiem* is Britten's *Satyagraha*; his "I have a dream" speech.

## Britten's World

Benjamin Britten was born in Lowestoft, England, a coastal town on the North Sea in 1913; he lived much of his life in Aldeburgh, about sixty miles south, and he died there in 1976. His father was an oral surgeon who built up a substantial practice. His adoring mother was a housewife and mother of four with a strong interest in music. She was, according to her son, Benjamin, youngest and most musically talented of the four, "a keen amateur with a sweet voice."

There were of course skeletons in the family closet and in Benjamin's developmental history. But accounts of his childhood are positive and enthusiastic. He was the proverbial happy child: physically adorable, bright and musically precocious, with loving and protective parents and mostly adoring older siblings. Occasionally he had to fight for the piano with his older brother Robert, who usually gave way, and he was not allowed to compose *all the time* by his mother, as he would have liked. At school he excelled at mathematics and was a decent athlete. He may have faced mild corporal punishment, perhaps sexual play and, in one highly speculative report, sexual harassment by a teacher. (Carpenter 1992, p. 557) What Britten remembered most, however, was the school music teacher who was pretentious and unhelpful, not willing or suited to enlist his student's extraordinary talent. But this lack was quickly made up by his parents, who hired Frank Bridge, one of England's preeminent musicians and composers, to further their son's musical education. Bridge, who had no other pupils, agreed to take Britten on upon hearing the thirteen-year-old's compositions.

Reading about Britten's childhood, I was struck by the essential goodness of it all. All of his teachers, friends, and even enemies invoke phrases like "golden boy," "good boy," "best boy," "great little man," "The Best Brought-Up Little Boy You Could Imagine" to describe him. (*Idem*)

His golden, innocent childhood, and his well-mannered, soft-spoken persona, did not match his music. Leonard Bernstein said Britten

> was a man at odds with the world. It's strange because on the surface his music is decorative, positive, charming and it's so much more than that. When you hear his music, really hear it, not just listen to it, you become aware of something very dark, gears that are grinding and not quite meshing. And they make a great pain. His was a lonely time. Yes, he was at odds with the world in many ways and he didn't show it." (Bernstein 1980, video 1158)

But the traditional scenario of childhood trauma writ large in his creative outpourings needs to be turned on its head. Bernstein touches on what seems to me to be the critical point: Britten was at odds with his world. The sweet innocence of his childhood is at dramatic odds with the collective psyche of the world in which he lived, and betrayed innocence is a major theme in his work. His world made him even a potential criminal because of his homosexual preference and his passionate commitment to pacifism. It also was a world that he saw as murdering his friends and peers in wars that he viewed as created by fathers, not sons, another prominent theme. The twentieth century was a psychotic time of unprecedented mass barbarity, which changed and *should have changed* the definition of sanity in conscious societies. Britten's artistry lies in the psychological and artistic forces that flowed through his music as he reflected upon and interpreted the darkest parts of his era. Ultimately his creative gift attracted listeners who might have otherwise shunned and denigrated him for his lifestyle and ethos.

Britten always wanted to be a composer, and the security he felt about composing ran very deep. He was extremely vulnerable to criticism; this was an extension of the life theme of betrayal (as if he couldn't abide the disparate messages from inner and outer world). As a child, and certainly as a mature composer, he was increasingly able to establish self-referential standards for his music. But to do this he required a sheltered world, one in which there was stability and support from like-minded colleagues. And this central need required wrestling with his homosexuality and his pacifism.

Britten probably did not fully accept the need to live out his sexual orientation until the beginning of his lifelong partnership with Peter Pears in late 1939, when he was twenty-four years old. Before that, he passively resisted actualizing his sexual orientation despite considerable self-knowledge and the powerful urgings of friends who knew him all too well. After studying composition at the Royal College of Music, Britten had found an intellectual home with other artists – left wing, many gay, some pacifist – in the theatre and in the government-funded GBO Film Unit. This provided a decent livelihood and a chance to expand his skills in programmatic compositions around political and social themes. The most significant influence was the powerful psycho-political effect of the worldly W. H. Auden and his radical circle.

In an early letter, Auden writes: "For my friend Benjamin Britten, composer, I beg that fortune send him a passionate affair." (Auden quoted in Carpenter 1992, p. 91) Later a poem, written to and for Britten, continued this theme:

Underneath the abject willow,
    Lover, sulk no more;
Act from thought should quickly follow:
    What is thinking for?
Your unique and moping station

Proves you cold;
Stand up and fold
Your map of desolation. (Auden 1936/1977, p. 160)

At stake, for the bossy, brilliant poet, was his friend's capacity for passion, without which he felt Britten's compositions would never fully emerge. Even after Britten and Pears were a couple, an Auden letter to him was still concerned about

> … the dangers that beset you as a man and as an artist. If you are really to develop to your full stature, you will have, I think, to suffer, and make others suffer, in ways which are totally strange to you at present, and against every conscious value that you have, i.e., you will have to be able to say what you never yet have had the right to say. (Mitchell and Reed, Vol. 2, 1991, p. 1016)

Auden's words were both warning and prophesy, for Britten's essential innocence and goodness was deeply challenged by the world around him. And as "a good boy," he had to transgress to compose and to live. According to Pears and his closest friends, Britten never fully accepted his own sexual orientation even as he lived it. (Pears 1980, video 1158) But the fact of his homosexuality, illegal in his country, was also the lifelong prod that kept Britten and his talents from folding into the golden, middle-class security that he understood so well. Homosexuality's pervasive influence on his feelings, including his feelings of acceptance in the public arena, forced him towards a lifelong moral exploration of such themes as the role of the outsider, that of the betrayer of innocence, the psychology of disgrace, and the plight of the innocent victim. Much of his music ruthlessly examined the collective psychology of the scapegoat and the trauma for the individual who is put in that position.

The other disjunction between Britten and the surrounding society was his fervent belief in pacifism. Whereas homosexuality was not a subject that Britten dealt centrally with in his music (except rather chastely in his final opera, *Death in Venice*), his views about war and violence were always at the forefront of his work. Pacifism in Britain was a popular cause among young intellectuals in the 1930s. World War I had exacted a terrible toll from British youth, and now the country was talking of rearming. With the violent patriarchy at it again, the young artists and writers wanted to fashion their own social vision. Britten was swept up in this social movement, although his profound anti-violent convictions certainly predated it. He declined to take part in his school's popular officers training program, and he wrote an impassioned essay indicting hunting and cruelty to animals, for which he was awarded no marks. His most influential teacher and mentor, Frank Bridge, pursued his own pacifist views in frequent conversations with Britten. What is extremely clear is that Britten's abhorrence of both public and private violence was a powerful motivator in his compositions, and that abhorrence guided rather than followed his musical outpourings. If Britten's homosexuality provided an underlying, if ambivalent, identification with the outsider and the scapegoat, pacifism, with its deep-rooted insistence on the disavowal of all violence, became a fully realized obsession.

Largely because of his views about the coming war, Britten, together with his at that time still platonic friend Pears, followed Auden and Isherwood (the former an avowed pacifist) to the United States in 1939. In the face of the Nazi threat, turning one's back on an England poised for war was an extremely unpopular act. Britten's musical life certainly gained from his exposure to American musicians. He renewed his friendship with Aaron Copland, whom he had known in London, and he met Boston Symphony Conductor Serge Koussevitzky, who commissioned several of his pieces, including the opera *Peter Grimes*. But he was also shunned by many of his countrymen even as his music was attracting notice. Musical critics in London abused him for his pacifist stance and "cowardly" self-exile, while grudgingly praising some of his new compositions.

Britten and Pears also felt a deep homesickness for their country. Confronted with actual war – begun by German invasions in central Europe and helped along by Britain's diplomatic acquiescence there – the young men were humiliated to be forsaking England in such a time of need. In 1942, Britten and Pears returned home. By then, the Atlantic was patrolled by German U-Boats, and embassy officials discouraged the trip. They would also have to petition, and be examined by, a formal tribunal to be granted conscientious objector status; otherwise, they would go to prison. Nevertheless, against the advice of many friends and supporters, they came home.

## Music in a Moral Key

Excerpts from Britten's statement to the War Board give us a picture of his convictions at twenty-nine years old:

> The whole of my life has been devoted to acts of creation (being by profession a composer) and I cannot take part in acts of destruction. (Mitchell and Reed, Vol. 2, 1991, p. 1046)

> I do not believe in the Divinity of Christ, but I think his teaching is sound and his example should be followed (*Idem,* fn.)

After some complications, his rather tortuous explanation of these religious beliefs led to full Conscientious Objector status.

The man who returned to England had learned a great deal about the power of the collective to affect his life. He also had learned how his musical talent could be used as a weapon, for there was little doubt that his increasingly recognized talent as a composer was seen by officials as valuable to a nation gripped by war.

Britten was already at work on the opera *Peter Grimes*. Grimes, a fisherman living in the small coastal village of Borough, was accused of abusing and killing his young apprentice boys by a community more hostile to his aberrant ways than his possible crime. Britten's portrait of the individual victim and the collective scapegoat is musically powerful and chilling:

> Who holds himself apart, lets his pride rise.
> Him who despises us we'll destroy.
> And cruelly becomes the enterprise.

Britten himself chose to live most of his adult life in Aldeburgh, an isolated fishing town on the forbidding North Sea. There he separated himself from the musical and artistic community in London. There was a canny self-knowledge in this decision. In Aldeburgh, Britten and Pears created a working collective that would nurture both for the rest of their lives. Britten knew that composing would require a special psychological environment, one that offered nurturance, not conflict; harmony, not diversity; inclusion, not intrusion or exclusion. In time he gathered around him people who could help him create and would not criticize his lifestyle or his values. Many were gay men with similar pacifist views. First among them was Peter Pears, who became his life partner and musical colleague. For Pears, Britten wrote all of his leading tenor vocal parts. Britten limited his ties with the great opera companies and musical artists and impresarios in London and instead created his own creative coterie, his own opera and musical companies, his own concert hall, and eventually his own music festival at Aldeburgh.

Perhaps most telling was his successful effort "not to hold himself apart" from the non-artists in the community in which he lived. He sought and obtained the involvement of the townspeople of Aldeburgh in every aspect of his work, using their chorus, and creating a children's chorus, using locals for their administrative and construction skills, using churches, town hall, and empty mills for his performances. He often composed for the community talent and community audiences and virtually created a new vocal form, the Chamber Opera, to fit local musical resources. The prestigious Sadler's Wells and other London companies and players were included only in so far as they worked for him and in his world.

This psychological orientation should not be reduced to a paranoid escape or regressive return to a doting family: rather it was a creative alloplastic solution to an inner dilemma, a way to reshape the world to match his vulnerabilities and his way of life. And because of his great talent, moral intent, and intense work and love relationship with Pears, it succeeded. Britten drew the musical talent that he needed to Aldeburgh. He organized his life in order to compose music, and from that secure but liminal space, the music he composed became a series of moral interpretations to the larger world.

*The Power of Music to Heal*

Almost twenty years passed before Britten wrote his *War Requiem*, finished December 20, 1961, and first performed in Coventry on May 30, 1962. During those twenty years, Britten composed the major body of his work.

Since the 1940s he had wanted to compose a major choral/orchestral piece – the standard of which, at least in the Western musical tradition, is the Mass and particularly the Requiem Mass. Characteristically, Britten wanted to write on a pacifist theme. He had earlier written an oratorio, *Mea Culpa,* in response to the dropping of the atomic bomb, and had already

thought of composing a Requiem in response to the assassination of Mahatma Gandhi. In 1962, the committee overseeing
the rebuilding of Coventry Cathedral, demolished by the Luft-
waffe, asked Britten to write and conduct a new work to mark
the reconsecration.

There is little doubt that Britten's "God" was not a traditional one: we already know his thoughts about a supernatural
God from his remarks to the Conscientious Objector Tribunal.
And his preparation ensured that the *War Requiem* would be
a vehicle for a theme of greater importance to Britten than
religion. His aim in this piece is first and foremost to deliver
an interpretation to the world about the pain and betrayal of
a century and the complicity of nations, religious institutions
and ourselves in the loss of life and hope that ensued. "A call
for peace" is what the Russian soprano Galina Vishneskaya said
Britten called it. (Vishneskaya in Cooke 1996, p. 26) We can
find this wish expressed in every part of the *Requiem*. With
obvious symbolism, the composer planned to write solos for
soprano, baritone and tenor singers from three different countries: Pears was his choice for British Tenor, the great Dietrich
Fischer-Dieskau was the German Baritone, and Vishneskaya
was to be the Russian Soprano. Vishneskaya was not allowed
by her government to sing at the opening, however, an ominous
and prophetic sign of the growing "cold" war.

Britten's choices were undoubtedly formed by knowledge
of the kind of voices he wanted. But the internationalism of
them was also a simple and profound attempt to heal Europe's
wounds, characteristic of his use of every element of the composition and presentation of the *Requiem* to serve the larger
moral intent.

273

*Elements of Composition*

Baudelaire once wrote that "music cannot pride itself on being able to translate all or anything with precision, as can painting or writing. But music translates in its own way and using means which are proper to it. In music ... there is always a lacuna which is filled in by the listener's imagination." (Baudelaire 1861/1964, p. 113) Richard Wagner said, "Where the speech of humankind leaves off, there the art of music commences." (Wagner in Fisk 1997, p. ix)

Most composers, including Britten, tend to begin their composition with nonmusical elements, especially when there is a programmatic requirement, as in an opera, or a structural requirement, as in a Mass. In preparing a libretto for the *War Requiem,* Britten pruned and edited Wilfred Owen's poems with great care, and struggled to interdigitate their lines and phrases with words from the *Missa pro defunct,* the Requiem Mass. He diagrammed a variety of structures that he would use to configure and integrate words, music, choruses, and orchestras. The way he found the music he poured into the nonmusical structures cannot be reduced or psychologized, and for that, his listeners can only be thankful.

Britten uses a very specific musical device, the tritone, as musical and ideological center of the work. This tritone interval, also known as the augmented fourth or diminished fifth, is the interval between the first and third successive whole tones in any scale: for example, the interval F-B, or C-F# (the first two notes of Bernstein's song "Maria" from *West Side Story*). This interval has long represented an "outcast" tone or "scapegoat" sound in the musical palette. The tritone was known as *diabolus in musica* and was actually banned from use in church music during the Middle Ages. Church leaders found it to be extremely dissonant, and they associated it with Satan, therefore deeming it unsuitable for Christian worship. Of course this "banned interval" also became a mythic shadow tone which was very attractive to dissenters! It was rumored to be used in "Black Sabbaths," midnight masses, and other "unnatural rites." Although daring composers gradually began to use it in secular works, the tritone still retains its aura of shadow.

Britten based much of the musical composition of his *Requiem* upon the tritone. It may seem strange that a simple vibrational interval can successfully hold the emotional center of the work, but the very imprecision of musical elements and the primitive emotionality of the language of sound are also the source of its power. The juxtaposition of tritone and poetry mocks the message of the Mass: liberation from death through Christ, and the inevitability of rebirth for the faithful. The Mass itself is a targeted symbol of Britten's pacifist attack on the culture of war: our dependency on religion, our unreflective acceptance and comfort in venerable tradition, he implies, are all powerfully connected to our acquiescence to War. The tritone echoes through Britten's composition like Chagall's ghostly fiddler swooping over a gigantic graveyard of soldiers.

### Owen and Britten in Duet

Wilfred Owen was considered to be one of the great poets of World War I, and it is to his poetry that Britten turned for his harsh words on war. Of strong pacifist beliefs, Owen still felt obliged to enlist in the British Army in a unit that was called "The Artists' Rifles." He was hospitalized for shell shock and neurasthenia in Edinburgh, where he met and was influenced by the poet Siegfried Sassoon, who was also a patient. Owen returned to the front and wrote war poetry from the foxholes. Seven days before the Armistice on November 11, 1918, he was killed in action leading his troops across the Sambre Canal near Ors in Northeast France. He was twenty-five.

Owen was a psychologically inspired choice, and not just for his poetry; he was an artist hero untainted by the questions of cowardice heaped on Britten during his exile in America. Owen is therefore Britten's soldier as well as his muse in delivering the message. In the title page of his score, Britten pays Owen special homage by quoting his famous preface (to a proposed compilation of poems) written shortly before his death:

> Above all I am not concerned with Poetry. My subject is War, and the pity of War. The Poetry is in the pity.... All a poet can do today is warn. (Britten 1962, frontispiece)

Britten's central concern in his *Requiem* was also War; War and the victims of War. He wanted the largest possible context for this pacifist work, and he wanted a hand in destroying, or at least subverting, the institutions that preserved war. He chose the Church and its great musical form to represent all the sanctified institutions which allow the Nations to send sons off to die. To do this, he went directly to the heart of the beast and challenged Christianity's ancient and sacred celebration of life after death: the Mass for the Dead.

## The Promise of Death

The centerpiece of the *War Requiem* is the *Offertorium* which contains the ancient promise of Abraham:

> *Sed signifier sanctus Michael*
> *Repraesentet eas in lucem sanctem:*
> *Quam olim Abraham promisisti*
> *Et semini ejus.*

> But let the standard-bearer, Saint Michael

Bring them into the holy light:
Which, of old, Thou didst promise
Unto Abraham and his seed.

*Quam olim Abraham promisisti,* the promise of Abraham, that ancient connection, is a moment of great power. *Long ago it was foretold and it has now come to pass in Christ* – that is the affirming message regarding Abraham's prophesies. Christianity has always been concerned with finding validation, whether from miracles or Saints or from the confirmation of prophesies contained in the Old Testament. Musically, this text of the Mass is often set in a fugue, a Renaissance music form perfected by Bach that multiplies and deepens the power of words through a complex interweaving of theme and variations. This music is almost always joyous. In Mozart's *Requiem,* it is a triumphant choral dance; Verdi sets it in a gorgeous operatic aria for baritone.

Britten has other ideas. The music begins with the boy's chorus in an almost mournful, monotonic chant, which becomes faintly pleading as it continues. This chorus represents the purity and innocence of youth, a prayer for the deliverance of the souls of the faithful "from hell, from darkness." The children's voices are broken into by the adult chorus singing *quam olim Abraham promisisti* to a theme incorporating the now familiar tritone. The musical line here is jaunty and irreverent, yet tension filled and increasingly discordant, carrying a hint of promise, perhaps a broken promise from God given in a former time. The effect is both ironic and confused; the hope of deliverance undercut and questioned. This section ends in a confident segue to another Owen poem, the content of which answers the musical question in no uncertain terms.

Owen's poem retells the familiar Abraham and Isaac story, which gave the basis of the promise itself. Owen's retelling uses the Sumerian name Abram, signifying a younger, less-developed

277

man than the later Abraham. Britten captures the pious young man's spirit in a musical line infused with the jaunty, sadistic clarity of a narcissist intent on a single, unmodifiable course. There is no love, no hesitation in either word or music as the sacrifice is described:

> So Abram rose and clave the wood, and went,
> And took the fire with him and a knife.

Isaac, the scapegoat, is not as sanguine as his father. He questions Abram about the absence of the sacrificial Lamb. His tenor musical line is suddenly gorgeous, lush but emanating an innocent and pathetic plea from trusting son to trusted father:

> My Father, Behold the preparations, fire and iron,
> But where the lamb for this burnt-offering?

The music turns dark as the narrator answers in a dark recitative:

> Then Abram bound the youth with belts and straps,
> And builded parapets and trenches there,
> and stretchèd forth the knife to slay his son.

The anachronistic words connote WW I technology as well as the frank sadomasochistic pleasures implied in the tools of sexual bondage; militant music brings us into the horrible present tense of trenches full of human sacrifice, including Owen himself. We are now in the space of War and its perversions, ready for the worst. But Britten allows a brief dramatic return to an earlier, more trusting, consciousness. The Lord, sung as a sweet duet in a major third between tenor and baritone, stays the father's hand and points out the Ram caught in a thicket by its horns:

> Offer the Ram of Pride instead of him.

And then the famous chilling lines sung in trenchant narration which speaks to the terror of sacrificial sons everywhere:

But the old man would not so,
but slew his son –
And half the seed of Europe, one by one.

These words, a dramatic deviation from all Abraham and Isaac stories before it, are shocking. Almost immediately the music and words disintegrate into an eerie trilogue among soloists, choruses and orchestra using the *quam olim* theme in weak and rhythmically disintegrating, fragmented lines: "half the seed" … "one by one." The boys' chorus begins mournful completion of the Latin liturgy now ironically transforming "prayer and praise" to the inevitable sacrifice as future soldiers:

*Hostias et preces tibi Domine*
*Laudis offerimus:*

We offer unto thee, O lord, sacrifices
of prayer and praise

The adult chorus once again takes up the fugue of promise, now a hypocritical and shameful boast: "*Quam Olim Abraham Promisisti*," the promise of annihilation.

Britten has achieved, in effect, an extraordinary choreography of Owen's poetry with Latin text, tenor and bass solo voices, adult and boys' chorus and symphonic and chamber orchestra. He had written nine operas by the time he composed the *War Requiem,* and the experience served him well. Owen's great text and its horrifying counterpoint of the adult chorus (we: the collective, the guilty?) and the boys (the innocents, the fatherless, the scapegoats?) inspire and contain what Britten creates. The boys pray and mourn, Isaacs pleads, but the Father Abram cannot stay his hand, and there is no counterforce to his desire for slaughter. God's six thousand year promise of protection is here transformed into a calculated betrayal by Elders seeking power and potency, and the betrayal is laid out in an unforgettable and unforgiving way. The hope for eternal life that religion offers both ritually and emotionally, through rebirth and renewal, the promise of God, that venerable covenant upon which Judeo-Christian civilization is based, is relegated to the darkest *abattoirs* of human history.

## The Question of Consolation

What, then, of the feminine in Britten's *Requiem*, of age and wisdom, of mercy and succor, of love? Although the text of the *Missa pro defunctis* itself brings no feminine figure or story to its liturgy, in practice there are often songs of a suffering and consoling Mary interpolated into the service. In the *War Requiem,* this kind of feminine voice is certainly not present in Britten's chosen texts nor in most of the solo soprano singing part (there is, for instance, no Mezzo represented). Although in the next movement, the *Sanctus,* a traditional hymn of faith, the soprano is given a major role, Britten has transformed her solo into the most desolate music in his *Requiem.* He introduces her lines:

> *Sanctus, sanctus Dominus Deus Sabaoth.*
> Holy Holy Holy, Lord of God of Sabaoth

with devilishly insistent bells, a mix of odd percussive sounds from vibraphone, glockenspiel, antique cymbals, and piano. The music is jagged, harmonies and scales change quickly, and the tritone is prominent, making her song of faith fierce and judgmental (compared, for example, with Mozart's joyous cosmic dance of the same text). The soprano returns with a mournful *Benedictus* sung on words that should symbolize salvation and eternal life.

*Benedictus qui venit in nomine Domini.*
Blessed is he who comes in the name of the Lord.

Help from the feminine gone, Britten uses Owen's words against any hope from the Elders or Earth:

Age?
When I do ask white Age he saith not so:
'My head hangs weighted with snow.'
And when I hearken to the Earth, she saith:
'My fiery heart shrinks, aching.
It is death.
Mine ancient scars shall not be glorified,
Nor my titanic tears, the sea, be dried.'

In the *Agnus Dei,* the penultimate movement of the *Requiem,* Britten shifts to a more somber mood. The Latin text requires it: glory and exultation in the Lord's coming gives way to the more earthly role of a forgiving God who must help a struggling humanity:

*Agnus Dei, qui tollis peccata mundi, dona eis requiem*
Lamb of God who taketh away the sins of the world, give us rest.

The tenor is center stage with a sad and beautiful song which is still undercut by Owen's brutal words:

And in their faces there is pride
That they were flesh-marked by the Beast
by whom the gentle Christ's denied....

And:

The scribes on all the people shove
And bawl allegiance to the state.

The "gentle Christ" is clearly present in the music and in the dynamics of its presentation. The tritone, C-F#, is still a dominant force, but Britten softens its dissonance by harmonizing the F# in B minor and the C in C major, in alternate measures. Britten ends this section by uncharacteristically deviating from the standard *Missa pro defunctis* liturgy and adding a familiar refrain:

*Dona nobis pacem*
Give us peace ...

which musically hints at resolution in C minor. It is as if, having deconstructed so much of Religion with the more powerful and morally devastating machines of War, Britten takes a musical breath ... and wonders where he is going. What does he want to say to a 1960s Cold War audience, representatives of a society that has been overwhelmed by violence, death, and loss and now is starting to rebuild its Churches *and* its War machines? Can he deny the Christian message that is his heritage, the sins of the world taken away by a gentle God? Can he persist in making that most subtle and devastating interpretation of all, that mankind will not change its warlike behavior as long as it is under the spell of the doctrine of rebirth and the promise of life after death, which the Catholic Mass (among other of Religion's rituals) explicitly offers? Britten pauses before the final movement and considers all this: "Give us peace!" he interpolates, but how? Despite the beauty of these ancient lines, there is still War looming behind and ahead with no hint of resolution.

*War Is Death without Rebirth*

His answer comes quickly and it is no surprise. The final movement *Libera Me* begins with the roll of drums, military drums, and crying voices which, though in Latin, can only be specters of dead soldiers. We are back on the battlefield, the place of death, the place where, for Britten at least, all questions about peace must be answered. The Latin text begins with an ultimate prayer in this regard:

*Libera me, Domine, de morte aeterna.*
Deliver me, O Lord, from death eternal.

The music moves from plea to a glimpse of the hell that is war, the drums again, the crack of whips, the words from the Mass

*Dum veneris judicare saeculum per ignem*
when thou shall judge the world by fire

that remind us of the real fire that killed these boys called soldiers. We hear echoes from a ghostly battlefield, a place with no answers and no God. And suddenly, out of dregs of that dark epiphany, a human voice begins to sing the last and most famous Owen setting, "Strange Meeting." The poem portrays two soldiers from opposing sides meeting on the battlefield. The first soldier, understanding nothing of his real situation, sings in familiar tritone the agonizing irony of denial.

'Strange friend,' I said, 'here is no cause to mourn.'

In this entreaty we meet, as Britten desires for us to do, our own selves and the world in denial, a world in which war is still a possibility even after World War II, the Holocaust, Hiroshima, Vietnam, and beyond.... The "friend" answers:

'None,' said the other, 'save the undone years,
The hopelessness. Whatever hope is yours
Was my life also: I went hunting wild
After the wildest beauty in the world.
For by my glee might many men have laughed;
And of my weeping something had been left,
Which must die now. I mean the truth untold,
The pity of war, the pity war distilled.'

Britten frames these wrenching sentiments in spare musical lines, often unaccompanied, beginning with the ominous tritone and gradually adding other intervals, then lyric lines and harmonies from other Britten anti-war pieces. There is sadness and also despair as if there is no more to be played or sung. But there is more sadness when we learn that this duet is between killer and killed:

> I am the enemy you killed, my friend
> I knew you in this dark ...

The two enemies now both know they are dead. Deadly enmity fueled by national causes and other irrationalities make no difference. "Let us sleep now," says one, and a duet of the soloists ensues on these sad, life-empty lines.

A Requiem Mass usually ends on a positive note, so a religious reprieve in the last bar lines is still possible. But we already know Britten will not offer this false hope. For these soldiers in the foxholes, sleep is but a brief respite from the finality of death; there is no step into eternal life on that killing field. The male soloists continue to sing "let us sleep now" while the boys' chorus and then the adult chorus begin the Latin burial text:

> *In paradisum deducant te angeli*
> May the angels escort you to heaven

Whatever hope *is* held in this beautiful ensemble is abruptly stopped by mournful bells and a long silent rest. Twice more, the ensemble begins and is stopped mid phrase by the bells. Reluctantly, then more firmly, the adult choir starts to intone the *requiem aeternam*, the tritone-based chant from the first movement. Now the original words of hope:

> *Requiem aeternam dona eis, Domine*
> Rest eternal grant unto them, O lord?

are replaced by a new text:

*Requiescant in pace. Amen*
May they rest in peace. Amen

The last musical notes of the piece, however, are the familiar tritone interval resolving to an F major chord, creating a question. Musically, emotionally, spiritually, and existentially we are left unsettled, unresolved, our longings for any kind of lasting peace unsated except for Britten's warning message to the world about War: a great composer, who spoke from the edge, the place of victims and prophets, interpreting his truth to all of us.

*Thank you for your help: Brian Baker, PhD, and Dr. Carl Johengen.*

– A.D.C.

## References

References to specific music text, Latin text, and poetry (excerpted from the work of Wilfred Owen) are taken from the full orchestral score of Britten's *War Requiem* (London: Boosey and Hawkins, 1962). Music selections referred to in the text of this paper can be heard on CD 414 383-2 *War Requiem, Opus 66* (London: Decca Records, 1963, 1985), and other recordings.

Auden, W. H. (1936/1977). "Poems 1931-1936, XXX (For Benjamin Britten)", in Mendelson, E. (Ed.), *The English Auden*. London: Faber and Faber.

Baudelaire, C. (1964), "Richard Wagner and Tannhauser in Paris" in *The Painter of Modern Life and Other Essays*. London: Phaidon.

Britten, B. (1962). *War Requiem, Op. 66*. London: Boosey and Hawkes.

Carpenter, H. (1992). *Benjamin Britten: A Biography*. New York: Scribner.

Colman, A. D. (1995). *Up from Scapegoating: Awakening Consciousness in Groups*. Evanston, Il: Chiron.

Cooke, M. (1996). *Britten, War Requiem*. Cambridge: Cambridge University Press.

Mahajan, A. (1989). *Ragas in Indian Classical Music*. New Delhi: Gian.

Mitchell, D. and Reed, P., eds. (1991). *Letters from a Life: Selected Letters and Diaries of Benjamin Britten*. Berkeley: University of California Press.

Montero, P. and Colman, A. D. (2000). "Collective Consciousness and the Psychology of Human Interconnectedness," *Group*. Vol. 24, Nos. 2/3.

*A Time There Was ... A Profile of Benjamin Britten* (1980). Video 1158, Kultur.

Wagner, R., in Fisk, J., ed. (1997). *Composers on Music*. Boston: Northeastern University Press.

# The Impulse to Destroy
# in Thomas Hardy's *Jude The Obscure*

*Arlene TePaske Landau*

In the twenty-seven years that have passed since I first saw a production based on Thomas Hardy's dark, melancholy, and fateful novel, *Jude the Obscure*, I have read and reread all of Thomas Hardy's novels and viewed films based on his novels many times. Over those years, events in my own life have made Hardy's work all the more significant. Both *Tess of the D'Urbervilles* and *Jude,* which end in murder, particularly strike home: murder, and particularly *parricidium* (the murder of a near relative), has touched my life in a profound way. Both my father and brother, my only sibling, were killed at their place of business in Beverly Hills twelve years ago.

Wolfgang Giegerich writes about the cosmic role of killing in soul-making:

> The soul first made itself through killing. *It killed itself into being.* That is why I consider sacrificial killing as primordial soul-making. The soul freed itself, *within* its immersion in the merely-biological, *from* this immersion – from an immersion, however, that continues to exist even after it has been overcome. (Giegerich 1993, p. 12)

Giegerich's thoughts find a deeply echoing chord within me. I was admitted into the training program at the Los Angeles Jung Institute just six weeks after the murder of my brother Harry, who was seven years younger than I, and my father Julius. By immersing myself in Hardy's works, which are so steeped in murder and murderous impulses, I have tried to make sense psychologically of these dark events about my family and my fate and the recent collective events that have so penetrated my soul. I am still trying.

Hardy shows us the nature of the human soul through the use of myth; he is a literary anthropologist who reaches for – and touches, sifts, ponders, and reveals – the deepest layers of the human psyche.

A summary of the plot of *Jude the Obscure* is offered as an appendix to this paper. In my exploration of the novel, I will identify the depth-psychological dimensions of the destructive impulses portrayed in *Jude* by applying Jungian archetypal perspectives to Hardy's symbols. I would like to stress at the outset the degree to which C.G. Jung's most all-embracing concepts, the collective unconscious, the archetype, and the individuation process, are reflected in, and pertinent to, a psychological understanding of Hardy's novel. Hardy's conceptions of an "Unconscious Will of the Universe," and "Nature's Holy Plan" are quite close to Jung's theory of the collective unconscious. Both Hardy and Jung understand, with horror, the effect and the affect of our technological age, wherein we become the "mass man" alienated from our native land, our myths, and our rituals. A striking feature of Hardy's multilayered novels is his highly perceptive references to the religious, mythical, and historical conditions of his contemporary humankind – references also shared and elucidated by Jung, to a striking degree.

Father Time (Jude's little son) is an unusual character who has a shocking impact in Hardy's novel: only an eight-year-old child, he kills his brother and sister and then hangs himself to spare his impoverished, unwed parents the continued burden of feeding, clothing, and sheltering them. Oddly, little has been written about him, whereas much has been written about Sue (Jude's cousin and illicit lover), Jude himself, and others in the novel. This lacuna around Father Time represents an academic disregard that is also hugely telling: It confirms in a way Father Time's proclamation that the world would be better off without children, or at least without wounded, neglected, orphaned children. Ian Gregor comments that the murder of the three little children describes the "most terrible scene in Hardy's fiction, indeed it might be reasonably argued in English fiction." (Gregor 1963, p. 22) Its dark vision brings Columbine to my mind. (On April 20, 1998, two high school students on a deadly rampage killed twelve Columbine High School classmates, a teacher, and finally took their own lives.) Columbine's murderers, however, seem sociopathic in the extreme, being overtly callous and showing no remorse, whereas Father Time seems to sense the very real poverty of spirit and love around him.

As Columbine shows, however, Hardy's vision of children killing children is prophetic. There have been several more of these school killings in the U.S. and a recent one in Germany. This epidemic brings to mind the contagion of suicide bombers – who are often barely out of teenagehood (or are still in it) and perhaps believe that there is no other solution than violent death and that what they are doing is spiritually connected to something larger than themselves. A poem in a Palestinian boys' seventh-grade reading book says, "I see my death, but I hasten my steps toward it." (Lehrman 2002, p. A5)

In *Jude the Obscure*, Little Father Time is the divine child and also the antithesis of the archetype of the divine child. He is a strange and peculiar little boy who looks like an "enslaved and dwarfed Divinity." (Hardy 1978, p. 219) Like the divine child, he is not sure of his parentage; he has no actual name and is wanted by no one. His epithet nickname, *Time,* refers to the devourer of all things. Jung notes the binary nature of the child archetype:

> It is a striking paradox in all child myths that the "child" is, on one hand, delivered helpless into the power of terrible enemies and in continual danger of extinction, while on the other he possesses powers far exceeding those of ordinary humanity." (Jung and Kérenyi 1963, p. 89)

The child archetype also applies to the character of Jude. When the story begins, Jude is an orphan who never knew his mother and who has lost his father a year earlier. At the story's end, Jude is still alone – even on his deathbed – and still an alienated orphan. According to Albert Guérard, *Jude the Obscure* explores

> the great theme of nineteenth- and twentieth-century fiction: the myth of the morally isolated individualist lost in a world he never made; who searches for freedom, though bereft of faith, and who wills his own destruction." (Guérard 1963, p. 159)

Hardy describes several of his characters as living a complete isolation that is coupled with utter restiveness. As Father Time travels on a train alone – having been rejected by his birth mother, Jude's former wife – to live with Jude and Sue, whom he has never met, his disparity from the rest of his companions (and even a kitten in a basket) is underscored:

> When the other travelers closed their eyes, which they did one by one – even the kitten curling itself up in the basket, weary of its too circumscribed play – the boy remained just as before. He then seemed to be doubly awake, like an enslaved and dwarfed Divinity, sitting passive and regarding his companions as if he saw their whole rounded lives rather than their immediate figures. (Hardy 1978, p. 218-219)

The enslaved, passive child is unable to experience any peace or light. "The train reached Aldbrickham, and the boy was deposited on the lonely platform beside his box." (*Ibid.,* p. 219) Little Father Time is vigilant and wakeful all the time, like abused and abandoned children who are always on the lookout for the next ill omen, who vigilantly search their parents' faces for signs of an incipient dark mood or sudden strike. Compounding the family pathology, his father Jude is an alcoholic, and Little Father Time bears the stigmata of an abused child of an alcoholic parent. Lawrence Jaffe has summarized the archetypal impact of parents:

> Edinger says that the memories of childhood enshrine the sacred object, and Jung writes that of all possible spirits, the spirits of the parents are the most important. That is to say, there is an unacknowledged religious dimension to our experiences in childhood, and the hold our childhood has over us is due partly to the fact that in our secularized society there is nothing to take the place of the people and things and locales that childhood has sanctified. (Jaffe 1990, p. 45)

Hardy describes the ancient qualities of Little Father Time:

> He was Age masquerading as Juvenility.... A ground swell from ancient years of night seemed now and then to lift the child in this his morning-life, when his face took a back view over some great Atlantic of Time, and appeared not to care about what it saw." (Hardy 1978, p. 218)

In his "ground swell" he is like Beloved in Toni Morrison's novel. Little Father Time is filled with gloom and despair; he has no inner vision of joy or love, no experience of play and lightheartedness.

Attending an agricultural show, Jude and Sue appear as young lovers: their real and spontaneous pleasure at the exhibit brings to mind young puppies. They hold each other's hands and almost skip from place to place. They are particularly pleased about the flowers. In poignant contrast, Father Time can only think about how quickly they will die. With his "octogenarian face," he represents death-in-life. The blight that is etched in his face will soon engulf the other children, and Jude and Sue as well – until, in a weird way, Jude and Sue become one with him, and his inner contagion spreads throughout the recesses of their already-damaged souls. As the story proceeds, Jude identifies more and more with Father Time. He gives his name to the boy and, like countless other parents, pins his hopes on him; Jude hopes to live out his unlived life through the boy's eventual admittance to the coveted Christminster University (a thinly disguised Oxford). Yet even as his hope for transcendence takes one final surge toward realization through his child, Jude also predicts the despair to come. He quotes Job: "'Let the day perish wherein I was born' … That's what the boy – my boy, perhaps – will find himself saying before long!" (*Ibid.,* p. 217)

When a parent "asks" the child, either directly or indirectly, to live out his or her unlived life (either the positive or negative aspects), the child usually ends up carrying a large psychic burden that proves to be too heavy.

In my own life I have observed a clear – and painful – example of this dynamic. My daughter studied ballet for many years; she was quite devoted to it, yet she also concentrated on her academic life. I noticed that many of the mothers of the pretty ballerinas in the dance school spent so much time making cookies for their daughters and sewing sequins on their costumes, that I wondered if they did anything else. Interestingly, these mothers, who seemed to have a life only at the ballet studio – and that, of course only vicariously – were almost all obese and their daughters suffered from anorexia and the "addiction to perfection" Marion Woodman has described in women with eating disorders. These mothers were clearly living out their own unlived sides while watching, hour after hour, the ephemeral sight of their daughters twirling and leaping across the dance floor. As the girls got older, a high proportion of them had ghost-like qualities; they were disembodied beings, while their mothers, who had hoped they would become stars, carried "all the weight."

Like these heavy mothers, Jude brings to mind Cronos, the devouring father who eats his own children. Even though Jude has a passive nature and certainly does not manifest a devouring personality, nevertheless the archetype he has not been able to integrate devours his young children. Edward Edinger has described what happens when the Cronos archetype is activated:

> Cronus [Edinger's spelling] was the Greek God who devoured his own children. In order to keep the child a child, and relatively impotent, the child is devoured or consumed, incorporated into the psychology of the [parent] and not permitted to have his or her own separate psychology. (Edinger 1995, p. 318)

Little Father Time feels just as Jude feels – that the day he was born was an evil day:

> I wish I hadn't been born! ... I think that whenever children be born that are not wanted they should be killed directly, before their souls come to 'em, and not allowed to grow big and walk about! (Hardy 1978, p. 263)

Little Father Time unconsciously lives out the dark aspects of Jude's own orphaned pain.

Even as a young boy, Jude saw the world as behaving cruelly toward its creatures; as manhood loomed, he glimpsed an even more threatening state of existence:

> All around you there seemed to be something glaring, garish, rattling, and the noises and glares hit upon the little cell called your life, and shook it, and warped it.

If he could only prevent himself growing up! He did not want to be a man." (*Ibid.*, p. 17)

In an article last year the *Los Angeles Times* described a Canadian community where

> sickness and death [are] spreading like a plague they can't control. More than half the town's 636 children say they have sniffed gas, used illegal drugs, or contemplated suicide. Nearly a quarter said they have tried to kill themselves. Three in the past year have committed suicide. (Farley 2000, p. A1)

Like Jude, many of the parents of these Canadian youths are struggling with alcohol problems, and like Little Father Time, many of the children seem to be carrying inherited burdens from which they seek all manner of escape.

The adults in *Jude the Obscure* feel their land and culture, their myth, has been taken away. It appears that Little Father Time, the inheritor of his father's dark internal world, is emblematic of an apocalypse whose stuff is universal gloom. After Father Time's death:

> The boy's face expressed the whole tale of their situation. On that little shape had converged all the inauspiciousness and shadow which had darkened the first union of Jude, and all the accidents, mistakes, fears, errors of the last. He was their nodal point, their focus, their expression in a single term. For the rashness of those parents he had groaned, for their ill assortment he had quaked, and for the misfortunes of these he had died. (Hardy 1978, p. 266)

It seems, finally, that Father Time, in his small frame and shrouded soul, carries the darkness of life – the inferior, worthless, and suicidal side of human creation – for all of us.

Christminster College, the object of so many projected fantasies throughout the novel, echoes with death for Hardy and his characters. Hardy even names one of the grey-stoned colleges "Sarcophagus College," describing it as "silent, black, and windowless" as it throws off its atmosphere of "gloom, bigotry, and decay." (*Ibid.,* p. 262) It is in a shabby room that looks out at Sarcophagus College that the fateful murders/suicide of Jude's children take place. Interestingly, the word *sarcophagus* is derived from words meaning "flesh" and "to eat" because its material [limestone] quickly dissolves the body. (de Vries 1984, p. 400) Jude is a pariah, a fatherless exile, an obscure man – interestingly, one meaning of "obscure" is "mildew," and it is on Mildew Lane, in an area just near the walls of the great University of Christminster, that his children die. Jude is further obscure in that he is a poor laborer of the lower class, a stone mason, and the dust and grits of the stone-dust follow him to his death. Bringing to mind Christ as carpenter, Hardy describes Jude's invisible persona with painful bluntness:

> He was a young workman in a white blouse, and with stone-dust in the creases of his clothes; and in passing him they did not even see him, or hear him, rather saw through him as through a pane of glass at their familiars beyond. (Hardy 1978, p. 70)

It should be noted that Jude's namesake, the apostle, St. Jude, is a faithful servant and friend of Jesus, and the patron saint of hopeless causes, of things despaired of. Even Jude's Christian name is uncommon enough to be called obscure – even though its Biblical origin is common knowledge. Jude is of the lineage of Christ, David, and Solomon – and is a name of the son of Jacob and Leah. And, of course, the name is also a designation simply for "Jew" itself. This association is particularly apropos to the novel's main character, whose story calls the myth of the Wandering Jew to mind. Like that fabled personification, Jude travels from town to town, forever without a home and forever destitute. With the novel's central character named for the Jews – a people too often alienated and misunderstood, but nonetheless the people from whose number Jesus Christ was born – the shocking image of his own son hanging dead, with his two other children beside him, associates Jude with the Crucifixion. From womb to tomb, Jude is made to carry a heavy cross, and the character is therefore associated with Christ and with biblical suffering generally. Even as he lay dying, Jude intones these lines from Job: "'Let the day perish wherein I was born, and the night in which it was said, There is a man child conceived.'" (*Ibid.,* p. 320) In his mixed associations with both Torah and New Testament, Jude embodies at once both the Jewish and Christian dispensations while never feeling at home or finding fulfillment in either of them. He recalls me to my own despair – never feeling at home with Judaism or Christianity – an opening that led me to Jung.

Little Father Time, who belongs really to neither of these traditions, is not even a child but an ancient death-like figure, archetypally a sort of Saturn. After the murder of all three children, Jude and Sue are in death's grip – "all falls like grain." At the graveyard where their children lie buried, Jude and Sue wander through the fog like "dead souls." From the same fog, Jude receives his deathblow; he returns from his last meeting with Sue and feels, as he says, the "chilly fog from the meadows of Cardinal as if death-claws were grabbing me through and through." (*Ibid.,* p. 312)

Little Father Time, however, has a face, an aspect that, to Hardy, suggests the future – not Father Time's own future, but humanity's. That Father Time is a symbol, a harbinger, of human evolution is made explicit when the doctor summoned to attend the three dead children, says,

> There are such boys springing up amongst us – boys of a sort unknown in the last generation – the outcome of new views of life. They seem to see all its terrors before they are old enough to have staying power to resist them." (*Ibid.,* p. 266)

The doctor concludes with the ominous prophecy that "it is the beginning of the coming universal wish not to live." (*Idem*) What is significant about Little Father Time is the scope of what he sees and understands and thinks about; his worldview has a peculiar hyper-conscious quality to it. Unlike the more familiar kind of children, who

> begin with the contiguous, and gradually comprehend the univer-
> sal, the boy seemed to have begun with the generals of life, and
> never to have concerned himself with the particulars. To him the
> houses, the willows, the obscure fields beyond were apparently
> regarded not as brick residence, pollards, meadows, but as human
> dwellings in the abstract, vegetation, and the wide dark world.
> (*Ibid.*, p. 220)

What is missing in such an abstracted existence is the particulars that lend joy and fascination to life and bring it meaning. When one writes down one's dreams, for example, it is the details that bring out the numinous, the feeling of the Self being constellated, that which makes life feel worth the suffering.

*Jude the Obscure* sounds the irrepressible note of sadness in an age as impoverished as ours, in which fate and individuation are the alternative possibilities to a life entirely without texture. What are the bodings of a novel as bleak in many ways as this? Are human beings spiraling down at a greater rate today, with their Columbines and suicidal communities, than in Hardy's time? We have known about vulnerable children being fed to machines, but now children are the ones feeding the machines. We can only ask, are children in the technological age, like Father Time, now taking their revenge? I know of teenagers who wash down Quaaludes with low-cost beer to see who can take the most, fall asleep quickest, and even become one with the unconsciousness of death the fastest. And where are Joseph's tears of recognition for his lost brother Benjamin now? Children, with sticks and stones, have destroyed the tomb of

Joseph in Israel. To what patriarch, what Benjamin, can we turn today? In Zurich (where the original Jung Institute was founded) there is today a nihilist movement whose motto is "no power for nobody;" only the state is invested with the right, the power, to let chaos ravage on. According to Amnesty International, "Around the world today, children are increasingly not only war's victims, but also its combatants. Some are as young as seven years old." (Amnesty International 2002) Little Father Time would feel at home in the postmodern world.

The background of Hardy's *Jude* also brings to mind the fateful progression of human cruelty that is built into our economic system. Children in rural societies or Third World countries often live close to the ground and are quite connected with the actual processes that control life and death on earth. There is a great abyss between the sentimentality of the divine child, the ideal child, and how children are actually treated. They have become the universal underclass, as they have no power and can be easily manipulated. Ownership and control are in opposition to idealization and sentimentality. Children have long had a gravitational and sentimental pull for politicians as well as artists (as evidenced by Edward Hicks' paintings of paradise). In an exhibit at New York University entitled "Child Labor and the Pictorialist Ideal" (Grey Art Gallery 2002), Lewis Hines's portraits of American child oyster suckers and mill workers capture the brutal conditions under which these young laborers grew up, offering a stark contrast to Clarence White's allegorical scene of Pan at his pipes." As Jung writes,

> The "child" is all that is abandoned and exposed and at the same time divinely powerful; the insignificant, dubious beginning, and the triumphal end. The "eternal child" in man is an indescribable experience, an incongruity, a disadvantage, and a divine prerogative; an imponderable that determines the ultimate worth or worthlessness of a personality. (Jung 1958, p. 44-45)

Where, however, is the "triumphal end" in Jude? Where does it reside in the depth of today's experience? The tension within this conflict between the drive toward life and the desire for death may be symbolized, Jung tells us

"The motifs of 'insignificance,' exposure, abandonment, danger, etc., try to show how precarious is the psychic possibility of wholeness, that is, the enormous difficulties to be met with in attaining this 'highest good.'" (Jung 1951/1959, par. 282, p. 166)

In this case, however, the orphan, the wild child, is a dead child, a "terminal creature." Jung writes: "The 'child' is ... both beginning and end, an initial and terminal creature ... the pre-conscious ... and the post-conscious essence." (Jung & Kérenyi 1963, p. 97)

Through their deaths, Jude and Little Father Time are linked and no longer alienated from Jude's promise of the possible. At the end of the novel, the curtain has fallen upon Jude's profoundly sad life. Jude strives toward individuation and consciousness, but the death of his children signals that it is an aborted attempt.

We think of children as victims, and Little Jude is certainly a victim, but he is also a killer with a purpose and a chilling precursor. Children who murder each other are the new contagion that is moving from town to town and from school to school. The war in Israel is not only a war of armies but also one of children. Now, as in Hardy's time, the traditional Christian worldview is being destroyed by reason, science, materialism, and technology. As Richard Carpenter has written,

The last novel Hardy wrote [*Jude the Obscure*] is also his most modern, turning away as it does from agricultural setting and pastoral myth to a restless world of cities and psychological insecurities." (Carpenter 1964, p. 130)

With the deaths of Little Father Time and his half-siblings, the world of Hardy's characters hits its nadir. We can only hope that with the deaths of all those victims of the now so many Columbines, the world psyche has hit its nadir, and that it is time at last for new life to emerge.

Jung warns us of the breach inherent when we dethrone the gods. Like Hardy, he experiences deep foreboding when he anticipates the coming "annulment of the human personality" (Jung 1951/1968, p. 170, p. 109), in an alienation of humankind from its roots in the divine. The great danger is that with the destruction of the God-image, the new "God" becomes the secular state. That this level of alienation is unbridled in our world is hardly in doubt. Only the details still serve to shock us:

> In the small native Innu Canadian community on Newfoundland's Labrador barrens Charles Rich, 11, was sniffing gasoline with his two brothers in their basement. His gas-soaked clothes exploded into flames. Fumes from his breath ignited, and the fire screamed down his throat to his lungs. He burned to death in front of his brothers. That should have been enough but brothers Carl, 11, and Phillip, 13, still sniff gas. (Farley 2000, p. A1)

The God-image in this story is in the fumes. My image of Little Father Time is as Yeats's black falcon, turning in an ever-tightening gyre. The image is linked in my mind to the black Hindu goddess Kali, who wears dead children as earrings. Little Father Time belongs to Kali Yuga, the Iron Age. In the Book of Revelation Christ returns carrying a rod of iron: "And she gave birth to a son, a male child, who is to rule all the nations with a rod of iron." (*Holy Bible,* 12:5) Yet another association is from the Book of Revelation:

> I looked and there was a pale green horse! Its rider's name was Death, and Hades followed with him; they were given authority

over a fourth of the earth, to kill with sword, famine, and pesti-lence, and by the wild animals of the earth. (*Ibid.,* 6:7)

It almost seems as though Little Father Time were an inverted Christ figure: as we have seen, he hangs himself in between his two nameless siblings, who dangle on either side. *Jude* ends with death, with these ashes of aborted strivings. There is no relief at the novel's conclusion, no solace, just bare tragedy. Perhaps it is up to us who read *Jude the Obscure* to fill in the theophany, like the audiences in ancient Greece, in order to experience a cathartic rebirth, a whole child in our own hearts. Our only hope is to be, each of us, nailed to the cross in the embodied world so that one will not be fodder for the universe, as Jude and Little Father Time are, but instead become a small star of consciousness to cast light in the *anima mundi,* the soul of the world. To be "obscure" is the really dark fate this novel cautions us to try to avoid, for that is to fail to coagulate in this world. Perhaps this failure is due to the unequal force of fate against the pull (be it strong or weak) toward individuation, but at the same time the apocalypse image must be constellated in order for the Self to manifest. Analysts following Jung have noted the child archetype often manifests when the Self con-stellates in psychological treatment. Where, therefore, is the "triumphal end" other than in our own soul-making psyches?

Jung does not mention Hardy in any of his work; neverthe-less, Hardy could be called an archetypal psychologist whose medium is poetry. And Hardy's vision is prophetic of Jung's; Hardy is at the same time a realist who does not sanitize the journey of self-discovery with conscious idealizations; rather, with nature as his template, he creates characters whose personalities mirror nature's bittersweet, never-ending cycles of change, its sound and fury, its fathomless stillness and tur-bulence. With all its gray shadings, Jude is prophetic of a new type of human anticipated by Hardy just before the beginning of the fateful twentieth century. Modern, existentialist, and even postmodern, Jude is wounded, displaced, restless, but also a personification of the possibilities of the urban psychological individual, whose reflective powers unfortunately too often bring little more to assuage the suffering of alienation than a ceaseless inkling of the larger Self.

After writing the preceding section, I dreamed that I adopted a little girl of color, about two years old, with blue eyes; she is sitting in a high chair in my kitchen and I am about to feed her some food. I feel that she is an aspect of the divine child and that she symbolizes a hopeful future for which I have accepted responsibility. The dream ends there. My conscious task is to redeem her from the shame of being one of unwanted millions of children of color who are marginalized and culturally expendable. She can be redeemed in time, for at age two damages can be undone. My analytic training teaches that when the number two appears in dreams, it may mean that something is emerging psychologically; it is two because it still lives in two worlds, that of unconscious possibility and conscious realization. The child's blue eyes, moreover, make her unusual; she carries the mixture of bloods, the opposites, in her small dark-tan frame. She is about to be given nourishment by a caring new mother who will love her. I am that adoptive mother. She is an image of the divine child; she is a foundling, and her origins are unknown. I know I must give her a chance to develop.

This is a contemporary dream inspired by Hardy's bleak novel, and her race is of an unknown mixture. It may not be out of context to mention that it was dreamed in Los Angeles, a city of angels that has also known many deaths. It brings to mind a story I was told about the new image of children in Los Angeles: they are a mixture of many races, and their origins are not discernible. They are neither black, white, nor tan; they are not Asian, African, Latino, or Caucasian. They are the new image of futurity. I call my child, born of my reading of *Jude the Obscure,* Hope.

## References

Amnesty International USA (2002). "Child Soldiers."

Carpenter, R. (1964). *Thomas Hardy.* New York: Twayne.

de Vries, A. (1984). *Dictionary of Symbols of Transformation and Imagery.* Amsterdam: Elsevier Science.

Edinger, E. F. (1995). *The* Mysterium Coniunctionis *Lectures.* Toronto: Inner City.

Farley, M. (19 December 2000). "Tribe Sends Kids Away to Dry Out," *Los Angeles Times,* p. A1.

Giegerich, W. (1993), "Killings," *Spring: A Journal of Archetype and Culture,* no. 54, p. 5-17.

Gregor, I. (1974). *The Great Web: The Form of Hardy's Major Fiction.* Totowa, NJ: Rowman & Littlefield.

Guérard, A. J., ed. (1963). "Introduction," *Thomas Hardy.* Englewood Cliffs, NJ: Prentice-Hall.

Hardy, T. (1978). *Jude the Obscure,* 3rd ed. New York: Norton.

*Holy Bible* (1989). Grand Rapids, MI: Zondervan.

Jaffe, L. W. (1990). *Liberating the Heart.* Toronto: Inner City.

Jung, C. G. (1951/1968). *Aion, Collected Works,* Vol. 9, ii. R. F. C. Hull, trans. Princeton, NJ: Princeton University Press.

Jung, C. G. (1951/1959). "The Psychology of the Child Archetype," in *Collected Works,* Vol. 9, i. R. F. C. Hull, trans. Princeton, NJ: Princeton University Press.

Jung, C. G. (1958). *Psyche and Symbol.* Violet de Laszlo, ed. New York: Doubleday.

Jung, C. G. and Kérenyi, C. (1963). *Essays on a Science of Mythology.* New York: Harper and Row.

Lehrman, E. (20 July 2002). "Children: Dreams of Becoming 'Martyrs,'" *Los Angeles Times,* p. A5. Grey Art Gallery, New York University (2002). New York.

*Appendix: A Summary of* Jude the Obscure

We meet Jude, an unwanted and abused orphan; his task is to chase rooks from the field like a solitary scarecrow. His world is almost devoid of brightness, be it from nature or from human contact. In *Jude the Obscure*, written in 1895, eleven-year-old Jude Fawley has a vision of leaving his rural village of Marygreen for a town called Christminster (Oxford, in reality) where he will take a university degree. As he grows older, he pursues this dream by teaching himself Latin and Greek and learning how to do ecclesiastic stonework to support himself. As a young man, he meets Arabella Donn, who lives with her parents on a pig farm. Their provocative first encounter is prompted by her taunting him and throwing a pig's penis at him while he is reading Latin and Greek. "It smacked him sharply in the ear." They begin a sexual relationship (Jude's first) soon thereafter, and within a few months Arabella has tricked Jude into marriage by pretending that she is pregnant.

There is a climactic and emblematic scene in which Jude and Arabella together slaughter their pet pig for food. Arabella is disgusted by Jude's compassion for the suffering animal. After a short time, she leaves him and voyages to Australia to start a new life. Relieved, Jude goes to Christminster, partly drawn there by his long-cherished academic dream but also to meet Sue Bridehead, a first cousin. He and Sue fall into a desperately complicated love that is loaded with unconscious archetypal forces. Sue's solution to her impossible dilemma is to marry Phillotson, Jude's former teacher, a dull but demanding man. Meanwhile, Jude is in despair over his loss of Sue and the fact that he is unable to gain entrance into the University of Christminster because of his humble working-class background.

Sue eventually divorces Phillotson, Jude divorces Arabella, and Sue and Jude live together in a nomadic existence, unable to marry for psychological reasons. Sue and Jude have been contaminated by the family myth that they should never marry because, it is said, marriages between people from their respective bloodlines end in suicide and or estrangement. Jude's mother drowned herself because she was so ill-used by his father. They are also first cousins. Despite these dire forewarnings, they have two children – out of wedlock. Jude is split between Sue and Arabella. Hardy attributes polar feminine qualities to Sue and Arabella: Sue is the goddess of the "starry heaven," while Arabella is allocated to the earth, pigs and instinctuality.

In Australia, meanwhile, unbeknownst to him Arabella has given birth to Jude's child. When the child, who is called Little Father Time, is five years old, Arabella sends him to Jude; Arabella has better things to do with her time than raise a child. Little Father Time, newly displaced to England and in the care of strangers (even though one is his father), overhears Sue talk despairingly about having too many children to feed and tend. Her words trigger a catastrophic reaction in Little Father Time – he hangs their two little babies and then himself. In unendurable anguish, Sue flees the household and returns to Phillotson; Jude submerges his horror in an alcoholic haze.

Arabella returns from Australia and, once again, tricks Jude into marrying her – remarrying her – this time, by getting him so drunk that he acquiesces. Jude, hung over and ill, marries Arabella in the miserable, little smoky back room of her father's pork shop. As time passes, Jude becomes increasingly ill. Though she realizes that Jude is about to die, Arabella nevertheless leaves his bedside to attend the town festival – and to captivate a new suitor. Jude dies alone. Hardy writes, "The bumping of near thirty years had ceased." (Hardy 1978, p. 321)

# Wrestling with God: From the Book of Job to the Poets of the Shoah*

*Naomi Ruth Lowinsky*

> ... the terrors of God do set themselves ... against me.
> — *Job (6:4)*

> No one is born just once. If you're lucky, you'll emerge again in someone's arms; or unlucky, wake when the long tail of terror brushes the inside of your skull.
> — Ann Michaels, *Fugitive Pieces,* p. 5

When terror strikes, our safe little world egg cracks open. Naked and vulnerable to the threatening sky, we are reminded, as was Job, of how small we are; what vast forces move in the universe; how little we control; how perverse our fate can be. Job speaks for all of us, especially after the terror attacks of Sept. 11th, 2001, when he says: "the thing which I greatly feared is come upon me."

---

* The word *Holocaust* has its origin in a sacred sacrificial ritual. It is a 'burnt offering' to a god. The Hebrew word *Shoah*, which means 'ruin or destruction,' seems much more appropriate to describe Hitler's genocide of European Jews.

In terror our numbing habits of mind, our routines that dull us to the numinous, are shattered. We cry out to God, as had the psalmist: "How long Lord, wilt thou hide thyself forever?" We are up against the archetypal world, and are, as Jung says of Job: "… in the immediate presence of the infinite power of creation, … trembling in every limb with the terror of almost total annihilation."

Terror, as a state of mind, can become a numbing habit, a paralysis. Terror was my familiar in childhood. It lived in the beleaguered air of a household filled with the ghosts of those who had died in the Shoah: the six million; my father's father and mother; Anne Frank. My grandparents' deaths were intertwined, in my young psyche, with Anne Frank's story and with the guilt that I lived and they didn't. Terror petrified me; made it hard for me to be a child, to play, to lay my claim on life.

Terror came roaring down the stairs, shouting in my father's voice. His fury was soul-murdering. He enacted Hitler. Terror came on the news at six. We listened as we ate dinner. It was 1952, in Princeton, New Jersey. My father was the first humanist to be invited to the Institute for Advanced Studies. His colleagues now were famous physicists – Oppenheimer and Einstein, the latter himself a refugee from the Shoah. On nightly newscasts we heard the terrifying voice of Joe McCarthy. The House UnAmerican Activities Committee, was about to go after Oppenheimer and Einstein. To my young mind the committee was the same as the pogroms against the Jews my paternal grandparents had fled in Russia, the Nazis they'd tried to flee.

I was stalked by terror, as by a big cat. I was the prey animal. How could I be wild, free, experimental with my life? I lived in a narrow world, hoping the beast wouldn't notice me. Perhaps, if I didn't really inhabit my life, I wouldn't be snatched out of it. This solution, of course, led me nowhere. Luckily I stumbled into a Jungian analysis in my late twenties. I learned slowly, picking my way through dreams filled with Nazis and Cossacks, that in order to grasp my own individual life, to have my own days and nights, suns and moons, to find my own path, I had to shake off the terrors of the six million, of Anne Frank, of my grandparents. I had to live in my own time and in my own culture.

Once I had grown roots into my own existence that were strong enough, I found that I needed to write about my family history of the Shoah. The chronicle entered my book, *Stories from the Motherline,* and many poems in my collection, *red clay is talking.* I discovered that I needed to follow the ancestral connections of my Motherline through what the Germans call *Die Schreckensjahre,* the "Terror Years." In writing *The Motherline,* I came to realize the obvious: I had been the first grandchild born in the New World after all the deaths and dislocations. No wonder I was so burdened, so marked, so tied to the only grandparent I knew, who was my mother's mother. It was in the writing of *The Motherline* that my father's mother, Clara, who died in a concentration camp before I was born, began speaking to me, and it was upon hearing her voice that I realized that I was haunted. In Ann Michaels' novel *Fugitive Pieces,* which is about survivors of the Shoah, she described how it was for me:

> my ear was pressed against the thin wall between the living and the dead ... the vibrating membrane between them was so fragile. (Michaels 1998, p. 31)

Through that fragile membrane, this grandmother continues to visit my life. She comes to me in glimpses: an image, a phrase, a thought that seems to come out of nowhere. Sometimes I experience her as a separate voice; sometimes she is a fugal voice that slips in and out of my own – deepened, opened up by her fierce spirit.

And though I have listened to the voices of this ghost and written about the life of the woman behind them, I made a decision years ago not to read the literature of the Shoah. I did not want to fill my psyche with images beyond those that were already there, and I certainly did not want to focus on Terror. So, when the call for papers arrived about this conference on Terror, I actually tossed it in the wastebasket. I'd paid my terror dues, I thought.

I thought wrong. My ghost grandmother appeared to me and insisted I address the topic once again. I was surprised. I had paid a lot of attention to her in *The Motherline*. I had written an entire poem in her voice. Shouldn't this have fed her? Shouldn't this have calmed her restless soul? Let me share with you part of her story, as I wrote it in *The Motherline:*

> On a sunny day in my forty-second year ... I receive a letter written before my birth. It is from my father's mother ... my grandmother, Clara. It was addressed to my mother and father and found in my father's safe deposit box, labeled "Mother's farewell letter." Because I am the executor of my father's estate, I received a copy of the letter ... The letter is in German ... [It] begins:
>
> "Dearest Giesele, dear Eli:
> "If you receive this, understand that it is a farewell letter. If, however, God lets me live until there is peace, then this letter will be superfluous ..."
> Clara was dying of cancer in a concentration camp in Holland ... What complexity of relationship lies behind the subtleties of this letter. Why is it that my mother is called dearest, *"liebste Giesele,"* while my father rates only a dear? ... My father is dead. But even in life there was no talking to him about such matters ... My mother ... is my only source of family history.
> "Your grandmother," she tells me, "was a very fine woman. She was kind, intelligent, even-tempered, loving ... But her life was full of suffering."

... [This grandmother] had known my mother since my mother was thirteen. My father was the piano teacher in my mother's family ... Here is Clara's voice, speaking to her daughter-in-law. "Dearest Giesele, how shortly I knew you. I wanted so much to see you develop. You are only a child yourself. I wanted so much to know your child. Who knows, maybe you're expecting?"

"You know," my mother says, "the time in which she wrote that letter was the time in which you were conceived. Nine months later you were born and she was dead."

The fog lifts from an unknown place in my soul. And on this soft spring day ... I learn that I am not only descended ... from my mother's side of the family. I am also descended from the mother of my father whose voice is so familiar ... She values development, she values continuity ... she greets the grandchildren who will never know her, and she bargains with God for a sense of meaning. "May God take all I have suffered," she writes at the end of her letter, "as a sacrifice for all of you, that your lives should be better. Then this will have had some meaning." (Lowinsky 1992, p. 133-4, 137-8)

Her blessing was a gift for me and my family. For years I would read it at Passover, so my children would know that they were blessed from the ashes of the Shoah. But that has not satisfied the ghost of my grandmother. It is not enough, she tells me. I remind her how she came to me in a poem I called "a grandmother speaks from the other side." It's in *"red clay is talking."* Here is the end of the poem, all in her words:

you have turned
       the age i was when everything
               stopped –

the train to auschwitz that took
your grandfather
the pyramid of skulls
that is
my grave

don't leave me out
i've let you be for many years
this is the time of life i never got to live
you need my eye
of grief i need your wandering eye
      that sees

          me –
          i'm here
          i've made my mark
               on you

(Lowinsky 2000, p. 18-19)

I think of my writing that poem as my covenant with her. Through it, she helped me understand that it did not serve *her* for me to live in a state of terror, of paralysis. What good would it be to her for me to lose my life as well? I promised her I wouldn't do that.

So, for many years I simply built a firewall between myself and the Shoah. I put terror away; I did not dwell with horror. I lived a personal life, enjoying the blessings of life in America, enjoying much the kind of security Job had when God was still on his side. This is how this state of being is described in the Book of Job.

> Hast thou not made an hedge about him and about his house, and about all he hath on every side? Thou hast blessed the work of his hands, and his substance is increased in the land. (Job 1:10)

But, after the events of September 11th in this country, I found myself in the grip of a strange feeling – one that felt blasphemous to say aloud. I felt relieved. Of what? Perhaps the isolation of my hedged-in, Job-like solution of security. Suddenly everyone around me inhabited a world I realized I knew from way back, a world that I shared with my ghostly grandmother, with my family, with my people, a world in which the terrible can happen at any moment. It was as though, during my period of feeling safely secure, I had somehow dissociated my being from its deeper truth, the truth of the world's suffering. That suffering, of course, did not end with the Shoah. In quite recent times in Bosnia, in Kosovo, in Sierra Leone, in Rwanda, in Northern Ireland, in Israel, in Palestine, in India, and in Pakistan, the legacy of what was done in the past has leapt into monstrous new instances of terror. Parents in these countries are telling their children what was done to their grandparents. And so the horror finds new ways to live and to repeat its terrible stories. As Ann Michaels puts it, "History is the poisoned well, seeping into the groundwater." (Michaels 1998, p. 161)

And, my ghostly grandmother is back, demanding my life energy, my ear for her mutterings, my wrestling with God and with the Shoah. She haunts me, she says, for a purpose:

> You have not yet looked the horror into which you were born in the face. You need to do this because it is your birthright. You were born in the middle of the catastrophe, summer 1943, as your kin were being herded into cattle cars, as they force a Rabbi to dance on the shoulders of his *Yeshivah bocher* (his students) and then knock him down. The Warsaw uprising had just been crushed. On the night of your birth Dresden was firebombed. You were born into a fire sign. How can you live out of your full fiery nature, if you don't face this awful history? When I wrote that letter to your parents I gave you all my blessing, and I meant it. I did not write the truth of my suffering, of what got broken between me and my God. Now you are strong enough to hear my agony. I cried out as did Job:

> God hath delivered me to the ungodly, and turned me over into the hands of the wicked. (Job 16:11)

> My face is foul with weeping, and on my eyelids is the shadow of death. (Job 16:16)

> I have said to corruption, thou art my father: to the worm, thou art my mother, and my sister. (Job 17:14)

313

Oh that I were as in months past, as in the days when God preserved me. (Job 29:2)

When the almighty was yet with me, when my children were about me. (Job 29:5)

Terrors are turned upon me: They pursue my soul as the wind: and my welfare passeth away as a cloud. (Job 30:15)

I cry unto thee, and thou dost not hear me: I stand up, and thou regardest me not. (Job 30:20)

Thou art become cruel to me: with thy strong hand thou opposest thyself against me. (Job 30:21)

When I looked for good, then evil came unto me: and when I waited for light, there came darkness. (Job 30:26)

What can your psychology say to those of us who faced such horror?

What can I say to a ghost from the Shoah, or to Job, about what happens in my quiet, comfortable consulting room, with its soft green chairs that rock; its rug from India? How can I describe the power of those stories of childhood terror; how agonies come back to life between me and my patient; how we must suffer them together, feel the horror in our guts, and hear the stories over and over again; how difficult it is to wrestle with that daimon that wants to keep any child imprisoned in petrified terror.

The ghost of my grandmother says:

You are working with those who are still in their bones and their flesh, whose hearts still beat. I am a ghost. My story can't be healed. My life can't be set to rights. I need you to live in the presence of that inconsolable grief: that you were never placed into my arms when you were a baby, that I never smelt your mother's milk upon your skin, that I died among strangers, all of us ripped out of our lives, severed from friends, family, from our kitchens, our gardens, our routines, our ways of talking to God. And when

I died there was no ritual, no burial, no Kaddish, no mourners, no grave, no headstone, for you to put a rock on. I am a restless hungry ghost. My connection to the eternal got ripped at my death. I can't find my way home.

You who live in physical space, in the six dimensions, who eat fine food and drink good wine, who play peek-a-boo with your grandchildren and watch their eyes fill with laughing light when your face returns to their sight, you who have had time to study psychology, Kabbala, Jewish mysticism, time to read and write poetry, what can you say to me about the catastrophe and God?

It makes one slightly feverish to be in the frequent company of a ghost: one feels somewhat beside oneself. I want to give my grandmother something powerful to calm her spirit, and thus to calm my own. I wonder, would Jung's *Answer to Job* be any help? It was published in 1952, soon after the war, when I was a child in Princeton, terrified by the voices of McCarthy and his cronies. I think Jung was wrestling with the Shoah at that time, and certainly with the place of terror and annihilation in the human psyche. Like a Jew, he was arguing with God. He wrote:

> We have experienced things so unheard of and so staggering that the question of whether such things are in any way reconcilable with the idea of a good God has becoming burningly topical. It is no longer a problem for experts in theological seminaries, but a universal religious nightmare. (Jung 1952/1969, par. 736, p. 453)

Jung was seventy-six when he wrote *Answer to Job*. It is a most unusual work for him. Instead of meandering all over intellectual creation, leaping from intuition to image, from idea to ancient text, as he does in most of his writing, *Answer to Job* is a concentrated dramatic onslaught of pure feeling. The long essay is opinionated, passionate, personal. He said himself:

> I found myself obliged to ... describ[e] a personal experience, carried by subjective emotions. I deliberately chose this form because

I wanted to avoid the impression that I had any idea of announcing an "eternal truth." The book does not pretend to be anything but the voice or question of a single individual. (*Ibid.,* p. 358)

In *Answer to Job,* Jung is wrestling with the difficult God who let the Devil have his way with Job, the same God who did not intervene in the Shoah. Jung sees the 'divine drama' as stemming from the very nature of this Hebrew God, Yahweh, which includes a dark side, but is, in Jung's view, unconscious and lacking in Eros. Jung says of Yahweh that "with brazen countenance he can project his shadow side and remain unconscious at man's expense." (*Ibid.,* p. 382) This God needs human beings to help him see his own nature. "Job," says Jung, "stands morally higher than Yahweh. In this light the creature has surpassed the creator." (*Ibid.,* p. 405) Only God doesn't really know this, because He lacks self-reflection.

Enter Sophia, whom God has forgotten but who was his equal in the old days. She brings feminine wisdom to divinity. Now Yahweh understands that he needs to become man. Sophia, later humanized as Mary, gives birth to Christ, who is both man and God. Jung writes:

[In] the despairing cry from the Cross: "My God, my God, why hast thou forsaken me?" … God experiences what it is to be a mortal man and drinks to the dregs what he made his faithful servant Job suffer. Here is given the answer to Job. (*Ibid.,* p. 408)

I tell my grandmother all this, but the ghost of my grandmother is restless. Jung's wrestling with God does not seem to settle her down. She tells me this is a Christian incarnation story, hardly an answer for a Jewish ghost of the Shoah.

I try to talk to her about what it means to me, how moved I am by Jung's appreciation of the Hebrew Bible, in which God's terrible nature is so evident. Jung even says that Job, a Jewish man, can see the unity of God, even though God is clearly "at odds with himself." (*Ibid.,* p. 369) Job tries to find in God an "'advocate' against God." Job gives us a picture of our human dilemma, Jews and Christians, that we need to be in relation to both the good and terrible aspects of God. But my grandmother is not interested. She only perks up when Jung invokes Sophia:

> [Sophia] describes herself … as the Logos, the word of God … As Ruah, the spirit of God, she brooded over the waters of the beginning … She is the mother-beloved, a reflection of Ishtar … this is confirmed by the detailed comparison of wisdom with trees, such as the cedar, palm, terebinth … olive, cypress. All these trees have from ancient times been symbols of the Semitic love and mother goddess. (*Ibid.,* p. 388)

My grandmother loves this passage. But, she argues, as Jung himself says, Sophia is originally a Jewish figure. She shows up in the Kabbala. Why does she have to be turned into Mary?

I tell my grandmother that Sophia is Jewish and Greek and Christian. I try to get her to see that Jung is writing, very personally, out of his own agony as a Christian, that he is actually quite critical of Christianity and its emphasis on perfection. Jung understands that when all the good is on God's side, human beings have to carry God's dark side. He even writes:

> It looks as if the attempt to secure an absolute and final victory for good is bound to lead to a dangerous accumulation of evil and thus to catastrophe. (*Ibid.,* p. 411)

Or, to put it in the terms of the mythological story Jung is telling:

> Christ … saw Satan fall like lightning from heaven … Satan is banished from heaven and no longer has any opportunity to inveigh his father into dubious undertakings … As a result of the partial neutralization of Satan, Yahweh identifies with his light aspect and becomes the good God and father. (*Ibid.,* p. 410)

My grandmother's ghost is not impressed.

It is all so grand and mythic. There was a time in my life when I would have been interested in such theological treatises. I was, you know, an intellectual. Your father got his brilliance from me! The Shoah removed all that. Listen, if Jung thinks it's such a good idea that the feminine is co-equal with God, and that God becomes a man, why don't I, a woman who died before my time, among so many other terrified, hungry, desperate souls, I who find my agony expressed so clearly in the ancient Book of Job, find a glimmer of my own experience in *Answer to Job?* Jung is so busy lecturing God he spends little time down in Job's mortal realm, with the grief and the physical agony. Could it be that Jung himself was afraid to climb down out of his myth into the broken human lives of the catastrophe? I'm not sure your Jung is much help to me in my Jewish quarrel with God.

And so, in the way of ghosts, my grandmother haunts, prods, tugs me toward the Jewish poets of the Shoah, especially to the poets Nelly Sachs and Paul Celan, and through them, she helps me understand her experience.

Though they were of different generations, lived in different countries, and had different experiences of what Celan referred to simply as 'what happened,' Nelly and Paul became important friends to one another. They met only a few times and conducted their passionate friendship primarily through letters and the exchange of poems.

Nelly Sachs was born in Berlin in 1891. She was of my grandmother's generation. Her upper-middle class parents felt thoroughly at home in Germany. John Felstiner, Celan's translator and biographer, has said of her experience:

> At seventeen, in love with a non-Jew, she was left by him and suffered severely ... Her neo-Romantic verse ... concerned Christmas and Easter, animals and landscape, Mozart, her parents ... With the Nazi advent in 1933, Sachs turned toward Biblical themes and Hasidic mysticism ... After 1938 she was threatened by the Gestapo; the man she still loved, now a resistance fighter,

was killed before her eyes. On 16 May, 1940 she fled with her mother to Stockholm ... and soon began translating Swedish poetry into German, meanwhile consecrating her own writing to "the suffering of Israel." (Celan and Sachs 1995, p. viii)

Though her books are out of print and she is little known in America these days, Sachs won the Nobel Prize for Poetry in 1966. Paul Celan, who is well known and highly regarded in American poetry circles, was born in 1920, the year my mother was born. He came from German-speaking Jewish parents and lived in Czernowitz, Bukovina, an Eastern outpost of the Austrian Empire that passed to Romania before Paul was born. He, like Sachs, was an only child, very close to his mother, and schooled in the great tradition of German poetry: Goethe, Heine, Schiller.

In 1941, the Romanian army and police joined the Germans in "obliterating a six-hundred-year Jewish presence: burning the Great Synagogue; imposing the yellow badge; plundering, torturing, and slaughtering community leaders and three-thousand others ..." (Felstiner 2001, p. 12-13) Celan and his parents escaped. But in the following year, when Celan was twenty-two and had had, by one account, a falling out with his father and stormed out of the house, he returned the next day to find his parents gone. They had been rounded up and deported. Paul never saw them again. (*Ibid.,* p. 14) His poetry is filled with the longing for his lost mother:

> Autumn bled all away, Mother, snow burned me through:
> I sought out my heart so it might weep, I found – oh
> the summer's
>     breath,
> it was like you.
> Then came my tears ...
> (Celan 2001, p. 15)

Leah Shelleda, in her important, but as yet unpublished book on art and terror in the 20th century, *In the Shadow of its Wings*, writes of Celan:

> [He] will live a perpetual, inconsolable 'yahrzeit' … the memory of catastrophe continued to reverberate. It was not dulled by time; there was no getting over it. To recover is to betray those one had lost.

The same note of inconsolable loss is sounded in a poem by Nelly Sachs called "Chorus of the Orphans." Celan found it in a journal in 1953 and wrote to Sachs, beginning their intense connection. Here is part of the poem:

> We orphans
> we lament to the world:
> At night our parents play hide and seek —
> From behind the black folds of night
> Their faces gaze at us
> Their mouths speak:
> Kindling we were in a woodcutter's hand —
> …
> We orphans
> We lament to the world:
> Stones have become our playthings,
> Stones have faces, father and mother faces
> They wilt not like flowers, nor bite like beasts —
> And burn not like tinder when tossed into the oven —
> (Sachs 1967, p. 29)

My grandmother's ghost carries feelings that are voiced in this poem. She too was orphaned: she lost her God, her home, her past, her future, her children, her grandchildren. And suddenly, listening to her suffering in Sachs' powerful imagery, I find myself beset by that difficult old question, one I've been protected from by the firewall I've put between myself and the Shoah, a question raised in the fifties by the critical philosopher Theodore Adorno: Is it barbaric to write poetry after Auschwitz? Does it make "an unimaginable fate" somehow meaningful? (Felstiner 2001, p. 188) Does it release us too easily from the horror?

My grandmother's voice leaps to respond:

> The poets give voice to the unthinkable, the unbearable, they give sorrow a voice, and lamentation. If there were only silence, song frozen by the horror, who would remember, who would mourn? Who would make wicked jokes, with "wild, cunning words" to resist the "crassness of the economic-miraculous" Germany (*Ibid.,* p. 191) as did Paul Celan in the early sixties? Who would remember the moment of my death? How it felt. Who was there. Who wasn't. God was supposed to be there when I died. No one was there. We all disappeared like smoke in the air. So says Celan, so says Sachs.

She is referring to the image of smoke that both Celan and Sachs used, before they knew one another's work. Celan wrote a poem in 1946, *"Todesfuge"* or *"Deathfugue"* which became perhaps the most famous poem of the Shoah, for its evocation of the horror of the death camps. Here is a section:

> Black milk of daybreak we drink you at night
> we drink you at midday and morning we drink you at evening
> we drink and we drink
> a man lives in the house your *goldenes Haar* Margareta
> your *aschenes Haar* Shulamith he plays with his vipers
> He shouts play death more sweetly this Death is a master from
>     Deutschland
> he shouts scrape your strings darker you'll rise up as smoke to
> the sky
> (Celan 2001, p. 31-2)

My grandmother, in response to this fugue, is rocking her ghost body in me, weeping, tearing her hair. The poem shouts her horror: the madness, the dance of death going faster and faster while the master from Deutschland, who loves music and high culture, evokes the Margareta of Goethe's *Faust* and the Shulamith of the *Song of Songs* whose hair is of ashes, in crazy company with vipers. If the poets don't say how it was, who will?

Nelly Sachs' poem is called "O the Chimneys" which became the title of her *Selected Poems*. The poem has an epigram from Job:

> And though after my skin worms destroy this body, yet in my flesh shall I see God – (Job 19:26)

Here is part of the poem:

> O the chimneys!
> Freedomway for Jeremiah and Job's dust –
> Who devised you and laid stone upon stone
> The road for refugees of smoke?
>
> O the habitations of death,
> Invitingly appointed
> for the host who used to be a guest –
> O you fingers
> Laying the threshold
> Like a knife between life and death –
>
> O you chimneys,
> O you fingers
> And Israel's body as smoke through the air!
> (Sachs 1967, p. 3)

My grandmother's ghost breath settles down in my body. She rests in me. The poem orients her. It is at once lamentation and accusation: "the host who used to be a guest" is the human being who takes the power of a god into his hands. To be part of Israel's body "as smoke through the air" is, strangely, consolation for a ghost.

We wonder, this ghost and her granddaughter, about Sachs' choice of that section of Job, "yet in my flesh shall I see God." We muse about Sachs as a religious poet. It was Nelly Sachs' goal, her longing, to see God. Celan believed she did and that in her company he, too, caught a glimpse. This happened in May, 1960, when, after many years of corresponding, the two poets met for the first time. Sachs was to receive the Droste prize in Germany. Though it had been twenty years since she had fled, she still could not bear to stay overnight in Germany and so met Celan in Zurich. (Felstiner 2001, p. 156) Celan was to write a poem about this meeting, "Zurich, at the Stork," which he dedicated to Nelly Sachs:

> On the day of an ascension, the
> Minster stood over there, it came
> with some gold across the water.
>
> Our talk was of your God, I spoke
> against him ... (Celan 2001, p. 141)

Celan was referring to the day of Christ's ascension into heaven, and to the sight of Zurich's great church reflected in the river. Both poets were steeped in Jewish mysticism, both had read Gerschom Scholem's translation of the *Zohar*. They understood the sacred meaning of light in the Kabbalistic tradition. Celan credited Sachs with showing him this light. She was a Jewish mystic with a deep connection to the sacred alphabet. She writes in a poem:

> Then wrote the scribe of *the Sohar*
> opening the words' mesh of veins
> instilling blood from stars ...
>
> The alphabet's corpse rose from the grave,
> alphabet angel, ancient crystal ... (Sachs 1967, p. 123)

Writing was Sachs' way to the divine, but she did not have an easy relationship with her God.

Neither did Celan. Though he claimed not to be a believer, many of his strongest poems wrestle directly with God. Both poets were beleaguered by darkness and psychological pain. Sachs suffered from a persecution mania that had a basis in reality. There was a Nazi revival in Sweden in the late 1950s. Her paranoia extended, however, to the noise from the water pipes in her apartment. She was hospitalized several times in her later life. Celan, who suffered from dark depressions, also was frequently hospitalized.

We wonder, the ghost of my grandmother and I, whether they were really crazy, or whether they were carrying the unbearable burden of their times, trying to digest what could not be digested. Were they, as poets, more permeable than others to the horror? It was their job to give sorrow a voice, lamentation words to say, their job to find images for the unthinkable. They were carrying something for us all. It was simply too much. Listen to Nelly Sachs:

> This is the landscape of screams!
> Ascension made of screams
> out of the bodies grate of bones ...
>
> Job's scream to the four winds ...
>
> O you bleeding eye
> in the tattered eclipse of the sun
> hung up to be dried by God ... (Sachs 1967, p. 129)

Hers is no Christian god of goodness and kindness. Neither is the God whom Celan addresses in his powerful poem, "Tenebrae." The title refers to a Catholic service during which candles are extinguished to symbolize the Crucifixion. (Felstiner 2001, p. 101) A gospel portion is read: *"Tenebrae factae sunt"* – "there was darkness over the earth."

Near are we, Lord,
near and graspable.

Grasped already, Lord,
clawed into each other, as if
each of our bodies were
your body, Lord.

Pray Lord,
pray to us,
we are near. (Celan 2001, p. 103)

The rest of the poem makes a clear, unbearable allusion to the manner in which people died in the gas ovens of the Shoah. Ann Michaels gives us a prose version:

When they opened the doors, the bodies were always in the same position. Compressed against one wall, a pyramid of flesh. Still hope. The climb to air, to the last disappearing pocket of breath near the ceiling. The terrifying hope of human cells. (Michaels 1998, p. 168)

The poem stands the whole idea of prayer on its head: God is supposed to pray to us. Our bodies, clawed unto each other in a terrible death, are God's body. Maybe Celan is saying something like what Jung was saying – that Job is morally superior to God, that God needs us humans to express the horrible aspect of the divine.

My ghost grandmother is making a loud noise in my heart as we read Sachs and Celan. It excites her to notice that certain themes that seem to come directly from those poets, appear in my poems, before I ever read them. It is as though they were floating about in that area of psyche Joseph Henderson calls the cultural unconscious, as though I was drawing from my poetic cultural lineage before I knew of it consciously.

For example in my poem called "Hera Reflects on the Anniversary of a Long Ago Dissolved First Marriage," which is in *red clay is talking,* there is a passage explaining the pressure I felt to have children young:

> ... all those ghosts
> fresh out
> of the ovens
> fresh out of
> mass graves
> they had
> no stones
> to lay down their heads
> no baskets
> for their bones
> no ground
> for their roots
> they spilled over
> oceans
> invading
> demanding
> new born
> baby
> bodies – (Lowinsky 2000, p. 41)

Sachs has a similar poem called "Chorus of the Unborn." Here is a section:

> Listen, you who are sick with parting:
> We are those who begin to live in your glances,
> In your hands which are searching the blue air –
> We are those who smell of morning.
> Already your breath is inhaling us,
> Drawing us down into your sleep
> Into the dreams which are our earth ... (Sachs 1967, p. 43)

"She's talking," says the ghost of my grandmother, "about you, your whole generation. And she's talking, as were you, about the powerful push for new life after so much death."

Celan wrote of poetry as "something standing open, occupiable, perhaps toward an addressable Thou." (Felstiner 2001, p. 206) I was possessed by this notion of an addressable you, before I had ever read Celan's poem, "Radix, Matrix."

> As one speaks to stone, as
> you,
> to me from the abyss, from
> a homeland con-
> Sanguined, up-
> Hurled, you,
> you of old to me,
> you in the Nix of a night to me,
> you in Yet-Night en-
> Countered, you
> Yet-You – : (Celan 2001, p. 167)

My poem, "You," published in *red clay is talking*, repeats the word "you" in a fashion similar to Celan's. Here is the last part of the poem:

> you
> break into my night –
> rattle my rib cage –
> make biblical claims
>               on my flesh –
>
>         you
>         two a.m. terror
>               lusting for what
>                     you have made –
>
>         lord of the apple tree –
>         angel with fangs –
>
>         i spit like an old jewish woman
>         water to dust
>         in your hands –

suddenly everything's
fire
on the mountain –

you –

burning
in me –

never
consumed

(Lowinsky 2000, p. 138)

So, it would appear that I was in receipt of a poetic legacy before having read it. As the ghost of my grandmother pushed and prodded me toward Sachs and Celan, I began to understand that I had kin in poetry, who had much to teach me about the cultivation of a religious attitude in the shadow of Terror.

Did these poets work out a relationship to their terror? I think they did, and in the only way my grandmother's ghost can understand – to know their terror as an aspect of divinity. To "wrestle with God" is not to repudiate or to deny the divine. It is a form of relationship to God. Jung grasps this: it is what *Answer to Job* is about. Sachs and Celan grasp it too, helped by Jewish mysticism and the Kabbala. What my ghostly grandmother, my familial Job, has helped me to understand, by her strongly voiced discomfort with Jung's *Answer to Job*, is that Jung, in following the train of his Christian thought, has not paid attention to how much God has changed in the Jewish tradition since the Middle Ages, especially through the Kabbala. Jung says that God wants to become human. But in the rich hermetic tradition of Jewish mysticism, as it is expressed in the Kabbalistic glyph of the Tree of Life, the lightning flash of God's ineffable being is traced from its most unknown and unsayable to its most touchable reality – in our human realm. The Kabbala shows God passing from masculine to feminine and back; from

328

severity to compassion; from energy to form. God becomes human, and we humans are revealed to be a part of God.

In this experience, God's ineffable femininity as an embodied creature is revealed. The indwelling of the Shekinah – the Sophia, the feminine face of God – is both process and goal of the journey down to the ground of manifestation and back up to the Mystery of Mysteries. This is a very different God from Job's God in the whirlwind; it is a God revealed to the poet, the mystic, the ecstatic. There is an echo of Dionysos in this vision.

To honor such a God is not to be protected from evil, from terror, from suffering. It is to expand our sense of the holy, as did the people of New York City, in declaring the site of the dismembered twin towers sacred ground. It is to follow within oneself the trajectory of light, as did Nelly Sachs, as did Paul Celan.

In his poem, "Psalm," Celan writes:

No one kneads us again out of earth and clay
no one incants our dust.
No one.

Blessed art thou, No One.
In thy sight would
we bloom
In thy
spite. (Celan 2001, p. 157)

To wrestle with God as 'No One' is of course a mystical idea, an existential counterpart to the "I am" that spoke to Moses out of the Burning Bush. It also expresses the despair of those who got no help from God in the catastrophe. The 'No One' who was there at my grandmother Clara's death is transformed by Celan's blazingly simple phrase combining the opposite faces of God: "Blessed art thou, No One."

Sachs, on the other hand, prefigures the return of the religious attitude in the Goddess religions, which will be revived to flood the western psyche soon after her death. Her simple, powerful images are the essence of the Shekinah:

> Like a milkmaid
> at dusk
> your fingertips pull
> at the hidden sources
> of light ...
>
> Dancer
> woman in childbirth
> you alone
> carry on the hidden navel-string
> of your body
> the identical god-given jewels
> of death and birth. (Sachs 1967, p. 149)

There is an echo of Hindu Krishna-consciousness here.

Both Sachs and Celan were often plunged into darkness – their own, their people's, and their time's. Both struggled in their poems to find their way back to the light. When Celan was in the psychiatric clinic, he had electroshock therapy and he read Freud. As far as I know he had no psychotherapy. But he read Gershom Scholem on the Kabbala. According to his biographer, in a moment of despair, he wrote out one of the sacred names of God in Judaism: "Shaddai! Shaddai!"

That something transformative happened to him in his encounter with the Kabbala is made evident by a poem he wrote while still in the hospital: "*Nah, am Aortenbogen*" or "Near, in the aorta's arch." It is such a short poem I will print it in its entirety:

> Near, in the aorta's arch,
> in brightblood
> the brightword.

> Mother Rachel
> weeps no more.
> Carried across now
> all of the weeping.
>
> Still, in the coronary arteries,
> unbinded:
> Ziv, that light. (Celan 2001, p. 303)

Celan moves from the physiology of human blood flow, (certainly an image of how God manifests in human form in all our lives), to the tragic history of the Jews ("Mother Rachel weeps no more"), to a Hebrew word that Gershom Scholem ascribes to the indwelling light of the Shekinah: *"Ziv."* (Felstiner 2001, p. 239) This, his biographer believes, is a word he has been waiting for and that has been waiting for him, a word for the light he first saw when he was in Zurich with Nelly Sachs, and saw again when Nelly visited him and his family in Paris. *Ziv,* a word for the mystery of becoming conscious and present to the divinity of human suffering.

But to find a way to move from the aorta's arch to the light — a way to translate the experience of God's incarnation through us — does not, it appears, necessarily resolve one's own agony as a human being who has gone through hell. At age fifty, Celan took his life by jumping into the Seine. He had written his last message to Nelly Sachs, who represented for him his lost mother, and the sister he never had: "all gladness dear Nelly, all light!" He was trying to pull her out of her darkness, even when he himself was about to drown in his own. She had written him: "the net of fear and terror that they threw over me hasn't yet been raised." (Celan and Sachs 1995, p. 35) And Celan answers:

> I think of you Nelly, always … Do you still remember, when we spoke for the second time of God, in our house … how a golden light shimmered on the wall? Through you, through your nearness,

331

such things become visible ... Look Nelly: the net is being drawn away! ... Look, it is getting light, you are breathing, you are breathing freely. You will not be lost to us ... (*Ibid.,* p. 36)

He is saying an incantation, to try to keep Nelly among the living, something he could not do for his mother, and, of course, for himself. Sachs died of cancer on the day Celan was buried.

Toward the end of her life, in her beautiful long poetry series: *"Glühende Rätsel"* – "Glowing Enigmas" or "Glowing Riddles," Sachs makes some peace with her "beloved dead."

Forgive me my sisters
I have taken your silence into my heart
There it lives and suffers the pearls of your suffering
heartache knocks
so loud so piercingly shrill
A lioness rides on the waves of Oceana
a lioness of pains ...

Weep away the unleashed heaviness of fear
Two butterflies support the weight of the world for you
and I lay your tears into these words:
Your fear has begun to shine – (Sachs 1967, p. 257)

In her poetry Sachs has created a transformation of terror into light.

I write you –
You have come into the world again
with the haunting strength of letters
that groped for your essence
Light shines
and your fingertips glow in the night
Constellation at the birth
of darkness like these verses – (*Ibid.,* p. 303)

With these lines, Sachs becomes a universal poet. You don't have to have a family connection to the Shoah to be haunted

by troubling ghosts. We all feel them in our bones these days
– whether they were ripped out of their lives in lower Manhattan on Sept. 11, disappeared in Chile and Argentina, blown up
in a house in Ramallah or a street in Jerusalem, torn out of
a village in Sierra Leone or Bosnia. So many taken violently,
shockingly out of their lives. They wail, they keen, they mutter
warnings. We tremble at the brink of a dangerous war with terrible unforseen consequences. The ghosts want our attention.

When you pay attention to your ghosts, by acknowledging
their terror, looking horror in the face, it is transformative. My
grandmother is shifting in me. She is going from ghost to light,
from a fearful presence I had not wanted to face to a bright,
fierce energy. She is a firebrand. *She* is a burning bush. She
comes to me as clarity, and I see why her name is Clara. She
has pushed me to wrestle with God in my poetry. She wants
me to end this record of our conversations with a recent poem
of mine, called "Psalm," in which I enter the territory of my forbears, Nelly Sachs, Paul Celan, and my grandmother Clara, in
order to face the terrors of our own time. Here is the poem:

**Psalm**

*death still celebrates*
*the life in you*
> Nelly Sachs, p. 213

descend upon me    you who are source
before source    fire in the sky    gleam
in the back of my skull    come in the wind
with wings    come in my breath    i cling
to the luminous stair    sing me your names –
spirit    void    darkening sea    world
tree –    when thunder speaks    come into my heart
where terrible stories are told –

333

                                                      the woman
whose womb has cast pieces of flesh       all over the streets
of Jerusalem        that son of your prophet      whose light
splintered   into thousands of dangerous
shards—    i gather it all for the altar
                        the blood    the rage    the weeping
                                        show me your face
                                                      in the fire


*References*

*The Book of Job, Holy Bible.* King James Version.

Celan, P. and Sachs, N. (1995). *Correspondence.* New York: Sheep Meadow Press.

Celan, P. (2001). *Selected Poems and Prose.* New York: W. W. Norton.

Felstiner, J. (2001). *Paul Celan: Poet, Survivor, Jew.* New Haven: Yale University Press.

Jung, C. G. (1952/1969). *Answer to Job. Collected Works,* Vol. 11. Princeton: Princeton University Press.

Lowinsky, N. (1992). *Stories from the Motherline.* Los Angeles: Jeremy Tarcher.

Lowinsky, N. (2000). *red clay is talking.* Oakland, CA: Scarlet Tanager Books.

Michaels, A. (1998). *Fugitive Pieces.* New York: Vintage International.

Sachs, N. (1967). *O the Chimneys. Selected Poems.* Philadelphia: The Jewish Publication Society of America (by arrangement with Farrar, Straus and Giroux).

# Jung, Spielrein and Nash:
# Three Beautiful Minds Confronting the Impulse to
# Love or to Destroy in the Creative Process

*Brian Skea*

## Introduction

Most of Jung's writings represent the creative outcome of his grappling with the dynamics involved in reconciling the oppo-sites within the psyche. In *Memories, Dreams, Reflections* (1961/ 1963) (*MDR*), as presented by Aniela Jaffé, Jung described the conflict between his personalities No. 1 and No. 2 in childhood, the one more rational and realistic, the other more grandiose and mystical, modeled on the split he observed in his mother's personality. He also described there the emotional coniunctios[1] he experienced in his significant relationships, for example, with mother, father or Sigmund Freud. In *Wandlungen und Symbole der Libido,* Jung defined two kinds of thinking, directed rational thinking versus non-rational fantasy thinking, corresponding to Freud's (1911) secondary (reality-principle) and primary (plea-sure-principle) process thinking respectively. In *Psychological Types* Jung explored conflicting modes of consciousness, extraversion versus introversion, thinking versus feeling, sensation versus intuition. In other works he discussed the love-hate dynamics within the psychotherapeutic coniunctio of therapist and client, as in *The Psychology of the Transference.* Within religion, as in *Answer to Job,* Jung considered the conflictual coniunctio between Jahweh and Job, representing Self and ego, where an omnipotent, ambivalent (both loving and persecuting) 'god' is confronted by a terrified mortal ego.

In his later years, Jung focused on the separation and synthesis of psychic opposites as revealed in alchemical symbolism. He began his last major work, *Mysterium Coniunctionis,* as follows: "The factors which come together in the coniunctio are conceived as opposites, either confronting one another in enmity or attracting one another in love." (Jung 1955/1963, par. 1, p. 3) Jung, following the alchemists, is here personifying the chemical combination of elements, and, by analogy, the tension between intrapsychic opposites, as an erotic attraction between lovers, or an 'aretic'[2] combat between warriors or lovers quarreling. Jung was well aware of the possible destructive outcome of the clash of opposites within an individual, for example, when the numinous energies of the Self overwhelm the ego, as in the case of Nietzsche. (Jung 1989a) He had also experienced destructive interpersonal outcomes with his father, with colleagues who became estranged rivals, such as Sigmund Freud, and in some of his therapeutic relationships, for instance with Sabina Spielrein, a relationship that will be explored here. Nevertheless, Jung and many Jungians have tended to paint an overly optimistic picture of the positive consequences of either intrapsychic or interpersonal coniunctio, postulating some creative transformation as the central outcome. Psychosis or suicide is a possible outcome of an inner coniunctio gone wrong; betrayal, manipulation or abandonment can represent an outer coniunctio gone wrong; and war, whether conventional, terroristic, or, since 9/11, 'against terror,' is often the result of an international coniunctio gone wrong. By 'gone wrong' I mean that the destructive and disintegrative energies of the Self have in the end outweighed the Self's creative and integrative energies, resulting not in a greater integrity or a creative transformation, but in chaos, death or dismemberment, whether literally or psychologically.

Though Jung conceded in *MDR* that the breakdown of his relationship with Freud plunged him into extreme depths of disorientation, he believed that the challenging process of self-exploration that led to his recovery, outlined in his *Red Book,* only now about to be published, laid the foundations of his future creative work. It is my impression, shared by a number of other authors, that Jung's other significant relationships, especially with women, were charged with ambivalence, but tended to be idealized by him, with his focusing on the creative outcome for himself while ignoring or minimizing the destructive outcome for the women involved.[3] I am thinking here of what has been said about his cousin, Helene Preiswerk, the subject of his medical dissertation, *On the Psychology and Pathology of So-Called Occult Phenomena* (Goodheart 1984; Kerr 1993; Skea 1995); of Christiana Morgan, the subject of his *Visions* seminars (Douglas 1993); and of Sabina Spielrein (Carotenuto 1982; Covington 2001). Spielrein's ideas on mythological aspects of psychotic regression closely paralleled Jung's own thinking, which he published as *Wandlungen und Symbole der Libido.*[4] At this time we await the publication of a biography of Toni Wolff to possibly disclose the full impact of her relationship with Jung with regard to his supposed mid-life breakdown.[5] All of these women were significant 'outer' women in Jung's life who contributed to his theory of the Anima.

Sabina Spielrein was a creative and imaginative Russian-Jewish woman who suffered a breakdown of almost psychotic proportions as a teenager following the death of her younger sister. After several unsuccessful treatments she finally came to the Burghölzli Hospital in Zurich where she became Jung's first psychoanalytic patient. The creative outcome of Jung and Spielrein's intense relationship, revealed in letters and journals analyzed by Carotenuto (1982), is certainly documented in her recovery and going on to train to become one of the first female psychoanalysts (Covington & Wharton 2003). Her longest published paper, "Destruction as a Cause of Coming into Being" (1912) creatively addressed from a psychoanalytic perspective the dark side of what Jung would later call the erotic coniunctio. In that paper she noted the risk of ego disintegration inherent in any passionate encounter between lovers. She then illustrated her thesis from a Zurich-School perspective, presenting clinical examples from her medical dissertation, "On the Psychological Content of a Case of Schizophrenia" (1911), amplified with parallels from mythology, literature and philosophy, notably the work and life of Nietzsche. Though her paper, except perhaps the 'Jungian' mythological section, was well received by Freud and his circle, her concept of a death or destruction instinct was not referred to by Freud until 1920, when he conceived his own Death Instinct in *Beyond the Pleasure Principle,* and even then he misrepresented her thesis. Jung, on the other hand, did cite Spielrein's medical dissertation frequently in *Wandlungen,* the book that occasioned his break with Freud, but strangely he did not refer there (or in any subsequent revisions) to her "Destruction" paper, which he had helped edit, and which was published in the *Jahrbuch* next to the second part of his *Wandlungen.*

Though Spielrein continued to work as a Freudian psychoanalyst in Zurich, Berlin and Geneva, mainly with children, and published several small papers, her contributions have only recently been recognized. (Carotenuto 1982; van Waring 1992; Covington 2001; Covington & Wharton 2003) The themes of death and destruction, however, continued to haunt Sabina. She returned to Russia at the end of the Civil War in 1923, just as Stalin was rising to power. She helped develop the State Psychoanalytical Institute in Moscow, where she worked as an analyst, teacher, and researcher, especially in the area of child analysis. After Stalin abolished, first, the Moscow Institute (1925), and then the Russian Psychoanalytic Society (1930), Spielrein defiantly continued her analytical work in her hometown of Rostov. In her personal life, Sabina almost lost her firstborn daughter, Renate, during pregnancy. Her husband left her soon after, returning to Russia, though they reunited later, following her return to Russia, and had a second daughter. All three of her talented younger brothers were killed in the Stalinist purges in the mid-thirties, her husband died suddenly in 1937, and Sabina and her two daughters were killed by the Nazis in 1942. (Ovcharenko 1999)

John Nash is a Nobel Laureate mathematical genius and the recent subject of the movie *A Beautiful Mind* (2001). This popular film is based on the 1999 biography of Nash by Sylvia Nasar, which details the onset, treatment, and his recovery from apparent schizophrenic psychosis. His schizophrenia seems to date as far back as his graduate school days at Princeton, where he wrote the paper that was later seen to be so important in the field of economics that it led to his receiving a Nobel Prize in 1994. It appears that as a young professor, he, like Jung, was an introvert with a rich inner life, peopled by sub-personalities and subject to visions. Unlike Jung, however, he did not find a way to integrate these manifestations of complexes and archetypes into his conception of himself, but rather projected them outside himself in the form of personified hallucinations, with whom he conversed and to whom he reacted within an elaborate, and increasingly paranoid, delusional system.

This was just after the Second World War, at the start of the Cold War, when many Princeton graduate students were being tapped by the U.S. government to work on classified material, including the possibilities for averting nuclear attack by breaking Russian communication codes. This was heady enough, but the way this real-life paranoid scenario became incorporated into Nash's delusional system led him towards more and more bizarre behavior. Starting at age thirty, he suffered a series of psychotic episodes, which led to psychiatric hospitalization, psychotherapy, medication, and treatments that included the then-popular insulin shock therapy, which was similar in its effect to electro-convulsive therapy. Over the next thirty years, however, only his relationship with his wife, Alicia,[6] the community support of colleagues at Princeton, and the intermittent capacity to do meaningful mathematical work, helped to permit some degree of sanity. The book and movie describe his long and painful partial recovery, culminating in his receiving the Nobel Prize in Sweden.

These three figures, Jung, Spielrein and Nash, all demonstrate the well-known relationship between creative genius and the risk of madness. All three were deep, original thinkers, where their creative products represented the positive offspring of dynamic coniunctios that were achieved within their psyches, based on their intuitive-thinking engagement with archetypal ideas and images. On the other hand, at the level of feeling and sensation, wild erotic and aggressive fantasies, and mood swings between omnipotent heights and impotent depths, threw them into inner turmoil, which was sometimes acted out in their intimate relationships. Many of these enactments, however inspiring, were not adequately contained, causing lasting wounds and scars throughout their own lives, and in those around them.

In the case of both Nash and Jung, there has been a tendency on the part of many of their supporters and followers to write this destructiveness off as the toll of their undoubted creative genius. In Spielrein's case, like many creative but non-conforming women of her time, this destructiveness met with societal disapproval, or at least ambivalence, and until recently, a lack of recognition of her creativity. Only recently have analytical psychologists begun to question Jung's tendency to idealize and mythologize the creative aspects of the coniunctio, and to minimize or deny the destructive aspects, even while emphasizing the reality of the shadow. This questioning has extended into a similar idealizing and mythologizing of Jung's personal life and relationships by both Jung (*MDR*) and his followers. The reflections that follow could be construed as continuing to raise these issues, but they do so less to question the integrity of Jung, Spielrein or Nash, than to inquire whether our present understanding of the coniunctio does not require further explication in order to do justice to this archetype's destructive potential.

### Four Aspects of the Self

In *Mysterium Coniunctionis,* Jung explored the various ways the alchemists metaphorically conceived the coniunctio and its opposite, *separatio,* from the level of chemistry to an unconscious 'psychology' projected onto matter, replete with mythology and spirituality. At the level of chemistry, these metaphorical processes represent the combining of chemical elements into compounds (coniunctio), and the separating of pure elements *out* of compounds and mixtures (separatio) by various processes such as distillation. However, these processes can also be understood as a symbolic psychology, trying to encompass the processes of psychic integration, dissociation, and transformation that depth psychologists in our time have explored in the consulting room. The alchemists' paired analogies, such as king and queen, Sol and Luna, and Logos and Eros, had obvious relationship to the union of Masculine and Feminine elements in the soul. The Chemical Wedding, an alchemical version of the motif of *hierosgamos,* can be seen ideally as a symbol of the Jungian Self. The transformative offspring of such a union can be symbolized as the Divine Child and realized in the life of the individuating ego in such creative products as art, music, literature, scientific theory or invention. The union of opposite elements, however, whether conceived of as a psychic or as a chemical conjunction, may equally result in a release of energy which cannot be contained, whether by the ego or a chemical container, and then it results not in a creative product but in a literal chemical explosion, as in dynamite or the fusion reaction of the hydrogen bomb. Even if overt destruction does not ensue, the product of such a union is not necessarily creative but may be a hermaphroditic monster, as in some alchemical drawings, or, in the current biomedical realm, a malformed embryo created by *in vitro* fertilization or a delusional system constructed out of a contact with the unconscious in the psychic realm.

Thus, the constellation of the Jungian Self through the archetype of the coniunctio does not always imply union and wholeness, but also disunion, fragmentation or even destruction of a unitary self. Jung explores this dark side of the Self in *Mysterium Coniunctionis* through his description of shadow sides of both Sol and Luna. The sun, though mainly for Jung a symbol of consciousness, has a shadow side – the *sol niger,* a symbol of unconsciousness, destructiveness and death, which presides over the *nigredo* and the *putrefactio.* (Jung 1955/1963, p. 95) In his earlier work, *Wandlungen,* Jung described the sun as "the only rational representation of God … the fructifier and creator … the source of energy of our world." But the sun "is not only beneficial, but also destructive…. it is the harmonious and inherent nature of the sun to scorch." (Jung 1916/1991, par. 201, p. 115) Jung in *Wandlungen* was focusing on the sun as a symbol of libido, its dynamic energy aspect, both creative and destructive, Eros and Ares, rather than its structural aspect as a symbol of consciousness, Logos. The moon also represents a form of consciousness, lunar or matriarchal consciousness, Mythos,[7] as against solar or patriarchal consciousness, Logos. (Neumann 1954) From a darker perspective, however, Jung, again in *Mysterium,* describes the moon in its changing appearance as representing the "changefulness of mortality, which is equivalent to death." The disappearance of the waning moon represents symbolically "the destruction of death." The moon can even 'corrupt' the sun through the phenomenon of the solar eclipse. We can understand how madness, lunacy, has been historically related to the moon, but in today's patriarchal cultures we can similarly speak of solar madness, a 'masculine' tendency to over identify with the Logos and Ares aspects of the Self, denying or dissociating Eros or Mythos aspects, and leading to narcissistic delusions of omnipotence or world domination, alternating with compensatory paranoia and delusions of persecution, as in the case of John Nash, and Jung to a much lesser extent. Contemporary Jungian analysts, Wieland-Burston (1992) and O'Kane (1994), have both spoken up for these dark or chaotic aspects of the Self as necessary to a dynamic conception of the Self, in its function of transformation and renewal of a stagnant ego stance.

The Western ego is understandably ambivalent about the transformative power of the Self. It knows all too well that transformation works through a partial destruction of what the ego has been. To that aspect of the ego which craves security

343

and order, the dark, chaotic transformations of the Self present occasion for dread and resistance. Nevertheless, the ego also craves stimulation and excitement, and hence is attracted to the dynamic archetypal forces associated with the Self. In earlier times, or in pre-literate cultures, where individual egos were less differentiated from the cultural matrix, chaos was even accepted as the *prima materia* from which all created beings originate, and to which they have naturally to return in death by a cyclic process. In her recent paper, "The Self as Violent Other" (2002, p. 438), Lucy Huskinson reiterates this theme:

> Violence therefore describes the destruction necessary to initiate the vital creative process of individuation, and the Self is "violent" because it is experienced as an overwhelming force that violates the self-containment of the ego, and forces the ego, often against its will, into a new identity.

In a previous paper, "The Trauma Paradox" (1999), I have explored the need for traumatic experience, or at least a traumatic imagination, to help develop a mature ego, capable of creativity, but also capable of developing defenses against possible future outer or inner trauma. In that paper I followed Jung's quote from *Aion* (p. 5):

> It [the ego] seems to arise in the first place from the collision between the somatic factor and the environment, and, once established, it goes on developing from further collisions with the outer world and the inner.

As the history of mankind's experience of an outer divine force, (whether given image as a fierce animal, or projected onto a natural phenomenon such as the sun, the moon, an earthquake, lightning, or a storm, or personified as an omnipotent father or mother) is one of numinous awe, wonder, but also possibly terror, so the inner god-image, the Self, in its many symbolic images, is experienced ambivalently by the ego, as all-loving, all-knowing, all-inspiring, but also as potentially all-destroying.

The opposing concepts, *Logos* and *Eros,* associated by Jung with the alchemical *Sol* and *Luna,* have come to be seen in Jungian tradition as representing two forms of experiencing, imagining, or understanding the world, Logos and Sol more demonstrated in the Western male ego, whereas Eros and Luna are more typical of the female ego. According to this Jungian theory, Eros in men exists unconsciously as a form of experiencing the world from the point of view of a functional complex, the Anima, usually portrayed in dreams as a woman, in compensation for the more conscious Logos ego position. The Animus in women then represents the equivalent uncon-scious Logos function, compensating her more conscious Eros ego perspective. If we recall, however, Jung's statement from *Mysterium Coniunctionis* that the opposites that come together in the coniunctio either confront "one another in enmity" or attract "one another in love," it becomes possible to conceive a dark side to both solar and lunar consciousness that adds back an unconscious and instinctual aspect to both Logos and Eros, an archetypal dimensionality that speaks to the dynamism and complexity of the Self underlying ego consciousness in both sexes.

In my diploma dissertation on the Celtic Masculine (1992), I argued that the concept Logos does not do justice to the image of "confronting one another in enmity" in the *Mysterium* quote above. This aspect of the masculine is better represented by the Greek god, Ares, god of war and aggressive destructive-ness. Jung himself had focused on the masculine's resistance to coniunctio, noting that men and the masculine in both sexes emphasize, rather, *separatio,* with the goal of achieving discrimi-nation, Logos. This, he felt, worked against the feminine goal of union, Eros. Separatio would seem to represent the strivings of the ego, in its goal of self-assertion and self-preservation, as opposed to an Eros that more blindly perpetuates the species through reproduction. This view corresponds to Freud's early view of aggressive impulses, which assimilated Adler's power drive into the "ego instincts." The early Freud, like Jung, leaves me unclear if the ego's will to power in the form of healthy self-assertion involves aggressive impulses that I would call Ares impulses, which include the urge to dominate and destroy the other. It was not until 1920 in *Beyond the Pleasure Principle* that Freud was to formulate a death or destruction instinct (Thanatos) separate from, and in opposition to, his original sexual libido concept (Eros), as underlying the will of the ego and its defenses. In that paper interestingly, Freud made glancing reference to Sabina Spielrein's 1912 paper, "Destruction as a Cause of Coming into Being," where she had postulated a destructive component within the sexual libido itself, not quite the separate instinct that Freud was now postulating.

A detailed study and analysis of the evolution of Freud's concept of aggressiveness and destructiveness can be found in the Appendix to Erich Fromm's *The Anatomy of Human Destructiveness*. (1973) Freud's original dualistic theory of life process as involving a battle between sexual desire (Eros) and the ego instincts was replaced by a second dualism, the battle between Eros and the death instinct. (The word *thanatos* for the death instinct was not used by Freud, but was introduced by Federn.) Unfortunately, according to Fromm, Freud made the death instinct concept

> so broad that as a result every striving which was not subsumed under Eros belonged to the death instinct, and vice versa. In this way aggressiveness, destructiveness, sadism, the drive for control and mastery were, in spite of their qualitative differences, mani-

festations of the same force – the death instinct. (Fromm 1973, p. 499)

I use the term Ares to describe these latter forces. The terms, death instinct and Thanatos, and the related concept, Nirvana principle, all speculate an urge of living organisms to return to an inorganic lifeless state, in opposition to the urge to live, grow, and reproduce (Eros). Thanatos might be reconceived as Ares, extraverted destructiveness, turned back on the self in the form of masochism or suicidal impulses; alternatively, Ares could be considered as redirecting the death instinct outwards towards the other.

In my dissertation, I offered a model of the Self that involved four overlapping archetypal aspects, *Logos, Mythos, Ares* and *Eros,* diagrammed as in Figure I.

This model permits a differentiation of types of coniunctio that moves well beyond the single coniunctio model (Logos-Eros in Jung, Eros-Thanatos in Freud) that the first depth psychologists had constructed. My model has as dynamic possibilities involving a play of opposites six, not one, possible coniunctios: Logos-Mythos, Logos-Eros, Logos-Ares, Mythos-Ares, Mythos-Eros, and Eros-Ares. For this reason, I believe it is a more comprehensive model. The diagram shows four quadrants, two upper, and two lower, corresponding to the spiritual and chthonic poles (Jung's "ultra-violet and infrared") of archetypal structure, and two left and right quadrants, corresponding to a 'masculine,' or left brain, bias and a 'feminine,' or right brain, bias. The Chthonic pole represents a grounded biological foundation to archetypal structure, and includes bodily instincts, emotions and sensations, while the Spiritual pole represents the realm of archetypal images, symbols and ideas, which impact on the human imagination with numinous power. The Chthonic and Spiritual realms overlap. Just as physical energy is bound within matter, so the psychic Chthonic

347

## Model of the Self

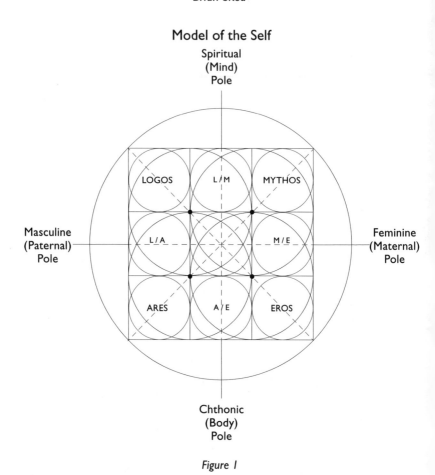

*Figure 1*

realm contains within it a Spiritual realm, though bound and embodied. Though partly spiritual, Eros and Ares are considered as archetypes residing mainly within the Chthonic realm. Likewise, Mythos and Logos are considered as residing within the Spiritual realm, with overlap into the Chthonic realm.

*Logos* represents the principle of universal order governing the world; the dynamic power of words, mathematics, thought and reason; the scientific perspective on the world; a theoretical, cognitive understanding of it. At the level of the Self, Logos is a numinous but nevertheless unconscious force. Integrated into ego consciousness, Logos represents Jung's solar rational consciousness.

*Mythos* provides the principle of spiritual connection and meaning, an intuitive and imaginative mythological belief system, conditioned by numinous archetypal images and symbols, which helps explain the origin and destiny of human culture. Mythos represents the spiritual aspect of Neumann's lunar matriarchal consciousness. Mythos is also expressed in music, art and dance. In addition, Mythos also represents the realm of dreams and fantasy; the mode of cognition in early childhood, where the undeveloped ego utilizes magical rather than rational thinking; the hypothesized realm of reasoning in primitive cultures, past or present, where individual logical ego consciousness is not developed, but is expressed in collective religious myths and folktales; and the realm of regressed ideation and imagery found in psychotic process.

*Eros* represents the principle of psychic relatedness, love, sexual attraction and attractiveness. Eros is the embodied chthonic aspect of matriarchal consciousness. At a biological level, Eros is the deep driving force behind sexual reproduction, needed to perpetuate the species. Eros is also the urge behind the nurturing instinct, required for parental care of children. Culturally (when integrated into collective consciousness) Eros extends to the nurturing crafts of agriculture and the raising of animals for food, and the cooking processes. I could have named this aspect of the Self Aphrodite, since she, as companionate mother to Eros, sometimes presented in mythology as her son, represents a similar function, but I chose the masculine image to avoid falling into the Jungian habit of viewing Eros as feminine, since there is a masculine Eros as well.

349

*Ares* is the embodiment of aggression, the god of war, thriving on conflict, rejoicing in the joy of battle victory, overcoming the fear of death and defeat; but also the restless and turbulent lover. At a deep biological level, Ares represents the aggressive energy required for the preservation of self, for the survival of the fittest in the face of competing members of the same or other species. In another sense, however, 'phallic' aggression is being described here, required for both lovemaking and warfare. Hence it plays a part in the reproduction of the species as well as the survival of the individual. Where Eros can be seen as Master of Life, Ares can be seen as Master of Death, in the ongoing evolutionary struggle for survival. Ares is the driving force behind the impulse to hunt animals for food, and hence behind the invention of weapons, which (when integrated in cultural consciousness) evolved into the technology of warfare. It is interesting that in Greek mythology the union between Ares and Aphrodite created four children: three sons – Phobos (fear), Deimos (terror), and in some versions, Eros – and a daughter, Harmonia (concord), revealing both the negative and positive consequences of such a union.

A main feature of this model is overlap between the four archetypal aspects of the Self, since their separate identity is an imagined fantasy. Only one small circle in each realm denotes the 'pure' experience of Logos, Eros, Mythos, or Ares. The central circle denotes maximum overlap or fusion between the aspects, while the four circles referring to Logos/Mythos (L/M), Mythos/Eros (M/E), Ares/Eros (A/E), and Logos/Ares (L/A) denote hybrid dynamics created by adjacent coniunctios.

Although this model does not pretend to completely circumscribe all the possible aspects of the Self, the model attempts to imply the totality of our experience of the Self as both unity *and* multiplicity; static order *and* potential creative (or chaotic) dynamism. Pointing to major archetypal dynamisms underlying the ego, this complex model of the Self's dynamics offers the ego a potential multiplicity of ways of unifying its consciousness. This complexity has its shadow side. The ability of the ego to align itself with different aspects of the Self may be helpful in different situations confronting the ego, but a multiplicity of extremely dissociated ego-states, as seen in Dissociative Identity Disorder (Multiple Personality Disorder), risk ego confusion and disorientation. (Noll 1989, but see Noll 1993, where he retracts his earlier views; Skea 1995; Curran 1998; Everest 1999) Schizophrenia is an even more drastic ego fragmentation and disintegration, with regressive introversion into the dynamic, but potentially chaotic, realm of the Self.

From the point of view of a valuing ego, each of these aspects of the Self can be experienced either positively or negatively. That is, each aspect has a shadow side. What I mean here is that, because the four aspects of Self-experience that I call Logos, Mythos, Eros, and Ares are archetypal, they are numinous from the point of view of an experiencing ego. That is, these states are either overwhelmingly attractive or frightening or repulsive to the limited ego position. Attraction to one or more aspects of the Self may lead to an over identification with those aspects, and even to the inflation of the ego by one or another aspect taken to an extreme.

Over identification with one aspect tends to lead to repression or dissociation of the compensatory remaining aspects of the Self, which normally would be available to help the ego maintain balance and some sense of objectivity with respect to how the energies of the Self are used. At the same time, the inflation of the ego by an aspect of the Self risks the possible overpowering of the ego as a center of conscious identity and action. Such overpowering may be experienced positively as euphoric and oceanic, including potentially creative imagery and ideation. But the lack of a stable ego point of reference leads inevitably to terror and confusion, and the Self may now flood an overwhelmed ego with destructive imagery. If the ego can emerge intact from such an experience, it may be strengthened and creatively stimulated. Lesser mortals with defensive egos that know their limits are more likely to fear and reject the possibility of over identifying with one or more aspects of the Self. This, however, may result in an alienated and impoverished ego, cut off from the potentially creative (even if also potentially destructive) energies of the Self.

The human ego has also the capacity to imagine itself as either subject or object, as 'mover' or as 'moved,' in relation to an 'other,' whether that other is an outer person or an inner aspect of the Self. Especially in the realms of Ares and Eros, it is possible for the ego to imagine itself either as aggressor or as the aggressed against, as lover or as the beloved. To have no capacity to identify with the aggressor and be able to own aggression may lead to fear of aggression, either from a real outer aggressive threat, or else from a split-off, intrapsychic Ares aspect of the Self (as in Kalsched's [1996] inner persecution system), or from that aspect projected out into the world (paranoia). Reaction may involve flight or "freeze" responses, rather than the affect of fight, which is the capacity to respond with appropriate defensive aggression. To freeze, which might represent dissociative flight, sets the victim up for further aggression, which may appear from the outside as masochistic repetition compulsion. Alternatively, an ego unable to identify with the victim of aggression, the persecuted, rather than the persecutor, may lead to entitled narcissism, and even to uninhibited violence and sadism, with no sense of remorse. Through unconscious compensation, a manifestation of the Self may come to persecute such an ego intrapsychically, via nightmares or frightening hallucinations.

In the realm of Eros, an ego deprived of outer love may not be able to access the Eros aspect of the Self, which can lead to chronic feelings of having been abandoned, of being unloved or unlovable. Or an Eros-deprived ego may exhibit an insatiable longing for love, exhibiting dependency, neediness or entitlement. Overexposing an ego to Eros, on the other hand, by smothering overprotective mothering, or by premature seduction by an adult in childhood, may lead to either a promiscuous Eros identification in adulthood or a phobic response to any erotic approach that might threaten the integrity of a vulnerable unstable ego.

In summary, the coniunctio of Ares and Eros better describes the *Mysterium* quote, "confronting one another in enmity, or attracting one another in love" than the more usual Jungian coniunctio, Logos and Eros. Similarly, the pairing, Logos and Mythos, better describes the two kinds of thinking – directed and fantasy thinking – with which Jung began his classic text, *Wandlungen und Symbole der Libido*, than does the classical Logos and Eros pairing. Ares of course represents that aspect of the Self most likely to be seen as destructive, from the point of view of the ego, because of its aggressive potential. More positively, however, especially when associated with Logos *(L/A),* it represents the Western ego asserting its individualistic heroic will on behalf of 'progress,' against more conservative forces of Nature and community, which seek to preserve a homeostatic status quo and which are often informed by, and more comfortable with a Mythos/Eros pattern of coniunctio of keeping the world together.

Logos would seem to represent that aspect of the Self most attractive to the Western ego, with its post-Enlightenment interest in rationality and order. However, the tendency of Logos towards abstraction may lead the ego to distance itself from the emotional life of the body (Eros and Ares*)* and from a

353

sustaining spiritual life (Mythos), leading to a false and ultimately alienating objectivity. Mythos is perennially attractive but also threatening to the Western ego, because of its irrational but intuitive and mystical call to transcendence, which challenges the Logos call to scientific rationalism. But the ego's identification with Mythos carries a particular risk of inflation, because of the latter's tendency to escape the confining but grounding sensations and emotions of the body (Ares + Eros), not to mention the reassuring logic of Logos. Eros is also attractive because of the pleasant aspects of "falling in love," which is often experienced as the merging with one's soul mate, dissolving the loneliness of the isolated ego, and offering the possibility of release of sexual tension in intercourse. Eros is also threatening to the integrity of the ego, however, just because of its call to dissolve ego boundaries in the love embrace. Practically speaking, each of these aspects of the Self, developed in moderation and balanced by the other three aspects, represents positive qualities the ego may identify with. It is over identification with one aspect, combined with under identification with the other three, via repression or dissociation, that leads to sterile rigidity and a restriction of the ego's capacity to represent in consciousness all aspects of the four-fold Self.

Finally, it should be mentioned that this model of the Self contains within it the potential for differentiation of the classic Jungian functional archetypal complexes, Persona, Shadow, Animus and Anima. For example, a male ego, identified at the Persona level with one aspect of the Self, say, Logos, may experience Mythos or Ares as Shadow, and Eros as Anima. But the model attempts to transcend the gender stereotypes invoked by the classical Jungian model. So, Eros, as a male god, could be shadow for a male ego, and Ares may for some men be an Anima image (associated, perhaps, with images of the Terrible Mother or the Amazon). In addition, Jung's four types of con-

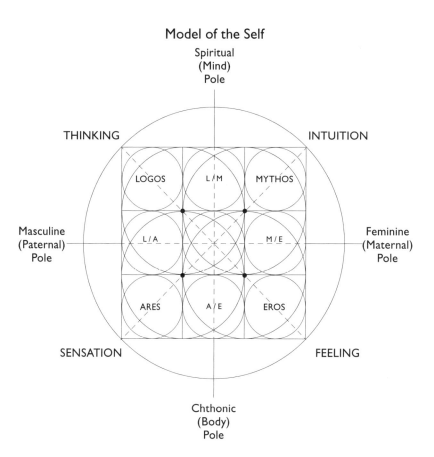

*Figure II: Jung's Psychological Types*

sciousness, thinking, feeling, sensation and intuition, can also be superimposed on this model, as shown on Figure II.

*Jung, Spielrein and Nash: Beautiful Minds in Peril*

Each of these three individuals experienced ego regression into the realm of the Self, an encounter with both creative and destructive consequences. All three have been described at one time or another as having experienced one or more breakdowns of psychotic proportions. Two – Spielrein and Nash – were hospitalized. The third, Jung, was a psychiatrist who encountered his own woundedness in what Ellenberger has called a "creative illness." (Ellenberger 1970) A study of their respective childhoods reveals a common tendency towards introversion and a rich fantasy life, implying that each, early on, developed an ego oriented to images from the Self rather than to an outer five sensory world of family, friends or work. It is not clear to what extent heredity plays a role in predestining such ego fragility. A genetic predisposition has been demonstrated most clearly in schizophrenia, more than in all of the other mental illnesses, although there is also compelling evidence for genetic predisposition to depression and to bipolar illness. Other, environmental factors, however, notably childhood developmental aberrations, are important in precipitating these disorders.

Trauma related to physical or sexual abuse, neglect, deprivation or loss of a parent or sibling plays a role in the development of an ego prone to dissociation or fragmentation and in stimulating regressive fantasy at the level of the Self. Such fantasy, Jungian analysis has demonstrated, can be both restorative (for example, mandala images) and further traumatizing (for instance, images of world destruction, or the inner persecuting 'alters' that Kalsched (1996), has described. The earlier the trauma occurs in childhood, the more vulnerable the developing ego will be to dissociation and fragmentation. The attachment context before and after the trauma has much to do with whether ego restabilization is helped or hindered after a traumatic experience. By 'attachment context' I mean both the security of the attachments to parental figures, both before and after the trauma, as well as the opportunities for processing the trauma afterwards, verbally or in play, in a relatively secure space. The social context may of course also be a traumatic factor, for example, the impact of war, famine, epidemic, natural disaster or poverty. The developmental histories of Jung, Spielrein and Nash all show some degree of trauma, either in their own childhoods, or else in their extended family backgrounds, which could have contributed to the predisposition of their 'beautiful minds' to psychotic breakdown, and also to the potential resiliency they were able to summon to overcome it.

## Jung

The history of Jung's psychological problems, including constitutional factors related to his family background, have been explored elsewhere. (*MDR*, Kerr 1993, Skea 1995, Kutek 2000) Winnicott (1964) has gone so far as to suggest that Jung suffered from schizophrenia during childhood, from which he recovered. I have argued (1995) that some form of post-traumatic or dissociative disorder is more likely. There is evidence of family psychopathology most clearly on Jung's mother's side, including his maternal grandfather, Samuel Preiswerk, his cousin, Helene Preiswerk, and his mother, Emilie.

On his mother's side, the Preiswerks, there was a long line of Protestant pastors, leading to Jung's grandfather, Samuel Preiswerk, also a pastor, who was an occultist with many eccentric beliefs and behaviors. Jung's mother, Emilie, was the youngest of thirteen children. She married Paul Jung, a pastor with a PhD in Oriental Studies, who was also the youngest of thirteen children sired by Jung's grandfather, Carl Gustav Jung, a medical professor who was himself the son of a physician. Three of Jung's uncles were pastors. There is no evidence of major mental illness in Jung's ancestral family background. Jung's mother Emilie was, like her father, interested in the occult. Together with the adolescent Jung, she attended séances, sometimes involving Jung's younger cousin, Helene, who was considered a talented medium. Jung's study of her became his medical dissertation, *On the Psychology and Pathology of So-Called Occult Phenomena*. He described her dissociated states from a pathological perspective as hysterical. From the vantage of present-day clinical understanding, there is evidence of a dissociative post-traumatic reaction to abuse from her father, as well as acting out within a positive transference towards Jung. (Goodheart 1984; Skea 1995)

The accounts in *MDR* provide hints of the family atmosphere. For Jung's parents there was financial hardship. Being the youngest of large prestigious families left them with aspirations but few resources. Jung's father never pursued an academic career beyond his PhD and ended up a poor pastor, which was somewhat of an embarrassment to both Jung and his mother. Jung's mother lost her firstborn son, Paul, at birth, two years before Carl was born. Her depressive breakdown and hospitalization when Jung was three must have been hard on the young boy. On return home she continued to be unpredictable with mood swings and was constantly in argument with Jung's father, who became progressively depressed until his premature death when Jung was in college. Though Jung felt close to his father in early childhood, he became increasingly disappointed in him in adolescence.

The traumatic aspect of Jung's childhood, I suspect, involved his witnessing his parents' constant quarreling and personal unhappiness, his mother's irrational moods, his sense of abandonment during her hospitalization, and finally his father's loss of faith in God. It is likely that all this led to deeply ambivalent feelings about his parents, between love and respect on the one hand and mistrust, fear and revulsion on the other hand. These ambivalent feelings extended to his religious imagination in childhood, for example, his conception of Jesus and of God himself. From the material recorded in *MDR,* we know that Jung struggled with his conflictual image of a loving Jesus devouring his "chicks" in a childhood prayer, his terror in reaction to his dream of an underground phallus (the "Man-Eater"), and his fear and shame in daring to acknowledge his dream in which the so-called all-loving God of Christianity was shitting on and destroying his cathedral. These images, from a clinical stand-point, reveal Jung's tendency to dissociate, project and deny his own infantile destructive rage. Images of himself as either omnipotent or impotent, as the creator/destroyer or the victim, continued throughout his childhood, for example, his building of castles of stones by the lakeshore, followed by their destruc-tion in "earthquakes" by his own hand, his miraculous recovery from a math-related school phobia, or his romantic fantasy of his No. 2 personality as a seventeenth century nobleman ver-sus the reality of No. 1, the poor parson's son. His ambitious strivings, encouraged by his mother, took the upper hand in late adolescence as he watched his father's crumbling faith and death. "He died in time for you" was his mother's comment, as he moved at age twenty-one into his father's room.

We have little information on Jung's psychosexual history. I sense no erotic attraction to his mother in early childhood. He does, however, mention an attraction to a young nurse who cared for him during his mother's hospitalization. We know nothing of masturbatory fantasies. He was shocked at the birth of a sister when he was nine, since his parents slept in separate rooms, implying that he did know how babies are conceived but had no image of the loving intercourse of the parental couple.

In adolescence he had a crush on a young peasant girl, but this seems very superficial and intellectualized. He confessed in a letter to Freud (McGuire 1974, 49J, p. 95) that a friend of his father's, whom he idealized, had molested him in some way when he was young, but of this (except for Jolande Jacobi's later assertion that this occurred when Jung was eighteen [Hayman 1999, p. 20]) we have no details. His relationship with his cousin, Hélène, mentioned above, shows unconscious erotic undertones on both sides not recognized by Jung at the time. We do not know if Jung had sexual relations with a woman before his marriage to Emma when he was twenty-eight.

As Jung moved into adult life, first as a medical student, then as an intern and researcher at the Burghölzli, he emerged as a capable and ambitious psychiatrist. He married Emma, the daughter of a wealthy family, with whom he fathered five children. Throughout most of his adult life, she remained his faithful companion and supporter, until her death in 1955, six years before his own. Emma, who also became an analyst, published papers on the animus and anima (1957) and the Grail legend (1986). Her financial wealth also enabled them to live very comfortably in the large house they built by the lake of Zurich and permitted Jung to give up his post at the hospital and university to devote his time to writing and private practice. No particular psychopathology is evident during these years, until mid-life, when he experienced the breakdown of his seven year relationship with Freud and the Psychoanalytic Movement, and the ensuing period of psychological disorientation that included a creative block and a series of extremely traumatic visions and anxieties, such as those described in his "Confrontation with the Unconscious" chapter of *MDR* and the ghostly visitations that led to his writing *VII Sermones ad Mortuos* (1916/1967).

Jung's supposed mid-life breakdown (1913-17) is described both in the 1925 seminar (Jung, 1989b) and in *MDR*, in the chapter, "Confrontation with the Unconscious." In the former, Jung stated, "I had the feeling that I was an over-compensated psychosis." (Jung 1961/1963, p. 44) In the latter, Jung said that after the break with Freud he was in a "state of disorientation," that he felt "totally suspended in mid-air." (Jung 1989b, p. 170) He had explained the myths of peoples of the past, he had written a book about the hero (*Wandlungen*) but he asked himself "What is my myth? ... At this point the dialogue with myself became uncomfortable, and I stopped thinking. I had reached a dead end." (Jung 1961/1963, p. 171) He had various disturbing dreams at this time, but they "could not help me over my feeling of disorientation.... At times this became so strong that I suspected there was some psychic disturbance in myself." (*Ibid.*, p. 173) After considerable reflection on his life, with particular attention to childhood memories, looking for a cause of his disturbance, Jung found nothing that satisfied him, so he "consciously submitted himself to the impulses of the unconscious." (*Idem.*) In the autumn of 1913 he had a set of dreams and visions that led him to the conclusion that he was "menaced by a psychosis." (*Ibid.*, p. 176) Dreams of corpses coming to life signaled the arousing of archetypal images in his unconscious. Then a recurrent vision of a giant flood, yellow waves, rubble and drowned bodies, turning to blood, covering northern Europe, and reaching up to the mountains of Switzerland, was interpreted by Jung as an imminent psychosis. Only later did he link these visions to the cultural and political situation in Europe that led to the outbreak of World War I in 1914. Jung fought to maintain his sanity, first by going back to his childhood game of creating buildings out of stones he found by the lake, then by writing down his fantasies and illustrating them with drawings, images representing emotions, often in the form of mandalas. One vivid dream portrayed himself in league with a primitive shadow figure (a brown-skinned savage) ambushing and killing the Germanic hero, Siegfried, an act that filled Jung with disgust and remorse. On waking, resisting the impulse to shoot himself lest he lose control of his violent impulses, Jung forced himself to understand his dream. He could see that Siegfried represented not only his own heroic ego's tendency to impose its will on others, but also the warlike impulse that was currently seizing Germany, and that this impulse had to die. Working out this problem led him to allow himself a more controlled egocide, by slipping down daily into fantasy, into the archetypal realm of the Self. In this world he imagined conversations with personified archetypes: Elijah, the wise old prophet, representing Logos in my model of the Self; a young blind girl, Salome, the prototype for Jung's anima, representing Eros; a large black snake, representing the shadow side of the hero archetype (Ares in my model of the Self); and the winged Gnostic pagan, Philemon, representing Mythos, who emerged as Jung's guru, or 'psychagogue' over the next few years. Philemon was later relativized by a figure that Jung simply called Ka, after the ancient Egyptian king's embodied soul, a "spirit of nature like the Anthroparion of Greek alchemy." This is shown in Figure III.

Towards the end of the First World War Jung gradually emerged from this period of "darkness." He had essentially given up teaching, reading or writing scientific work for three years. He now regarded the written fantasies and collection of drawn mandalas that he had accumulated as a set of "cryptograms concerning the state of the self." A woman colleague was encouraging Jung in her letters to consider this material as art.[8] Jung, however, rejected this "seductive voice of the anima," instead seeing the psychological importance of the material as representing his discovery of the necessity for himself as depth psychologist to abandon the superordinate position of the ego, in order to allow a process of circumambulation of the Self that he named individuation. This chapter of *MDR* in which these

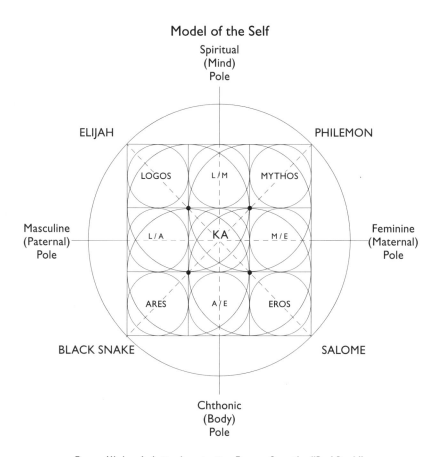

Figure III: Jung's Active Imagination Figures from the "Red Book"

reflections are recorded ends with him saying, "The years when I was pursuing my inner images were the most important in my life – in them everything essential was decided.... It was the *prima materia* for a lifetime's work." (Jung 1961/1963, p. 199)

Ellenberger (1970) has described this as a period of "creative illness," in analogy to the formation of a shaman's identity as a healer, by experiencing both breakdown and healing following a traumatic event. Jung himself said that his differences with Freud both led to their split and to his determination to become another sort of healer. Freud was phobic about spirituality, the realm of Mythos, except for the Oedipus myth, instead insisting that Eros (sexuality, taken in Freud's writings from a Logos perspective) underlies all human psychology. Only after the break with Jung did Freud add Thanatos (Ares in my model). Jung, on the other hand, saw a Logos of Mythos as equally fundamental as a Logos of Eros or Thanatos. However, neither in the 1925 seminar nor in *MDR* did Jung speak of the impact of the loss of Freud's personal friendship on his breakdown. Nor did he speak of the loss of his intimate relationship with Sabina Spielrein, or voice any sense of betrayal by her going over to Freud's camp. It has to be admitted that others have made more of these events than Jung did, and there is a lingering feeling that Jung handled them by an inner withdrawal that minimized their importance to him.

We will look shortly at Jung's relationship with Sabina Spielrein, in the years after her hospitalization in 1904-5, when Jung continued his relationship with her, as part intimate friend, part informal outpatient therapist, and part mentor of her medical school dissertation and "Destruction" paper. This ambiguous situation was complicated by an intensely enacted transference/countertransference that Sabina interpreted as their falling in love, as revealed in her journal, and in their letters, to each other, and to and from Freud. (Carotenuto 1982; Kerr 1993; Wharton 2001; *Freud/Jung Letters* 1974; Lothane 1996, 1999; Covington and Wharton 2003) After their "love affair" was exposed in 1909, Jung became more conventionally professional, and their relationship became platonic and collegial, especially by 1911, when Jung had become involved with Toni Wolff, and Sabina had affiliated with Freud's group in Vienna.

It is unclear to me why Jung minimized Spielrein's theoretical contribution in *Wandlungen,* not mentioning her "Destruction" article in that or any subsequent edition (*Symbols of Transformation*). He may have seen her contribution as derivative to his, but, in my opinion, this is perhaps the most telling evidence that Jung downplayed the destructive aspect of the coniunctio. Jung also could not fully confess to Freud his own role in the breakdown of his intimate relationship with Sabina; he blamed the erotic nature of their relationship on her transference to him, rather than it being a mutual attraction, or at least one in which his own positive countertransference was stirred. And he could not mention to Freud how quickly he had replaced Sabina, as early as 1911, with Toni Wolff, his new protégé. Nor does Jung admit in these recorded reminiscences available to us how much impact Toni, and the marital situation that ensued with her arrival on the scene, played in the development of his mid-life breakdown and subsequent creative recovery from it.

In Jung's relation to Spielrein and Wolff, many, including myself, have found evidence of some narcissistic character formation, of the kind not uncommon in celebrity geniuses, involving omnipotence, entitlement, manipulation and using of others, lacunae of both empathy and guilt, and repressing or dissociating feelings of impotence and destructive rage. (Austin 1999; von Raffay 2000; Colman 2002) Despite his claimed preference for an introverted life, Jung clearly derived self-esteem from the love and admiration of others. It has been pointed out by other analytical psychologists, who have critically addressed the quality of his relatedness, that Jung was prone to over idealize at the start of an intimate relationship, followed later in the relationship by disillusionment and feelings of betrayal and abandonment, especially following the wounding of his narcissistic pride. (Satinover 1985; Douglas 1993)

## Sabina Spielrein

Sabina Spielrein's hospital record at the Burghölzli (1904-1905; Steffens 2001) reveals a formal diagnosis of hysteria, which was seen as constitutional, in that many of her relatives, her brothers, both parents, and their families, were also judged as hysterical.

Hysterical traits in the Spielrein family included her father's violent outbursts and suicidal threats, her mother's obsessive compulsiveness (shopaholism), and her brothers' various tics, fits of weeping, anger outbursts, melancholia and masochism. Sabina herself on admission displayed many of these family traits, and many more, including delusions and hallucinations, wild mood changes between laughter and crying, involuntary movements of her tongue, head and legs, many somatic complaints, and suicidal ideation and threats. She showed deep ambivalence about her father in particular, related to memories and fantasies of sexual excitement during masturbation, combined with disgust and revulsion, stimulated by being spanked by him on her bare buttocks as a child and young adolescent. In earlier childhood she had tried to restrict bowel movement by pressing her heel against her anus. Jung and Freud both saw this as anal eroticism, and Freud anticipated that this would lead to an obsessive-compulsive character in adulthood, which may in fact be true of her later years, although a hysterical or cyclothymic character style was more evident in the period Jung knew her. We have minimal information on her personality style during the years spent in Russia, from 1923 to her death in 1942.

Not all of Sabina's ancestors were what were called at the beginning of the twentieth century hysterics. In her diary (Carotenuto 1992, p. 21-23) she described her maternal grandfather and great-grandfather as highly honored rabbis. Her grandfather as a young man fell in love with a Christian woman, but his father prohibited their relating, and selected a suitable Jewish woman for him to marry, Sabina's grandmother. Sabina's mother, the only daughter, was her grandfather's favorite, was sent to university, even to study the "Christian sciences." She became a dentist. She too struggled to find the right person to marry. She became engaged to her first love, but his parents disapproved of her, causing him to "hurt her with his ridiculous suspicions," which led her to angrily break off relations with him, "not wanting to be his relatives' plaything." Another man fell in love with her, but he was a Christian. She said "she would never marry a Christian, because that would destroy her parents." The next day he shot himself. Sabina's father was then presented to her mother by Sabina's grandmother. Like Sabina's grandfather, her mother accepted the arranged marriage. Sabina's mother turned to affairs with other men throughout her marriage.

In writing about her case, Jung uses most frequently the term 'psychotic hysteria.' Others who have reviewed the material reach various diagnoses. Carotenuto surprisingly judged her breakdown as "a genuine schizophrenic episode" (1982, p. 144) despite his acknowledgement of her consistent ability to observe and reflect on her delusions and hallucinations, an ego capacity not usually seen in schizophrenia. In the foreword to Carotenuto's book, Bettelheim (p. xvi) postulated "either a schizophrenic disturbance or severe hysteria with schizoid features." Minder, who had access to the medical records (2001, p. 51-53), noted the presence of "borderline paranoid states" but that "a true symptomatology of psychosis is not present ... pronounced disturbances of affectivity ... depressive episodes ... masochistic features ... anxiety attacks ... physical complaints.... negativistic infantile behavior" which led him to confirm the diagnosis of hysteria. He felt that her symptoms had their roots in childhood traumas connected with her parents' violence. (p. 54) He added, "It seems highly astonishing to me that incest was never brought into the discussion, either by Jung, or later by Freud." There is no mention of a physical examination in the records. Hoffer (2001, p. 123) concluded, "It is my impression that if she was admitted to an American hospital today, she would be diagnosed as a young woman in an adolescent turmoil, not psychotic, but probably suffering from a borderline personality disorder." While I can empathize with this last impression, I feel that, while such an adolescent's behavior resembles BPD, especially the transient psychotic states, acting out, suicidal ideation, anger, mood swings, and identity confusion, it was not yet firmly established in her as an ongoing personality style. She had performed well at school throughout this time, received the gold medal, and had the goal of becoming a medical doctor – which in fact she became, and her identity and commitment in that role remained consistent.

Today she might be diagnosed as having had some form of dissociative or post-traumatic disorder. My own study of Spielrein's diary and letters in the years subsequent to her hospitalization reveals both hysterical and cyclothymic features, pointing to both bipolar disorder and dissociative disorder. Certainly the reality of dissociated identity states is attested to in her conversations with various component parts, some positive, like her guardian angel, some pathetic like her "damp poodle," and some fearsome, like the wolf-like face she encounters in the mirror. (Carotenuto 1982, p. 19)

It is not clear to me what finally precipitated Sabina's breakdown at eighteen, leading to her hospitalization at the Burghölzli. In the article where he first outlined her case ("The Freudian Theory of Hysteria," 1908/1961), Jung suggested that it was caused by the conflict between her normal adolescent erotic strivings towards young men, her teacher, for example, and the revulsion aroused by associated memories of anal-eroticism in relation to her father's spanking her.

Up to adolescence Sabina masturbated to fantasies of her father hitting her or her brothers. At fourteen, her six-year-old sister died from typhoid, and Sabina retreated from friend-ships into a depressive isolation. In mid adolescence, however, it seems that Sabina started to show an interest in men, beyond the "painful love" she felt for her father, as she began to emerge from her depression. She fell in love with her history teacher, after initially feeling a deep revulsion.

> … my eagerness for knowledge opens up a whole new world, and simultaneously my crush on the man who opened up to me previously unknown vistas grows by leaps and bounds. I want to make some sacrifice for him, I want to suffer for him. (Carotenuto 1982, p. 25)

She invited him to her house, where she wanted to be alone with him, but at the same time was afraid to not include her mother. In time she became bored with him, at which he switched his attention to her mother. "He had come to love her, too, and when she left for Paris, he jumped out of a window, intending to take his own life. He was diagnosed as suffering from Dementia Praecox." (*Ibid.,* p. 26) Sabina switched her infatuation to her uncle Adolf, who also finally fell in love with her mother. In 1910, when Sabina wrote this history, she had been studying Jung's "Significance of the Father" (1909/1949) essay, and clearly saw these relationships, as well as her infatua-tion with Jung, as examples of 'father-transference.'

When Jung met her at the Burghölzli as an inpatient in 1904, he focused exclusively on her neurotic symptoms of anal eroti-cism, which receded quickly after their long sessions together. At least, that is how he presented her case in 1907 (published in 1908) when he was still considerably influenced by Freud's psychoanalytic theory and method. In that report, although he diagnosed her case as "psychotic hysteria," he did not outline the psychotic symptoms, delusional states, and hallucinations that are recorded in her medical record. (Steffens 2001, p. 15-42) Jung's treatment must have had an effect, however, for these symptoms abated and she was discharged within a year, and enrolled as a medical student. Though Jung was aware that Sabina had fallen in love with him, and considered transferring her case to Freud (Report of 9/25/05, *Ibid.*, p. 67-72), nevertheless he continued to see her informally on an outpatient basis. Although the success of her inpatient therapy represented to Jung a classic Freudian father-transference cure, it has to be pointed out that it was also due to the way that Bleuler ran the Burghölzli, as a therapeutic community, and to this authoritative psychiatrist's ability to block the intrusive, incestuous, and regressive influence of her parents. At the Burghölzli, patients with gifts like Sabina's were encouraged to work, do research (such as helping administer the word association test), and even enroll as medical students, and go on to become psychiatrists.

Spielrein began her medical dissertation, "On the Psychological Content of a Case of Schizophrenia (Dementia Praecox)" (1911), based on her work with a schizophrenic woman, Frau M, much in the style of Jung's study of B in his "Psychology of Dementia Praecox" (1907/1960). At that time Jung and his colleagues at the Burghölzli were attempting to apply psychoanalytic concepts to the content of schizophrenic delusions, with the help of the word association test. Although erotic complexes were found, much else was discovered, which could not be so easily linked to Freud's theory of libido and his hypothesis that psychosis is the result of withdrawal of libido from objects, but which more resembled the fantasy thinking found in dreams, myths, poetry, alchemy, and "folk superstition," suggesting an intensified cathexis of the inner world. Jung and Spielrein recognized their own fantasies and dreams as resembling such psychotic thought, leading them both to postulate a layer of universal archaic mythological thinking that resides in everyone, accessed in states of profound introversion. In her dissertation, Spielrein called it the "species-psyche," as against the "ego-psyche;" Jung would later call it the "collective unconscious." In the face of conflict at the level of the personal ego (or because of a constitutional fragility in that ego) the psychotic person regresses to a collective level, relating to the world, not from an "I" perspective, but from a "We" or even a "They" perspective. While this dissolving of ego responsibility for feelings and action may be pleasurably oceanic to one aspect of the ego, from another aspect, that of the ego's sense of responsibility and agency, the dissolution is experienced as death or dismemberment. Spielrein spoke of how her patient used psychosis, from which she apparently did not recover, to avoid facing the ego task of divorcing her abusive and philandering husband. Like Jung, Spielrein saw the layer of psyche to which her patient had regressed, as in itself valid, the source of creative transformation, and hence as potentially positive to the ego of someone recovering from delusional thinking. In *Wandlungen*, Jung quotes Spielrein's dissertation:

> Thus a symbol seems to me to owe its origin to the striving of a complex for dissolution in the common totality of thought ... The complex is thus robbed of its personal quality.... This tendency towards dissolution or transformation of every individual complex is the mainspring of poetry, painting, and every form of art. (Spielrein 1911, quoted in Jung 1912. For Hinkle's translation, see 1916/1991, par. 234, p. 137)

Both Jung and Spielrein recognized that 'falling in love,' especially from their own recent experience, also resembled a psychotic episode, in which the ego gives itself up to the Eros and Mythos aspects of the Self. But there had also been a scene, early in 1909, involving the constellation of Ares, including an

371

encounter between them in his consulting room involving a knife, and the drawing of blood, Jung's, when he took the knife away from her. (Hayman 1999, p. 206) It is not clear whether Sabina was intending to stab Jung, or herself in his presence. This was followed by Jung turning eventually to Freud for moral support, and the hot transference/countertransference relationship was sublimated into Logos: Jung's connection with Spielrein became that of a collegial relationship, discussing and editing their respective papers for the *Jahrbuch*.

Spielrein had worked on her ideas about a death or destructive instinct as early as 1906 or 1907 (Spielrein 1906/1907, p. 155-171), mentioned these in a letter to Freud in 1909 (Carotenuto 1982, p. 108), discussed them with Jung (Diary, Sept., Oct. 1910 [Carotenuto 1982, p. 20, 29]) and referred to them in her medical dissertation (the case study of a schizophrenic), published in the 1911, Part 1 edition of the *Jahrbuch*. She first became concerned about Jung plagiarizing her ideas as early as 1910 (Diary, Nov 26, 1910), but her concern heightened in the summer of 1911, when she sent Jung a final draft of her "Destruction" paper to edit. Jung made various reassuring comments as to her ideas being prior to his (letter of 8/8/11, Wharton 2001), though he had not yet finished reading the draft. That was just before the Weimar Congress in September, 1911, which Jung was organizing. Spielrein was due to present her medical dissertation (the case study of a schizophrenic) but at the last minute did not attend, due to psychosomatic pain in her feet, much to Jung's disapproval. (See letter of 9/21/11.) However, Jung did hand out copies at the conference. It is not clear what the true reasons for her non-attendance might have been.

Jung sent back Spielrein's "Destruction" draft in November, 1911, having still not finished reading it; she needed it for her presentation to Freud and his group in Vienna. (Nov. 26, 1911)

Jung promised to make reference to her new paper in his *Wand-lungen, Part II*, which he was still finishing. He never did, nor did he refer to it in subsequent editions, including the considerably rewritten 1952 edition, *Symbols of Transformation*. In that edition, in the chapter entitled "The Dual Mother," Jung made a single reference to Spielrein's idea of the death instinct, but not to her seminal paper putting forth this idea. He was describing mythological symbols of "the Terrible Mother who devours and destroys, and thus symbolizes death itself" and appended the following footnote:

> This fact led my pupil Dr. Spielrein to develop her idea of the death-instinct, which was then taken up by Freud. In my opinion it is not so much a question of a death-instinct as of that "other" instinct (Goethe) which signifies spiritual life. (Jung 1952/1967, p. 328 n. 38)

Jung is presumably talking here of regressive introversion of libido from the world, which can end in destructive psychosis or be transformed in a sublimated artistic or spiritual form.

In December 1911, Jung responded to Spielrein's being downcast at the delay in publication of her "Destruction" paper. She had hoped it would be printed in the 1911, Part 2, issue of the *Jahrbuch* (which was not in fact published until March, 1912). Jung heartily congratulated her on the success of her presentation of her paper before Freud's group. It seems that it was only in March, 1912, when Jung really took the time to read her paper thoroughly and to notice the "uncanny parallels" with his own work (letter of 3/18/12). He confessed that he had been misreading the title as 'distinction' instead of 'destruction.' Nevertheless, Jung promised that her paper would be published before his in the next *Jahrbuch* (1912, Part 1). In answer to a presumably angry letter from Sabina, Jung (3/25/12) made one more apologetic and reassuring reply, "the death tendency or death wish was clear to you before it was to me, understandably." In fact, the issue was not published until September 1912, with Jung's paper, *Wandlungen*, Part II, printed before Sabina's "Destruction" paper!

Nevertheless, Sabina's professional development clearly evolved out of her intimate relationship with Jung, and we have to inquire why. Jung and Spielrein's mutual attraction began while she was an inpatient in 1904-1905, but blossomed in the subsequent outpatient years, 1905-1909, when they were meeting, often secretly, as friends, mutual therapists, and possibly lovers (Carotenuto 1982; Wharton 2001, p. 173-199), though this is not by any means a documented fact. The *apparent* manifestations of a love affair and its discovery have been well documented by Carotenuto (1982); Kerr (1993); Appignanesi & Forrester (1992, p. 211-215, but see note on p. 504, questioning whether the affair had been sexually consummated). Lothane (1996) at first assumed a conventional consummation had occurred, but in a later publication expresses his doubt that it did. (Lothane 1999) In describing their affair in her journal, Sabina used the ambiguous term 'poetry' to describe what she and apparently Jung were using to describe their behavior. She took this term from her psychotic patient, Frau M, who used the term in her delusions, where 'poetry' referred to a blend of sexual, artistic and religious meanings. (See Spielrein, 1911.)

Jung's wife, Emma, has been suspected as the one who in an anonymous letter notified Sabina's parents about their increasingly unbounded relationship. There is no direct evidence of this. But the story also involved Freud, whom Jung finally confided in a few weeks after the knife episode, when it appeared that Spielrein would stain his reputation. Freud at first colluded with Jung's defense against Spielrein's 'allegations,' that she had "kicked up a vile scandal solely because I (Jung) denied myself the pleasure of giving her a child." (McGuire 1974, 133J, p. 207-209; see also 144J, p. 228-230) Later, however, after Jung had finally confessed the truth, that his action in "imputing all the ... wishes and hopes entirely to my patient without seeing the same thing in myself ... was a piece of knavery" (*Ibid.,* 148J, p. 236-237), Freud aligned with Spielrein against Jung. It is still not clear if Jung was confessing to frank seduction or a seductive countertransference that stopped short of actual sexual enactment.

The attraction between Jung and Spielrein seems to me to be based less on lust or Eros than on their recognizing how similar they seemed to be in an almost miraculous way, a mutual narcissistic mirror transference involving their shared discovery of the importance of Mythos. On the surface, both exhibited strong, if narcissistic, egos that were ambitious and scientifically curious in a Logos way about the realm of Mythos. They marveled at the similarity of their insightful analyses of their own and their patients' dreams, their fantasies, their love of romantic poetry and visionary philosophy (particularly Hölderlin and the writings of Goethe and Nietzsche). Both, moreover, had retreated as children from a disturbed outer family constellation into a private fantasy world, which, however pathological, they could both remember and reflect on in great detail as adults. (Jung *MDR*; Spielrein 1912, "Contributions to the Knowledge of the Child's Psyche") And both were struggling to bring what had been relegated to the realm of art and literature into the science of psychology.

From a more neurotic, Freudian, perspective, as children they had been both curious and phobic about the realms of Ares and Eros. Jung's early memories, as we have already seen, are full of references to his fears of violence and destruction. His relation to Eros is similarly shadowed by his late nineteenth century parsonage upbringing, in which sex was largely in shadow, even though he would claim that as a country boy he took in the facts of life 'naturally.' He does not appear to have had what would later be understood as an oedipal mother, whom he experienced as fat and unattractive. His parents slept in separate rooms, so he saw little evidence of intimacy between them. At the age of nine, he did not notice his mother's pregnancy, and he was surprised when a sister was born. We do not know if Jung discovered masturbation as a child. We have seen that he was apparently approached sexually by an older man in his late adolescence, and we know that this shocked him. (McGuire 1974, 49J, p. 94-95) He was aware of sexual attraction to young girls in late adolescence, but he may well have had no sexual experience until marriage.

Spielrein was protected from knowledge of the facts of life by her mother, who nevertheless exposed her daughter to stories about her affairs with other men. She was also stimulated in the anal and genital region by spankings from her father, which led to masturbatory fantasies of an anal-erotic nature, which combined feelings of pleasure with those of disgust. Nevertheless she loved her father, "painfully," and transferred these oedipal feelings, however masochistic, in turn to an uncle, a teacher, a doctor prior to Jung, and then to Jung himself. It is not clear if, as a girl, Sabina was ever directly sexually molested by her father, uncle or brother. If so, she apparently dissociated or repressed such knowledge. Kerr (1993, p. 68) suspects that even after her analysis with Jung she still did not know the details of sexual intercourse until medical school.

Sabina's relation to Ares and Eros, especially when fused in a coniunctio *(A/E),* was a masochistic one, and this was recognized by Jung, who, like many later psychoanalysts, generalized this to most women. In an early passage in *Wandlungen,* he described the prevalence, in the dreams of women, of sexual intercourse being imaged as violent assault, for example, "a robber breaks open her door noisily and stabs through her body with a lance." (p. 10) Jung focused on the mixture of lust and anxiety that is being expressed in such dreams, rather than on the aggressive nature of the man in such a sex act, however masochistically experienced by the woman. Spielrein opened her "Destruction" paper with a similar statement about a woman's anxiety about sexual intercourse. She then followed this with an appreciative quote from Jung's *Wandlungen*, exploring the social aspects:

> Passionate longing, that is, the libido, has two aspects: it is the power that beautifies everything and in certain cases, destroys everything. Often, one cannot recognize the source of this creative power's destructive quality. A woman who, in today's society, abandons herself to passion soon leads herself to ruin. (Jung 1912. For Hinkle's translation see Jung 1916/1991, par. 188, p. 103)

Here Jung was talking about the social stigma involved if a woman, like Spielrein, gets sexually involved with a married man, like Jung. Society was more likely to condone the man involved.

At that time Jung was influenced by Otto Gross, another early patient and colleague (see Heuer 2001), who was advocating polygamy and free love. In fact Spielrein did not seem to fear condemnation if her affair with Jung was to become public, and her parents were also surprisingly open-minded. They were more concerned about Jung's taking no responsibility for his part in the affair, how he had tried to blame the parents' not paying a fee as the reason he felt entitled to change the contract from psychotherapy to a personal relationship. Studying the Jung/Spielrein letters, it could be said that Jung was talking more about his own near ruin from giving way to his passion for Sabina. This was not only true in an outer sense – the scandal of his affair with a patient could most certainly have ruined his career – but it also reflected the inner chaos that his passion for Sabina plunged him into, which he did not hesitate to reveal to her in a letter:

My mind is torn to its very depths. I, who had to be a tower of strength for many weak people, am the weakest of all … Give me back now something of the love and patience and unselfishness which I was able to give you at the time of your illness. Now I am ill…. (Jung in Wharton (trans.) 2001, p. 177, letter, 12/4/08)

Sabina, for her part, did not want to be Jung's mistress; she wanted to be his wife and mother of their child, "Siegfried." She accurately saw that Jung was not going to leave his wife, and she also had compassionate feelings towards Emma, despite the suspicion that it was she who had brought the affair to her parents' attention. Somehow Sabina was able to transform her love for Jung and her hopes of their future together into a collegial relationship, which found its flowering in her dissertation (1911) and her "Destruction" paper (1912). She continued to correspond with Jung long after she had affiliated with the Freudian group, up to 1919. She channeled her erotic energies into her marriage to Paul Scheftel and the birth of her daughter, Renate. Did Jung in fact also transform his erotic feelings into his work, as he suggests in a letter written in 1919?

> *The love of S. for J.* made the latter aware of something he had previously only vaguely suspected, namely of a power in the unconscious which shapes one's destiny, a power which later led him to things of the greatest importance. The relationship had to be 'sublimated,' because otherwise it would have led to delusion and madness (a concretization of the unconscious).
> Sometimes we must be unworthy to live at all. (Jung 2001, letter 9/1/19, p. 194)

It is interesting to note how Jung refers to their relationship in the third person, indicating, for all the feeling in this letter, a detachment that is almost dissociative in its irony. He also does not acknowledge his love for her, J for S, although that is implied. Neither of them in fact truly sublimated their love into their work, but rather displaced it onto other partners.

Sabina rushed into what turned out to be a problematic marriage. And Jung quickly replaced Spielrein with his new protégé, Toni Wolff, with whom he was intimately involved for the next thirty years. Apparently it was his relationship with her, as positive anima, "mother for the other side of men's thinking" (Jung, 1989b, p. 33) that is, carrying his Mythos function, which the practical Emma could not, and which helped him to emerge from his mid-life breakdown.

Jung seemed to believe that he, like Spielrein, was a self-sacrificing kind of person, but I sense he was much more self-serving than he was willing to admit. If self-sacrifice in Spielrein's case can be connected to masochism, the fusion of Eros with Ares, turned against the self, then can we not link Jung's self-serving narcissism to a kind of psychological sadism – Eros turned to the self, with Ares turned outwards towards others, however subtly disguised? An example would be Jung's consistently, and, I think vengefully, omitting Spielrein's theoretical contributions in her "Destruction" paper in subsequent editions of *Wandlungen*, including the final revision, *Symbols of Transformation*.[9]

Yet it was through Jung that Spielrein was able to publish her medical dissertation and her "Destruction" paper in the *Jahrbuch*. He also introduced her to Freud and his circle, which enabled her to publish in psychoanalytic journals such as the *Zentralblatt*. Study of Sabina's diary and letters in 1912, as she awaited the publication of her "Destruction" paper, reveals nothing of how she met and quickly married Paul Scheftel, a Jewish Russian doctor. She has written almost nothing of their relationship. According to Appignanesi and Forrester (1992, p. 221), "he had a progressive disease, which first drove him insane and eventually killed him ..." My suspicion is that their marriage was arranged by her parents; certainly it is reminiscent of their marriage. After the birth of their first daughter, Renate, in 1913, Scheftel left Sabina, returning to Russia; she herself did not return to her homeland until 1923. Sabina lived in Moscow, while her husband lived in Rostov. In 1924, she discovered that he had fathered a daughter by another woman. Sabina moved back to Rostov, integrated this woman and her daughter into the family, and she and Paul had another daughter, Eva. They apparently remained married until his death in 1937. We have no diary or letters from that period, so we have little sense of her personality or any psychopathology during those years. In a 1923 questionnaire she wrote "I enjoy my work ... and without it I see no other meaning in my life." (Ovcharenko 1999, p. 365) Her niece, Menicha, has reported that her aunt Sabina once stated in the early thirties that she could "undoubtedly have been able to cure Lenin," who was by then long since dead and lying in a mausoleum (*Ibid.,* p. 367) In a 1983 interview, Menicha had this last thing to say about her aunt: "She was a completely impractical person. She gave an impression of being pliant but also inwardly strong. She had character; I liked her terribly much." (Carotenuto 1984 edition, p. xi). Dr. Sabina Spielrein and her two daughters were executed by the Nazis in 1942.

## John Nash

In the Prologue to her biography of John Nash, *A Beautiful Mind*, Sylvia Nasar suggests that "Nash's genius was of that mysterious variety more often associated with music and art than with the oldest of all sciences," mathematics, in that Nash used non-rational intuition rather than logic. "Nash saw the vision first, constructing the laborious proofs long afterward." (Nasar 1999, p. 12) From the perspective of my model of the Self, Nash's ego drew on the area of overlap between Logos and Mythos (L/M). In 1959, when Nash was hospitalized at the age of thirty for his first major psychotic episode, involving delusions about aliens from outer space, a visitor asked, "How could you, a mathematician, a man devoted to reason and logical proof ... how could you believe that extraterrestrials are sending you messages?" Nash replied, "Because the ideas I had about supernatural beings came to me the same way that my mathematical ideas did. So I took them seriously." (*Ibid.,* p. 11) Nevertheless, Nash's "faith in rationality and the power of pure thought was extreme.... His heroes were solitary thinkers and supermen like Newton and Nietzsche. Computers and science fiction were his passions." (*Ibid.,* p. 12) Thus his conscious focus was the Logos of pure mathematics, though he drew on the realm of Mythos for his inspiration. His colleagues, many of whom could be described as eccentric 'geeks,' found Nash especially strange, aloof, and haughty. However, "his remoteness was punctuated by flights of garrulousness about outer space and geopolitical trends, childish pranks, and unpredictable outbursts of anger." (*Ibid.,* p. 13) From the standpoint of my model of the Self, Nash could be considered ungrounded in the realms of Ares and Eros, in his head, out of his body, and unrelated to others. Certainly he was vulnerable to unconscious outbursts from those realms, getting into physical or verbal fights with fellow students, or else developing irrational crushes on them, which included his making homoerotic advances. He later found himself attracted to caring and nurturant women, a nurse, Eleanor, the mother of his first son, John David, and his wife, Alicia, the mother of his second son, also named John (but with distinguishing middle names, Charles Martin). He treated Eleanor poorly and did not acknowledge or support her son, until she forced him to. His actual treatment of Alicia, who adored him, and who was an attractive, intelligent physicist, daughter of a prestigious immigrant physician from South America, was not much better. He saw his second son, John Charles Martin Nash, only sporadically, because of the many hospitalizations and separations that took place during this boy's growing up, beginning with his birth in 1959, which coincided with Nash's first hospitalization.

My impression, from reading Nasar's biography, is that Nash was a social and intellectual snob. He believed he was descended from Southern upper class families of superior intelligence and education. There is, in fact, minimal truth to this assertion, from a review of both his mother's and father's family background, as researched by Sylvia Nasar. There is no evidence of a family history of major mental illness that might point to John's pre-disposition to paranoid schizophrenia. His paternal grandfather, Alexander, was also a strange and unstable individual, unhappily married, a philanderer, who abandoned his wife and three children. John's father, John Sr., grew up fatherless, though admiring of his brave mother, who worked and raised the children by herself. John Sr. had compensated for his wayward father by becoming a serious, conservative, responsible, hard-working husband and family man, but he was emotionally distant from John and his younger sister. John seems to have combined elements of his paternal grandfather's irresponsible acting out with his father's emotional detachment.

John's mother, Virginia, grew up in a stable affluent family in Bluefield, West Virginia. She was deaf in one ear as the result of Scarlet Fever, and she lost three out of four siblings through childhood illness or accident. She went to college, became a schoolteacher, but devoted herself after marriage to her children's education. She led an active social life, at church and the local country club. Only much later, after the death of her husband, did Virginia become depressed and develop an alcohol problem.

Unlike his younger sister, Martha, John was, from an early age, solitary, reclusive, antisocial, preferring to read books or play by himself. At elementary school, he displayed many symptoms of Attention Deficit Hyperactivity Disorder. His handwriting was illegible, possibly from having been forced by his father to switch from his left to his right hand. He was, however, a scientifically curious child, experimenting with electrical gadgets; in adolescence, he made bombs out of homemade explosives. Though handsome and physically strong, he hated sports and was awkward in the presence of girls. In high school, his intuitive gift for mathematics was recognized, but he intended originally to follow in his father's footsteps by pursuing the study of electrical engineering. (His father had served in World War I in France, which precluded his attending college.) John began college at Carnegie Tech in Pittsburgh in 1945, being too young to serve in World War II. He graduated in 1948 and received a scholarship to study for his PhD in theoretical mathematics at Princeton. Fears of war had continued into the post-war era, and John was well aware of the possibility of being drafted into the Korean War when he graduated in 1950.

Though much of his later work would be on pure mathematical topics, Nash's famous Equilibrium Theorem, completed in his first year at Princeton, and which led to his Nobel Prize, was in applied mathematics. It was John von Neumann who had first recognized in 1928 that game theory could be applied to rivalries, including those that occurred in business or in war. (von Neumann 1944) He gave mathematical solutions for games that are two-person "zero-sum" games, that is games in which one person's gain is another's loss. But in the field of economics, and in the late 1940s and early 1950s, especially, the game of strategic nuclear deterrence had become much more complicated, involving compromise, cooperation, and mutual gain between protagonists. Nash created a mathematical solution through which every player could independently choose his best response to the other person's best strategy, yet arrive at a solution that speaks more to interdependence and cooperation than competition. His paper, published in 1950 in *Econometrica*, was entitled "The Bargaining Problem."

After a summer spent at the Rand Corporation in California, "where brilliant academics pondered nuclear war and the new theory of games" (Nasar 1999, p. 104), Nash returned to his hometown, to renew his draft exemption (for which he qualified because of the important nature of his work for the government), then went on to Princeton, where he completed a pure mathematical theorem on manifolds, which he hoped would lead to an academic position. Nasar believes that at some deep level Nash could not have psychologically tolerated the regimentation, loss of autonomy, and communal living with strangers that military life would have involved. On the surface, however, he was preserving his academic career, fully aware that the early years of a mathematician's life are often the most, if not only, creative years. In 1951 Nash was hired, not by Princeton, much to his disappointment, but by MIT, where he spent the next eight years, until his first hospitalization in 1959.

Although Nash could be a helpful mentor and teacher to those individual students he regarded as talented, he was in the main an irresponsible classroom teacher, and greatly disliked. His colleagues tolerated his arrogance and eccentricity as the price for genius. Parallel to his brilliant mathematical career, Nash secretly delved into the realm of intimate relationships during the MIT years. "Nash became emotionally involved with at least three men. He acquired and then abandoned a secret mistress who bore his child. And he courted – or rather was courted by – a woman who became his wife." (*Ibid.*, p. 167) He struggled with the reciprocal nature of intimate relationships, which was ironic in view of his knowledge of this from the theoretical perspective of his PhD thesis. Although he could access his emotional needs in relation to others, he seemed unable to empathize with or meet the needs of others or grasp his effect on others. "He had in fact no more sense of "the Other" than does a very young child." (*Ibid.,* p. 168) (Diagnostically at that time, he could be considered a narcissistic, if not schizoid, personality.)

Nash's breakdown occurred in 1959, at the age of thirty, just after he had been given tenure at MIT and just before the birth of his second son, John Charles. It is unclear whether one of these life events was the determining precipitating factor, or whether it was his attempt to solve the notorious and previously unsolvable Riemann Hypothesis that tipped him over the edge. All we know for sure is that by that time he was sending letters to all the embassies in Washington, stating he was forming a world government. He turned down the offer of a chair at the University of Chicago, saying that he was instead scheduled to become Emperor of Antarctica. One can hear that as a symbolic statement of the imperative to address emotional needs of the Self that lay below his frozen, schizoid coldness rather than simply move on to greater outward achievement.

Now delusions of grandeur alternated with intense feelings of persecution and powerlessness, representing the combination of omnipotence and impotence characteristic of a beautiful mind in breakdown, the theme we have already met in relation to Jung and Spielrein. The dynamics in this more clearly psychotic manifestation are different, however. Nash's conscious over-identification with the Logos aspect of the Self, albeit inspired by ideas sprung from the Mythos realm, fully gave way to a compensatory flood of images and affect from the realms of Mythos, Ares and Eros. Nash's previous interest in the logic of numbers, for instance, gave way to a superstitious belief in numerology. Yet even when psychotic, he could do incredible manipulations with numbers. Once he punched in Khrushchev's birth date and transformed it via the Dow Jones average of that day into the social security number of the Princeton chairman of mathematics, much to the latter's astonishment. Cambray (2002) sees this as an example of the emergence of a synchronistic occurrence to someone in a psychotic state, "the psyche's desperate attempt at self-organization, trying to make links to the external world in a bid to reconnect to life." (p. 131)

Religious ideas, which he had previously scorned, calling himself an atheist, now filled his psychic world. "I am the left foot of God on earth," (Nasar 1999, p. 275) he once declared (as against, I suppose, the nurturing right hand of God). At other times, wandering around the Princeton streets and campus, he would strike up conversations with others he met, referring to himself, obliquely, and usually in the third person, as one Johann von Nassau, and discuss his ideas on world peace and world government. This name, a condensation of his predecessor in game theory, John von Neumann with that of Nassau Street, the main street of Princeton, is reminiscent of the psychotic condensations described by Jung and Spielrein in relation to their patients B and Frau M at the Burghölzli.

There is no room here to detail the thirty years of Nash's struggles with symptoms of paranoid schizophrenia, interspersed with periods of lucidity, in which, despite severe bouts of apathy and depression, he did useful work. During this period the psychiatric diagnosis of Schizotypal Personality Disorder might be more appropriate than Paranoid Schizophrenia. He traveled to Europe many times in a delusional state, attempting to give up his US citizenship, apparently in relation to fears of being drafted and fears of being implicated in a US-organized war, and in preparation to lead some kind of world government.

During the early years, his wife went with him or followed him to Europe, leaving their son with her mother. This son was not baptized or even named until his second year. John Charles grew up to be a rather intense adolescent, with an aptitude for mathematics, like his father, but with a deep religious commitment to fundamentalist Christianity. He also suffered a breakdown, was hospitalized, and was diagnosed with paranoid schizophrenia. By young adulthood, he had recovered enough to go to Rutgers where he obtained both an undergraduate degree and a PhD in mathematics. He relapsed, however, in his first academic position at Marshall, and to this day is unable to work, remains on anti-psychotic medication, and lives with his parents. Nash's older son by Eleanor has no obvious psychological problems; Nasar did not investigate the family background of John Charles' mother, Alicia, but her older brother, Rolando, was apparently "confined to an institution." We have no further details of his fate. Nash himself has mostly recovered from his symptoms and lives today without any medications relatively schizophrenia-free.

*Concluding Remarks*

As the various types of breakdown experienced by Jung, Spielrein, and Nash suggest, encounters with the Self by an inflated ego can take on destructive characteristics, which can be relieved with the help of various therapy measures, but also from a strong act of will on the part of a "beautiful mind." Often it seems as if the previously inflated ego has been forced to surrender under the wounding, deflating and fragmenting powers of the Self, releasing other potential aspects of the Self for conscious access by the ego. In the case of Jung, Spielrein, and Nash, recovery was aided by work, therapy, and caring relationships. For Jung, the least manifestly disturbed and the most resilient of these three, this involved his theoretical writing, his self-therapy via active imagination, but also relationship with his wife, his children, and his patients and colleagues who stayed with him after the break with Freud. His unique and enduring theoretical contribution is his development of a theory that places the ego in a humble but discriminating position in relation to an underlying Self "as moved to the mover." For Spielrein, beyond her inpatient and subsequent outpatient analysis with Jung, recovery involved not just the relationship with Jung but the giving up of the fantasy of having Jung's child, "Siegfried," who represented for her the literal offspring of her mutual infatuation with Jung and Freud, sublimating it by writing her seminal 'Destruction' paper, and taking up her responsibilities as wife and mother, while still working as a Freudian analyst and teacher. For Nash, beyond any benefit he received from medication or the various inpatient and outpatient therapies he underwent, healing involved conscious acknowledgement of his wife's love, Eros, as key to his recovery, together with his attempting to reach out to both of his sons in a more related way. He also renewed his work on previous mathematical projects, abandoned in his delusional times. Nash learned to avoid anything geopolitical or religious, now fully aware of the danger of stimulating delusional or paranoid ideation.

All three of these beautiful minds, in other words, managed to restore balance, moving past a particular inflating coniunctio and developing other coniunctio possibilities. Yet each also seems to me limited in the degree of recovery from his or her version of the drama of the gifted child. (Miller 1996; Jung 1946/1954) Jung sacrificed his connection with what Freud represented, a belief in the primacy of libidinous Eros and Ares energies in determining human destiny, instead focusing mainly on the more spiritual aspects of the quest for individuation, beginning with his *Wandlungen* paper. He said in his autobiography that he still honored Eros, but in a spiritual way. (*MDR*, p. 168) Though he did not specify Ares, or Freud's Thanatos, he did acknowledge the "other face of God, the dark side of the God-image," that is, the destructive aspect of the Self, as well as the creative or loving aspect, which he explored in his mature religious and alchemical writings.

Spielrein's sacrifice was more restrictive. She gave up her connection to Jungian archetypal theory in her move to the Freudian camp. Though she continued to do creative work as an analyst, researcher, and teacher as she moved from Zurich via Berlin to Geneva (she worked briefly with Piaget) and Moscow, her work never again, so far as we know, showed the fertile coniunctio of Jung and Freud. Sadly, she did not continue to publish. In leaving Zurich, the Burghölzli, and the Jungian circle, she turned away from her previous interest in psychotic process. Her marriage, a sudden development in 1912, coincided with her alliance with the Freudians, and the publication of her "Destruction" paper. It served her developing sense of responsibility, but it does not seem to have been based on love. She seemed drawn back slowly but surely to her roots, Russia, and her family of origin. Her two talented daughters, as young adults, never married, but remained with Sabina until their deaths, in this sense at least, unindividuated. Spielrein, in a last letter to Jung in 1918 (Carotenuto 1982, p. 90) conceded that she remained a "saviour or sacrifice type," as Freud had described her, "one who depicts her desires in symbols that express complete dissolution of the personality, like, for instance, all the great heroes who die for their ideals, like the sun-god, Siegfried."

Today, Nash still works in the Mathematics Department at Princeton. In television interviews he seems sad and passive, dependent on his ever-present wife. Is there not perhaps a down side to his having turned away completely from Mythos in the form of geopolitics and religion? I wonder what he might be thinking of the World Trade Center bombing, or the ongoing Islamic extremist terrorist threat today. His "paranoid" delusions were in a way prophetic, reminiscent of Jung's own visions of destruction just before World War I. One wonders what might have happened if Nash had been treated by a Jungian, rather than by the more pragmatic neo-Freudian.

*This paper is dedicated to my wife, Brooke. Thanks to my friend, Keith Knecht, for his assistance in drafting the diagrams. Thanks to Joseph Cambray, Thomas Kirsch, and Sonu Shamdasani for their feedback to earlier drafts of this paper.*

## References

Appignanesi, L. & Forrester, J. (1992). *Freud's Women.* New York: Basic Books.

Austin, S. (1999). "Women's Aggressive Fantasies," *Harvest,* Vol. 45, no. 2, p. 7-28.

Cambray, J. (2002). "Synchronicity and Emergence," *American Imago,* Vol. 59, no. 4, p. 409-434.

Carotenuto, A. (1982). *A Secret Symmetry; Sabina Spielrein Between Jung and Freud.* New York: Random House.

Colman, W. (2002). "A Response to Barbara Stephens," *Journal of Analytical Psychology,* Vol. 47, p. 492.

Covington, C. (2001). "Editorial," *Journal of Analytical Psychology,* Vol. 46, p. 1-9.

Covington, C. and Wharton, B. (eds.) (2003) *Sabina Spielrein: Forgotten Pioneer of Psychoanalysis.* London and New York: Brunner-Routledge.

Curran, R. T. (1998). "'Cat Burglar' in the Topkapi Palace: The double binds of therapy with dissociative identity patients" Parts 1 & 2. *Quadrant,* XXVIII (1&2) p. 31-50, 65-80.

Douglas, C. (1993). *Translate This Darkness.* Princeton: Princeton University Press.

Ellenberger, Henri (1970). *The Discovery of the Unconscious.* New York: Basic Books.

Everest, P. (1999). "The Multiple Self: Working with Dissociation and Trauma." *Journal of Analytical Psychology,* Vol. 44, p. 443-463.

Freud, S. (1911). "Formulations Regarding the Two Principles in Mental Functioning," *Jahrbuch für psychoanalytische und psychopathologische Forschungen,* Vol. III, p. 1-9.

Freud, S. (1920). *Beyond the Pleasure Principle*. Standard Edition, Vol. 18, ed. J. Strachey. London: Hogarth Press.

Fromm, E. (1973). *The Anatomy of Human Destructiveness*. Greenwich: Fawcett Publications.

Goodheart, W. B. (1984). "C. G. Jung's First Patient: On the Seminal Emergence of Jung's Thought," *Journal of Analytical Psychology*, Vol. 29, p. 1-33.

Hayman, R. (1999). *A Life of Jung*. New York and London: WW Norton.

Heuer, G. (2001). "Jung's Twin Brother; Otto Gross and Carl Gustav Jung," *Journal of Analytical Psychology*, Vol. 46, p. 655-688.

Hoffer, A. (2001). "Jung's Analysis of Sabina Spielrein and His Use of Freud's Free Association Method," *Journal of Analytical Psychology*, Vol. 46, p. 117-128.

Huskinson, L. (2002). "The Self as Violent Other," *Journal of Analytical Psychology*, Vol. 47, p. 437-458.

Jung, C. G. (1902/1957). "On the Psychology and Pathology of So-Called Occult Phenomena," *Collected Works*, Vol. 1.

Jung, C. G. (1907/1960). "The Psychology of Dementia Praecox," *Collected Works*, Vol. 3.

Jung, C. G. (1908/1961). "The Freudian Theory of Hysteria," *Collected Works*, Vol. 4.

Jung, C. G. (1909/1949). "The Significance of the Father in the Destiny of the Individual," *Collected Works*, Vol. 4.

Jung, C. G. (1912). *Wandlungen und Symbole der Libido*; *Beiträge zur Entwicklungsgeschichte des Denkens*. Leipzig and Vienna: Franz Deuticke.

Jung, C. G. (1916/1991) *Psychology of the Unconscious*. [English version of Jung (1912)] B. Hinkle (trans.) *Collected Works*, Supplemental Volume B.

Jung, C. G. (1916/1967). "VII Sermones ad Mortuos" London: Stuart & Watkins.

Jung, C. G. (1921/1970). "Psychological Types," *Collected Works*, Vol. 6.

Jung, C.G. (1946/1954). "The Gifted Child," *Collected Works*, Vol. 17

Jung, C. G. (1946/1966). "The Psychology of the Transference," *Collected Works*, Vol. 16.

Jung, C. G. (1951/1968). "Aion," *Collected Works*, Vol. 9, pt. ii.

Jung, C. G. (1952/1967). "Symbols of Transformation," *Collected Works*, Vol. 5.

Jung, C. G. (1952/1969). "Answer to Job," *Collected Works*, Vol. 11.

Jung, C. G. (1955/1963). "Mysterium Coniunctionis," *Collected Works*, Vol. 14.

Jung, C. G. (1961/1963). *Memories, Dreams, Reflections.* Ed. Aniela Jaffe. New York: Pantheon.

Jung, C. G. (1976). *The Visions Seminars; From the Notes of Mary Foote.* Zurich: Spring.

Jung, C. G. (1989a). *Nietzsche's Zarathustra: Notes of the Seminar Given in 1934-39.* Vols. I & II. Ed. J. L. Jarret. London: Routledge.

Jung, C. G. (1989b). *Analytical Psychology; Notes of the Seminar Given in 1925.* Ed. W. F. Princeton: Princeton University Press.

Jung, C. G. (2001). Wharton, B., (trans.) "The letters of C. G. Jung to Sabina Spielrein," *Journal of Analytical Psychology,* Vol. 46, p. 173-199.

Jung, E. (1957). *Animus and Anima.* Dallas: Spring Publishers.

Jung, E. and Von Franz, M-L. (1986). *The Grail Legend.* Boston: Sigo Press.

Kalsched, D. (1996). *The Inner World of Trauma; Archetypal Defenses of the Personal Spirit.* London: Routledge.

Kerr, J. (1993). *A Most Dangerous Method.* New York: Knopf.

Kutek, A. (2000). "Jung and His Family – A Contemporary Paradigm," in *Jungian Thought in the Modern World.* Ed. E. Christopher and H. M. Solomon. London/New York: Free Association Books.

Lothane, Z. (1996). "In Defense of Sabina Spielrein," *International Forum of Psychoanalysis,* 5:203 – 217.

Lothane, Z. (1999). "Tender Love and Transference: Unpublished Letters of C. G. Jung and Sabina Spielrein," *International Journal of Psychoanalysis,* Vol. 80, p. 1189-1204.

McGuire, W., ed. (1974). *The Freud/Jung Letters.* London: Hogarth/ Routledge.

Miller, A. (1996). *The Drama of the Gifted Child,* rev. ed. New York: Basic Books.

Minder, B. (2001). "Sabina Spielrein; Jung's Patient at the Burghölzli." Trans. B. Wharton. *Journal of Analytical Psychology,* Vol. 46, p. 43-66.

Moore, R. & Gillette, D. (1990). *King, Warrior, Magician, Lover.* New York: Harper Collins.

Nasar, S. (1999). *A Beautiful Mind.* New York: Touchstone.

Nash, J. (1950). "The Bargaining Problem," *Econometrica,* Vol. 18, p. 155-162.

Neumann, E. (1954). "The Moon and Matriarchal Consciousness," *Spring,* p. 83-100.

Noll, R. (1989). "Multiple Personality, Dissociation, and C. G. Jung's Complex Theory," *Journal of Analytical Psychology,* Vol. 34, p. 353-370.

Noll, R. (1993). "Multiple Personality and the Complex Theory; A Correction and Rejection of C. G. Jung's 'Collective Unconscious,'" *Journal of Analytical Psychology,* Vol. 38, p. 321-323.

O'Kane, F. (1994). *Sacred Chaos; Reflections on God's Shadow and the Dark Self.* Toronto: Inner City Books.

Ovcharenko, V. (1999). "Love, Psychoanalysis and Destruction," *Journal of Analytical Psychology,* Vol. 44, p. 355-373.

Satinover, J. (1985). "At the Mercy of Another; Abandonment and Restitution in Psychosis and Psychotic Character," *Chiron,* p. 47-86.

Schultz, D. (1990). *Intimate Friends, Dangerous Rivals.* Los Angeles: Tarcher.

Shamdasani, S. (1990). "A Woman Called Frank," *Spring,* Vol. 50, p. 26-56.

Shamdasani, S. (1998). "The Lost Contributions of Maria Moltzer to Analytical Psychology," *Spring,* Vol. 64, p. 103-119.

Shelburne, W. (1988). Mythos *and* Logos *in the Thought of Carl Jung.* Albany: State University of New York Press.

Skea, B. R. (1992). *Cuchulainn and his Celtic Fathers; Ancient Models of Masculinity for Modern Men.* Diploma Thesis, C. G. Jung Institute of New York.

Skea, B. R. (1995). *Trauma, Transference, and Transformation; A Jungian Perspective on the Dissociability of the Self and the Psychotherapy of Dissociative Disorders.* Paper presented at the C.G. Jung Education Center of Pittsburgh, (www.cgjungpage.org/articles/skea.html).

Skea, B. R. (1999). *The Trauma Paradox.* Paper presented at the National Conference of Jungian Analysts, Santa Fe, NM, (www.cgjungpage.org/traumap202.html).

Spielrein, S. (1906/1907?). "Unedited Extracts from a Diary." Trans. J. Moll, P. Bennett, B. Wharton. *Journal of Analytical Psychology,* Vol. 46, p. 155-171.

Spielrein, S. (1911). "On the Psychological Content of a Case of Schizophrenia (Dementia Praecox)." Trans. K. McCormick (1992), personal communication. Originally *Jahrbuch für psychoanalytische und psychopathologische Forschungen,* Vol. III, p. 329-400.

Spielrein, S. (1912). "Destruction as a Cause of Coming into Being." Trans. K. McCormick (1994), *Journal of Analytical Psychology,* Vol. 39, p. 155-186. Originally *Jahrbuch für psychoanalytische und psychopathologische Forschungen,* Vol. IV, p. 465-504.

Spielrein, S. (1912). "Contributions to the Knowledge of the Child's Psyche," *Zentralblatt fur Psychoanalyse und Psychotherapie,* Vol. II, p. 57-72.

Spielrein, S. (1913-1930). "Various Short Papers by Sabina Spielrein." Trans. C. J. Wharton, P. Bennett, & B. Wharton, *Journal of Analytical Psychology,* Vol. 46, p. 201-214.

Steffens, D. Trans. (2001). "Burghölzli Hospital Records of Sabina Spielrein," *Journal of Analytical Psychology,* Vol. 46, p. 15-42.

van Waring, A. (1992). "The Works of Pioneering Psychoanalyst Sabina Spielrein," *International Review of Psychoanalysis,* Vol. 19, p. 399-414.

von Neumann, J. & Morganstern, O. (1944). *Theory of Games and Economic Behavior.* Princeton: Princeton University Press.

von Raffay, A. (2000). "Why It Is Difficult to See the Anima as a Helpful Object," *Journal of Analyical Psychology,* Vol. 45, p. 541-560.

Wieland-Burston, J. (1992). *Chaos and Order in the World of the Psyche.* London/New York: Routledge.

Winnicott, D. (1964). "Review of Jung's *Memories, Dreams, Reflections,*" *International Journal of Psychoanalysis,* Vol. 45, p. 450-455.

Wolff, A. (1956). "Structural Forms of the Feminine Psyche." Trans. P. Watzlawik. Students Association, C. G. Jung Institute, Zurich.

## Notes

1 *Coniunctio,* an alchemical term for the conjunction of elements achieved through chemical combination, was used by Jung as an analogy for the union of individual personalities that occurs within a psychological relationship.

2 This is an adjective I have coined, from the god Ares, in analogy to 'martial' from the god Mars.

3 An interesting exception to this supposed pattern is Miss Frank Miller, whose published poems and reveries were used by Jung in *Wandlungen und Symbole der Libido.* Rather than idealize her, Jung pathologized her, predicting a schizophrenic breakdown which apparently did not occur (Shamdasani, 1990).

4 *Wandlungen und Symbole der Libido* was originally published in *Jahrbuch fur psychoanalytische und psychopathologische Forschungen* in two parts in 1911 and 1912. It was first translated into English in 1916 by Beatrice Hinckle and published as *Psychology of the Unconscious.* Jung subsequently issued a considerably rewritten edition in 1952, entitled *Symbole der Wandlung,* translated in 1956 as *Symbols of Transformation,* now Volume 5 of the Collected Works.

5 Jung first mentioned Toni Wolff in a letter to Freud, indicating she was one of several women (others included his wife, Emma, Sabina Spielrein, and Maria Moltzer) he was bringing to the Weimar Congress in 1911 – "a new discovery of mine, a remarkable intellect with an excellent feeling for religion and philosophy." (McGuire 1974, 269J, p. 440) Two years earlier, at

the age of 21, she had begun inpatient treatment with Jung at the Burghölzli Hospital, for depression, a condition aggravated by the recent death of her father. She blossomed under Jung's care, and became his research assistant, working on his *Wandlungen* project (Schultz, 1990). Less ambiguously than with Spielrein in the preceding years, Jung and Wolff became romantically involved, out in the open, with Jung overriding his wife, Emma's, objections. Wolff remained in a romantic triangle with Jung and his wife for more than thirty years, usually entertaining Jung at her house every Wednesday, yet maintaining some kind of friendship with Emma. Like Emma, Toni Wolff became an analyst and served as president of the Psychological Club in Zurich. She published several papers, including 'Structural Forms of the Feminine Psyche' (1956), where she extended Jung's dual image of the Feminine archetype, Mother and Hetaira, to the four-fold Mother, Hetaira, Medium, and Amazon. According to some undocumented accounts, based on Zurich gossip, Wolff's personal situation soured when she unsuccessfully sought marriage to Jung. Rejected, she turned to alcohol, and several other affairs, and died in 1953 at age sixty-four, two years before Emma's death (Schultz, 1990).

6 In actual fact Nash and Alicia were divorced for most of this period, only remarrying much later. Alicia was his second significant relationship with a woman; he never married Eleanor, the mother of his first son.

7 This term is taken from Shelburne(1988).

8 Among others, McGuire, as editor of the 1925 Jung lectures (1989b), has suggested that the "insidious anima voice" that tried in 1918 to persuade Jung that his *Red Book* illustrations were art, was Sabina Spielrein. Sonu Shamdasani (personal communication) doubts this assertion, believing that Maria Moltzer, an early member of the Analytical Psychology Club, is the more likely candidate (see also Shamdasani 1998).

9 Another example would be the way Jung made use of Miss Frank Miller's writings in *Wandlungen* for his own purposes, pathologizing her, without making any attempt to communicate with her before publishing. In 1925 (Jung 1989b, p31) he wrote, "I found a lump of clay, turned it to gold and put it in my pocket. I got Miller into myself and strengthened my fantasy power by the mythological material."

A further example would be statements he made later about animus-possession in women. Rather than acknowledge the conscious Logos aspect of many of the women who worked with him, he focused on women in general, whom he saw as having only unconscious access to Logos. To me he reveals an underlying fear of and hostility towards the Logos power of women, which he had to denigrate, reducing it to the unconscious Animus.

In women ... Eros is an expression of their true nature, while their Logos is often only a regrettable accident.... No matter how friendly and obliging a woman's Eros may be, no logic on earth can shake her if she is ridden by the animus. Often the man has the feeling – and he is not altogether wrong – that only seduction or a beating or rape would have the necessary power of persuasion. (Jung 1951, para 293, p. 187-188)

A few sentences before this astonishing published remark appears, Jung concedes that men can be in the grip of an irrational complex of their own when dialoguing with animus-ridden women, their "anima possessed and transformed into the animus of their own anima." (*Idem.*) This seems as close as Jung ever came to admitting that men, too, can become 'animus-possessed.' But the underlying fault is still assigned to their possession by their unconscious Feminine animas, rather than to unconscious male sadism, or to phallic narcissism – the masculine complex that Jung's childhood underground phallus dream had warned him to watch out for.

# CNASJA Affiliations of Contributors to this Volume

*John Beebe* is an analyst Member of the C. G. Jung Institute of San Francisco.

*Clarissa Pinkola Estés* is an analyst Member of the Inter-Regional Society of Jungian Analysts.

*Jacqueline Gerson* is an analyst Member of the Asociación Mexicana De Analistas Junguianos.

*Judith Hecker* is a Candidate in the C.G. Jung Institute of Los Angeles.

*John Dourley* is an analyst Member of the Ontario Association of Jungian Analysts.

*Beverley Zabriskie* is an analyst Member of the New York Association for Analytical Psychology.

*Mary Dougherty* is an analyst Member of the C. G. Jung Institute of Chicago.

*Thomas Singer* is an analyst Member of the C.G. Jung Institute of San Francisco.

*Samuel Kimbles* is an analyst Member of the C. G. Jung Institute of San Francisco.

*Sherry Salman* is an analyst Member of the New York Association for Analytical Psychology.

*Arthur Colman* is an analyst Member of the C. G. Jung Institute of San Francisco.

*Arlene TePaske Landau* is an analyst Member of the C.G. Jung Institute of Los Angeles.

*Naomi Lowinsky* is an analyst Member of the C.G. Jung Institute of San Francisco.

*Brian Skea* is an analyst Member of the Inter-Regional Society of Jungian Analysts.

The Jungian Analytic Associations, Societies, and Institutes listed above are all North American Member Groups of the International Association of Analytical Psychology (IAAP). To learn more about the IAAP and its Member Groups on the Internet, go to www.iaap.org/groups.html

# Acknowledgements

Permission to quote from *The English Auden* (1977) was granted by Curtis Brown, Ltd., New York, and Faber and Faber, London.

Permission to quote here from Paul Celan's *Selected Poems and Prose* (2001) was granted by W. W. Norton, New York.

Certain concepts in Dr. Clarissa Pinkola Estés's keynote speech, entitled "Explaining Evil," first delivered at the 2002 North American Conference of Jungian Analysts and Candidates, were taken from a larger unpublished manuscript called *The Other Leviathan*. "I wrote the latter," the author explains, "in contrast to an idea in a work, also called *Leviathan*, of Thomas Hobbes (1588-1679). He posited that humans are inherently wicked. He thought they might best be ruled by an absolute monarchy, a government that would force all people to behave in certain ways. This kingship would rule like Leviathan, the sea monster (which for several thousand years had been associated with domination and predation). I wanted to pursue another way of thinking about human nature, as blessed, and desirous of finding one's way to a greater, as well as to an individual, good. –CPE"

Permission to quote here from Naomi Ruth Lowinsky's *red clay is talking* is granted by Scarlet Tanager Books, Oakland, California.

Permission to quote here from Czeslaw Milosz's *New and Collected Poems* (2001) was granted by HarperCollins, New York.

Permission to quote here from Nelly Sachs's *O the Chimneys; Selected Poems* (1967), was granted by the The Jewish Publication Society of America , who first published this collection by arrangement with Farrar, Straus and Giroux, New York.

"Blood Payments" was splendidly read at the Conference itself, when Sherry Salman was unable to attend, by Elizabeth Strahan, who also led the lively discussion that followed.

# Index

## John Fraim
### Battle of Symbols
Global Dynamics of Advertising, Media
& Entertainment

Symbols increasingly dominate international communication. The events of 9/11 and the ongoing war against terrorism demonstrate their power.

*Battle of Symbols* examines 9/11 and current events in light of global symbolism. While 9/11 represented the beginning of the war against terrorism, the real "battle of symbols" started long before September 11th and will continue long after the fall of Osama bin Laden or Saddam Hussein.

The book defines current global symbols and observes the response of the American symbolism industry to the events of 9/11. As Fraim notes, the events of 9/11 offered a rare opportunity to observe how American symbols are *created* (by Madison Avenue advertising and Hollywood entertainment), *communicated* (by New York media) and *managed* (by Washington public relations).

432 pages, illustrated, ISBN 3-85630-620-X

### Cambridge 2001

The Fifteenth Triannual Congress of the International Association for Analytical Psychology (IAAP) took place on the grounds of St. John's College in Cambridge, England from August 19-24, 2001. It was a memorable occasion both in its preparation and its incarnation and the present volume is meant to preserve at least a portion of what transpired: the papers comprising the program. The presentations and events were more far-reaching and all-inclusive than ever before, incorporating numerous political and intercultural issues and including representatives from psychoanalysis and other fields of endeavor for the first time.

768 pages, illustrated

ISBN 3-85630-609-9

## Recent Titles from Daimon

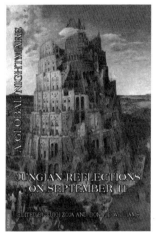

**Jungian Reflections on September 11**
A Global Nightmare
*Edited by Luigi Zoja and Donald Williams*

Seldom has an event in the world had such a pervasive and all-encompassing effect as the brutal terrorist attacks on New York and Washington in September, 2001. Has our world become a different place as a result? If so, in what ways? Along with the tragic aspects, what might this "global nightmare" have to give us, the human inhabitants of this world? What is there for us to acknowledge and what old and new wounds have been opened? Beyond the obvious scars, what sort of a legacy has it left behind?

224 pages, ISBN 3-85630-619-6

*Luigi Zoja*
**Drugs, Addiction and Initiation**
The Modern Search for Ritual

Luigi Zoja argues that the pervasive abuse of drugs in our society can in large part be ascribed to a resurgence of the collective need for initiation and initiatory structures: a longing for something sacred underlies our culture's manic drive toward excessive consumption. In a society without ritual, the drug addict seeks not so much the thrill of a high as the satisfaction of an inner need for a *participation mystique* in the dominant religion of our times: consumerism. From its critique of drug cures based on detoxification to its discussion of the esoteric-terrorist cult of the Assassins, Zoja's work is a classic in the field of psycho-anthropology.

144 pages, ISBN 3-85630-595-5

## English Titles from Daimon

*Available from your bookstore or from our distributors:*

*In the United States:*

Bookworld Trade Inc.
1941 Whitfield Park Loop
Sarasota FL 34243
Please order on the web: www.bookworld.com
Fax: 800-777-2524  Phone: 800-444-2524

*In Great Britain:*

Airlift Book Company
8 The Arena
Enfield, Middlesex EN3 7NJ
Phone: (0181) 804 0400
Fax: (0181) 804 0044

*Worldwide:*

*Daimon Verlag    Hauptstrasse 85    CH-8840 Einsiedeln    Switzerland*
*Phone: (41)(55) 412 2266    Fax: (41)(55) 412 2231*
*email: info@daimon.ch*

*Visit our website: www.daimon.ch*
*or write for our complete catalog!*